ROYAL HISTORICAL SOCIETY
STUDIES IN HISTORY
SERIES
No. 36

LAW, LITIGANTS, AND THE LEGAL PROFESSION

Recent volumes published in this series include

For a complete list of the series please see pp.234-5.

LAW, LITIGANTS AND THE LEGAL PROFESSION

Papers presented to the Fourth British Legal History Conference at the University of Birmingham 10-13 July 1979

Edited by
E.W. Ives
and
A.H. Manchester

LONDON: Royal Historical Society
NEW JERSEY: Humanities Press Inc.
1983

347.9
B862l

The Society records its gratitude to the following,
whose generosity made possible the initiation of this
series: The British Academy; The Pilgrim Trust;
The Twenty-Seven Foundation; The United States
Embassy's bicentennial funds; The Wolfson Trust;
several private donors.

British Library Cataloguing in Publication Data
British Legal History Conference (*4th: 1979: Birmingham*)
Law, litigants and the legal profession. –
(Royal Historical Society studies in history series; no. 36)
1. Law – Great Britain – History and criticism
– Congresses
I. Title   II. Ives, E.W.
III. Manchester, A.H.   IV. Series
344.1'009   KD606

84-4446

First published in Great Britain in 1983 by Swift Printers (Publishing) Ltd, London EC1
for The Royal Historical Society
and in the U.S.A. by Humanities Press Inc., Atlantic Highlands, NJ 07716

Printed in England by Swift Printers Ltd. London EC1

CONTENTS

vi

NOTE ON THE CONTRIBUTORS

J.N. Adams
Senior Lecturer in Law, University of Kent at Canterbury

J.L. Barton
Fellow of Merton College, Oxford

R. Campbell
Senior Lecturer in Law, University of Melbourne, Australia

D. Duman
Lecturer in the Department of History, Ben Gurion University of the Negev, Israel

J.A. Guy
Reader in History, University of Bristol

R.F. Hunnisett
Public Record Office, London

C.U. Ilegbune
Senior Lecturer in Law, University of Nigeria (Enugu), Nigeria

L. Knafla
Professor of History, University of Calgary, Canada

P.S. Lachs
Associate Professor of History, Bryn Mawr College, U.S.A

M.K. McIntosh
Assistant Professor of History, University of Colorado at Boulder, U.S.A.

J.B. Post
Assistant Keeper, Public Record Office, London

E. Powell
Downing College, Cambridge.

R.B. Pugh
Late Emeritus Professor of English History, University of London

A.W.B. Simpson
Professor of Law, University of Kent at Canterbury

H.R.T. Summerson
Historian to the City of Carlisle

B. Touhill
> Associate Vice-Chancellor for Academic Affairs, University of Missouri, U.S.A.

D. White
> Attorney-at-Law, Senior Lecturer in Law, University of the West Indies, Cave Hill, Barbados.

NOTE ON THE CONFERENCES

Professor Dafydd Jenkins convened the first British Legal History Conference at Aberystwyth in 1973. A selection of the papers which were given at that conference was edited by Professor Jenkins and published by the University of Wales Press under the title *Legal History Studies*. In the light of the success of that conference further conferences were held at the University of Cambridge in 1975 and at Edinburgh University in 1977. Dr. J.H. Baker has since edited a selection of the Cambridge papers under the title *Legal Records and the Historian* in the Royal Historical Society's Studies in History Series. Professor A. Harding has prepared a selection of the Edinburgh papers for the same series under the title *Law-Making and Law-Makers in British History*.

The Fourth British Legal History Conference was held at the University of Birmingham from 10 to 13 July 1979. The papers which make up this volume were offered to that conference. In addition the conference had the benefit of hearing the following papers:

Professor P. Landau
> The Origins of the Systematic Decretal Collections and Schools of Canon Law in the Twelfth Century

Professor R.V. Turner
> Twelfth and Thirteenth Century Royal Justices and the Public Service

Professor M.D. Gordon
> The Elizabethan Perjury Statute of 1563

Professor A. K. R. Kiralfy
A General Theory of Absolute Liability in the Law of Contract

Mr. D. Sugarman
The Transformation of English Company Law 1750-1900

Professor B. Z. Beinart
The History of the Law of Associations

Mr. J. Styles
From 'an offence between man to an offence against property'

Dr. N. Narayanan Nair
Indian Legal History as an Integral Part of British Legal History

Professor D. Giesen
The Law and Religious Minorities in Post Tudor Ireland

Professor E. F. J. Tucker
Shakespeare's Knowledge and Dramatic Use of Law and Equity

A symposium was also held on the Teaching of Legal History. It was led by Dr. J. H. Baker and was based upon his collation of the response to a questionnaire which he had circulated to all universities.

The Birmingham Conference was held at the invitation of the Faculty of Law. The Faculty's conference committee was composed of Professor B. Z. Beinart (Dean), Dr. E. W. Ives, Dr. A. H. Manchester (Convenor), Mr. P. J. Cook and Mrs. V. Edwards (Deputy Convenors). At that time the Conference Continuation Committee was composed of: Dr. J. H. Baker (Cambridge), Professor W. H. Bryson (Richmond, Virginia, U.S.A.), Dr. M. T. Clanchy (Glasgow), Professor A. Harding (Liverpool, formerly of Edinburgh), Professor D. Jenkins (Aberystwyth), Dr. A. H. Manchester (Birmingham). A further conference was convened at the University of Bristol in July 1981 by Mr. Hugh Beale and Dr. J. A. Guy, and the sixth is to be held at the University of East Anglia in July 1983, organised by Miss Michele Slatter and Dr. Roger Virgoe.

Since the Birmingham Conference was held Professor B. Z. Beinart has died. We trust that the universal recollection of both the breadth and depth of his scholarly interests as well as of his personal kindliness will be stimulated still further by the publication of these wide-ranging essays which are the fruits of a conference over whose arrangements he presided with his usual charm and skill.

ABBREVIATIONS

Manuscript Sources

Manuscripts are cited by location, class mark and call number, except for material in the Public Record Office which is cited by class mark and call number only, according to the following schedule.

ASSI35	Clerks of Assize, Indictments
C1	Chancery, Early Proceedings
C44	Chancery, Files, Judicial Proceedings (Common Law Side), Tower Series
C47	Chancery, Miscellanea
C66	Chancery, Patent Rolls
C67	Chancery, Patent Rolls, Supplementary
C78	Chancery, Decree Rolls
C144	Chancery, Criminal Inquisitions
C145	Chancery, Miscellaneous Inquisitions
C244	Chancery, Files (Tower and Rolls Chapel), *corpus cum causa*
C260	Chancery, Files (Tower and Rolls Chapel), *recorda*
CO96	Colonial Office, Papers, Gold Coast, Original Correspondence
CO137	Colonial Office, Papers, Jamaica, Original Correspondence
CO280	Colonial Office, Papers, Tasmania, Original Correspondence
CO408	Colonial Office, Papers, Tasmania, Entry Books
CP40	Common Pleas, Plea Rolls
E41	Exchequer, Treasury of Receipt, Deeds, Series AA
E404	Exchequer of Receipt, Writs and Warrants for Issue
JUST1	Justices Itinerant, Eyre Rolls, Assize Rolls, Etc.

JUST2	Justices Itinerant, Coroners' Rolls
JUST3	Justices Itinerant, Gaol Delivery Rolls
KB9	King's Bench, Ancient Indictments
KB27	King's Bench, Coram Rege Rolls
KB29	King's Bench, Controlment Rolls
KB140	King's Bench, Miscellanea
KB145	King's Bench, Files, Recorda
LR11	Exchequer, Land Revenue, Estreats of Court Rolls
SC2	Special Collections, Courts Rolls

Printed Sources, etc.

AmJLH	*American Journal of Legal History*
Anglo-AmLR	*Anglo-American Law Review*
APC	*Acts of the Privy Council*
BIHR	*Bulletin of the Institute of Historical Research*
BL	British Library
BPP	British Parliamentary Papers
CalChR	*Calendar of Charter Rolls*
CCR	*Calendar of Close Rolls*
CPR	*Calendar of Patent Rolls*
CSPDom	*Calendar of State Papers, Domestic*
EcHR	*Economic History Review*
EHR	*English Historical Review*
ERO	Essex Record Office
HMC	Historical Manuscripts Commission
HMSO	Her Majesty's Stationery Office
ICLQ	*International and Comparative Law Quarterly*
JLJ	*Jamaica Law Journal*

KRO	Kent Record Office
LQR	*Law Quarterly Review*
PRO	Public Record Office
Rot. Parl.	*Rotuli Parliamentorum*
SR	*Statutes of the Realm*
SS	Selden Society
TRHS	*Transactions of the Royal Historical Society*
YB	*Year Books*

INTRODUCTION

A.H. Manchester and E.W. Ives

(i) Towards a Modern Perspective

An academic conference usually has a distinctive character of its own. It is compounded in part of place and of personality, but it also reflects the programme on offer. From the start, the papers which were offered to the Fourth British Legal History Conference, a selection of which form the present volume, were seen as cautiously innovatory. Substantial time was allocated to what has always been the medieval bedrock of the subject and to that more recent outcrop, the legal history of early Modern England. But while it is clear that interest in these periods remains high and that contributions maintain their customary high scholarly standards, the conference also sought to reflect the increasing attention which has been given in recent years to newer fields. In particular there was an interest in both comparative legal history and modern legal history, especially that of the nineteenth century.

Of course an interest in comparative legal history is not new, although it has been little developed in recent years. Such a relative lack of interest in the contribution which this country's concept of law and of the legal system made to the administration of the largest empire which the world has ever known is surely remarkable. Certainly there have been some valuable studies of the impact of the common law upon early colonial legal systems, especially in the U.S.A.[1] We look forward to similar studies being undertaken in other countries. We look forward also to studies of the manner in which like systems and concepts have developed, and differed, in different countries within a common legal culture. After all it is now some years since Robert Stevens reminded us that nobody – 'with the possible exception of the officers of the American Bar Association and editors of the Law Quarterly Review – now believes that, because some substantive rules are couched in similar terms in the United States and England, the two legal systems are thereby made the same.'[2] Stevens looked forward especially to comparative studies of legal institutions.

Nor can anybody who is familiar with nineteenth-century legal reform possibly be ignorant of the flow of information and of ideas

[1] G. Haskins, *Law and Authority in Early Massachusetts* (New York, Macmillan 1960).

[2] R. Stevens, 'Unexplored Avenues in Comparative Anglo-American Legal History', *Tulane L.R.* 48: (1973-74) 1086.

between countries during that period. One does not think only of correspondence between individuals e.g. Scott-Story or Pollock-Holmes, important although that is. Many Royal Commissions and Select Committees made considerable efforts to learn how well overseas legal institutions and legal rules worked. Other countries, not only within the empire, sought to learn from us. For example, our criminal procedure – and especially our jury system – was of considerable interest to other countries in Western Europe at the beginning of the nineteenth century. Nor can those whom the interaction between law and opinion fascinates, fail to be engaged by the extra dimension to that interaction which stems from the fact that the country whose law is under examination is but a colony and so subject to numerous influences from the mother country.

Rather more attention has been given in recent years to modern legal historical studies. How they will develop is another matter. In the U.S.A. Willard Hurst has placed considerable emphasis upon the in-depth study of a particular topic, most notably in his exhaustive analysis of the Wisconsin Lumber industry.[3] Yet others, some of whom owe something to Hurst, have also been ready to adopt a rather broader approach to the study of modern American legal history.[4] In England one of the editors of this volume has chosen to link the study of modern legal history with that of law reform with a view to illuminating the social processes of the law.[5] Truly the possibilities for further study in these areas are both exciting and numerous. Legal history is flourishing, therefore. Indeed, the attendance at the Birmingham conference of a number of legal historians from Western Europe, in addition to our friends from the English speaking world, illustrates the opportunities which exist for extending the boundaries of our study of comparative legal history.

To what extent the promising condition of legal historical scholarship is reflected in the popularity amongst undergraduate students of the subject is uncertain. Certainly, a symposium at the conference upon the teaching of legal history did offer some grounds for optimism. Yet scholarship cannot fail to contribute to that necessary enthusiasm for the subject which alone will foster a fresh generation of enthusiasts, no matter how they define their subject, and no matter

---

[3] W. Hurst, *Law and Economic Growth: The Legal History of the Lumber Industry in Wisconsin, 1836-1915* (Harvard; 1964).

[4] L. Friedman, *A History of American Law* (Simon and Schuster, 1973) M. Horwitz, *The Transformation of American Law* (Harvard 1977).

[5] A.H. Manchester, *A Modern Legal History of England and Wales 1750-1950* (1980).

what their personal philosophy of legal history may be.[6] To that end
the British Legal History Conferences will continue to make a
valuable contribution.

(ii) Law, history and society: an eternal triangle

The year which sees the publication of these papers from the fourth,
and the assembling of the sixth British Legal History Conference, sees
also the seventy-fifth anniversary of the death of F.W. Maitland. No
one who knew him as a teacher and scholar can be still alive – a
majority of the legal historians practising today hardly, if at all, knew
his successors Holdsworth and Plucknett – and yet we recognise
Maitland as the Cortez of our profession. What would he make of us
today? He would, doubtless, be amazed by the vitality of legal history;
Maitland hardly expected to be the inspiration of a growth industry!
The sophistication of early legal studies would gratify him, in many
ways reflecting, as it does, the continuing impetus of his own work. In
1884 and 1888 Maitland wrote on itinerant royal justice, in 1885 on
the seisin of chattels, in 1889 on ancient demesne, in 1909 his lectures
on equity were published — all subjects continued in the essays in this
collection.[7] He would without question welcome increasing concern
in recent years with post medieval law, where his pioneering interest
was frustrated by premature death. The famous questions of *English
Law and the Renaissance* lie behind all the exploration of Tudor
equity discussed below by J.A. Guy :'The Shallows and Silences of
Real Life' remains a prescient comment on aspects of a Victorian law
reform which is only now, as we have seen, receiving serious attention
from legal historians.[8] Maitland, we can be certain, would also
applaud as long overdue the signs in this (and the previous) volume of
conference papers of a retreat from English common-law myopia by
admitting the Scots, and an abandonment of British insularity by
bringing in the law of former imperial and colonial territories.[9]

[6] For a recent survey see G. Parker, 'The Masochism of the Legal Historian',
University of Toronto Law Journal 24. (1974) 279.

[7] *Pleas of the Crown for the County of Gloucester before the Justices Itinerant,* ed.
F.W. Maitland (1884); *Select Pleas of the Crown,* ed. F.W. Maitland, SS 1 (1888);
F.W. Maitland, 'The seisin of chattels', in *LQR* 1 (1885), 324-41; *Select Pleas in
Manorial Courts,* ed. F.W. Maitland, SS 2 (1889); F.W. Maitland, *Equity;* also, *The
Forms of Action at Common Law,* ed. A.H. Chaytor and W.J. Whittaker (Cambridge,
1909).

[8] F.W. Maitland, *English Law and the Renaissance* (Cambridge, 1901); F.W.
Maitland, 'The Shallows and Silences of Real Life', in *The Reflector,* 1 (1888), 113-
117.

[9] See below, and *Law-Making and Law-Makers in British History: Papers presented
to the Edinburgh Legal History Conference 1977,* ed. A. Harding (London, 1980).

4

Maitland might, thus, be pleased with us. On the other hand, he would probably feel that the bringing together of the teachers of law and the teachers of history had only partially resolved the tension between the two disciplines which he discussed in his inaugural lecture at Cambridge in 1888 when he spoke of:

> different logics, the logic of authority, and the logic of evidence. What the lawyer wants is authority and the newer the better; what the historian wants is evidence and the older the better.[10]

He had in mind, it is true, the contrast between legal historian and legal practitioner. It is also true, as J.H. Baker has argued recently, that there is positive benefit in bringing together different approaches.[11] Nevertheless, legal historians trained in law and legal historians trained in history (a breed which Maitland found inconceivable) do often start from different positions and with different expectations.[12] Legal history is a Siamese twin.

It is easy to appreciate this if the positions are stated in an extreme form. The lawyer is trained to think of the past in a vertical fashion, from the root in earlier generations to the flower – or weed – of today. When he approaches legal history his instinctive course is to trace the growth of seisin, *assumpsit* or the like, or, alternatively, to chronicle the development of a jurisdiction. Should he choose instead to investigate a legal problem in a particular historical context, he will still tend to think in terms of a local answer to a generic problem — contract, tort, the family and so on. By contrast, historians follow what is distinctively a lateral fashion of thinking: their brief is to write about the past, as Ranke said, 'as it actually happened'. They are brought up to ask what significance events have at a particular period in the past and to be suspicious of categories which presuppose the right way of looking at a problem. If adopted in its full rigour, such an approach would even see the title of Maitland's inaugural – 'Why the History of English Law is not written' – as nothing less than the invocation of a chimera. Only in a very obvious sense has there been a continuing history of English law to write about – the label on the can ignores the wide variation of the contents. To the legal historian trained in law such a posture must appear that of the observer of an assembly line who is so fascinated with the mechanics of one process that he fails to notice either the remaining stages or the growing vehicle which the

---

[10]F.W. Maitland, 'Why the History of English Law is not written', in *Collected Papers,* ed. H.A.L. Fisher (Cambridge, 1911), i. 491.

[11]*Legal Records and the Historian,* ed. J.H. Baker (London, 1978), p. 1.

[12]Maitland, *Collected Papers,* i. 486, 493-4.

track carries. Reverse the positions, and the lawyer may appear like the erstwhile professor of history who ended every lecture on political ideas with the equivalent of: 'However, it was not what Machiavelli wrote at the time which was important so much as the stimulus he gave to other thinkers.'

Actuality has not mirrored these extremes for a number of reasons, not least that few historians have maintained, or would maintain that lateral thinking, the distinctive feature of their discipline, is also the exclusive mode proper to historical discussion. The study of change through time is integral, too. Thus, constitutional historians have had a viewpoint close to that of legal historians trained in law, and studies of institutions read much the same whoever holds the pen. But where the Siamese nature of legal history is a serious problem is in the study of society. To the social historian the lateral dimension takes priority over the chronological, and when he turns to the law he finds himself asking questions of a new and disturbing kind. The law obviously exercises a formative influence over society, but what does the law represent? Even if we allow, with Thrasymachus, that justice represents the interest of the strongest, or agree with Marx that systems of law embody and support the interest of the dominant economic class, we still have to explain how such influences operate. The contemporary mechanism would be the control and enforcement of legislation, but this was not a major factor in English legal history until the nineteenth century and later – although it would include rare episodes such as the granting of Magna Carta, Edward I's statutes and the occasional instance of royal high-handedness both in making and applying the law. Yet if there was no well-articulated procedure for legislation and policing, how was legal change effected? Since case law dominated the system, this question requires us to explain what it was which caused judges in one generation to extend, modify or even reject the judgements of their predecessors. What, too, of those numerous procedural changes which were too small and too technical even for judicial decision, still less for any legislation, but were of crucial importance in making movement possible; where did these originate? Furthermore, society undoubtedly changes under the impact of factors other than law. Surely such change must in turn put law under pressure to accommodate the new situation. The law shapes society certainly, but is it not itself shaped by society, a relationship of both cause and effect? And if so, how does this pressure operate? Questions of this kind are complex, difficult and subtle, but they are the questions which social history asks of law.

By the nature of things, the relationship between society and law will be most revealingly demonstrated when either one or the other or both are changing. This was the case in England between, say, 1490 and 1740 when major social, economic and political changes were accompanied by a major reconstruction, or rather, major reconstructions of the law. Some commentators have felt that a Marxist analysis makes the most sense of this. It is, after all, the case that the arrival of chancery protection for the mortgagee early in the seventeenth century and the development of the strict settlement in a somewhat later period, made England a country safe for aristocrats. There is, too, the striking contrast between the encouragement given to charities by courts and parliaments before the Civil War and the atmosphere surrounding the 1735 Mortmain Act which stigmatised charitable endowments 'rather as an act of injustice towards the heir-at-law, than an act of charity in the donor'.[13] As for the legal profession, is it not notorious that lawyers were archetypal capitalists?

The motivation of legal change is, however, more complex than may first appear. For one thing, the law is almost a third party in any change, along with lawyers and legislators. To take again the example of the law of charity. Judges and politicians in the eighteenth century might feel reluctant, but the weight of settled case law in favour of charity was such that 'the inherited, generous conception of legal charity' had to be respected.[14] Analogous to this authority of established principle has been the sanctity of due process. The courts of Henry VIII could not deny Thomas More's right to argue a motion in arrest of judgement, however damaging, any more than the Interregnum government could dispose of John Lilburne unheard.[15] It is, furthermore, important to note that in case law and in legislation, change can sometimes be forced on the courts. Just as during the Industrial Revolution developments in fields as diverse as banking and railway travel brought to the judges issues of a new kind to which they had to apply existing concepts as best they might, so in the earlier period, bills of exchange, joint stock companies, enclosures and similar issues put their predecessors on the spot.[16] Nor is it correct to suggest that the class prejudice of the profession made the outcome inevitable. Not only was class often irrelevant, for example in litigation about negotiable instruments, but even given a man like Edward Coke

[13] G. Jones, *History of the Law of Charity, 1532-1827* (Cambridge, 1969), p.111.
[14] *Ibid.*, pp. 106-7.

[15] J.D.M. Derrett, 'The trial of Sir Thomas More', in *EHR* 79 (1964), 450-77. For a substantial demonstration of the respect for due process see G.R. Elton, *Policy and Police: the Enforcement of the Reformation in the Age of Thomas Cromwell* (Cambridge, 1972).

[16] For common-law litigation on bills of exchange in the sixteenth century see *The Reports of Sir John Spelman*, ed. J.H. Baker, SS 93, 94 (1977, 1978), ii. 286.

whose judgements, opinions and prejudices are well documented (along with their fluctuations), it has proved impossible to confine him within a coherent definition of economic or class interest.[17] Still less is it possible to categorise a bench of judges deeply involved as individuals in purchase and exploitation of land, which nevertheless, as the sixteenth century drew on, extended to tenants a protection at common law against landlords which had previously only been available in equity.[18] The relationship between society and the law is anything but simple.

The value of asking 'social history' questions of the law has already been demonstrated in recent studies of crime in early-modern England.[19] We are now able to see that the way in which pleas of the crown are recorded in the archives of a court tells us not about crime but about the bureaucratic despatch of offenders in custody, and only about that.[20] On the one hand, neither the date and nature of the offence given in an indictment, nor the description and place of origin of the offender are necessarily correct; these were entered according to the way in which judges and court clerks decided, agreed or were persuaded to designate both crime and criminal. On the other hand, whether an individual was convicted and hanged, still more, whether he was or was not prosecuted in the first place, and on what charge, depended, we now realise, on the feelings of the victim and the sympathies and attitudes of the community. Judges and juries were sensitive (as they had always been) to the circumstances and to the character of the accused; it is no accident that of thirty-seven people charged with felony at sessions of gaol delivery for the borough of Colchester between 1575 and 1577, only, perhaps, two were hanged, the one guilty of bestiality and the other of a particularly bloody domestic killing.[21] Furthermore, the decision to prosecute, and the vigour of any prosecution depended on the victim, and victims often would not press their case, or would make a lesser charge, or would proceed by civil process or would decide to take no action at all.

[17]Cf. D.O. Wagner, 'Coke and the rise of economic individualism', in *Economic History Review* 6 (1935), 30-44, and B. Malament, 'The "Economic Liberalism" of Sir Edward Coke', in *Yale Law Journal* 76 (1967), 1321-58.

[18]*Reports of Spelman*, ii. 256.

[19]For a survey of recent work, see E.W. Ives, 'English law and English society, 1450-1700', in *History* 66 (1981).

[20]J.S. Cockburn, 'Early-modern assize records as historical evidence', in *Journal of the Society of Archivists* 5 (1975), 215-31 and 'Trial by the book? Fact and theory in the criminal process 1558-1625', in *Legal Records and the Historian*, pp. 60-79.

[21]J.B. Samaha, 'Hanging for felony: the rule of law in Elizabethan Colchester', in *Historical Journal* 21 (1978), 763-82.

8

Felony, misdemeanour, trespass, civil and criminal – the safe categories collapse around us. The consequence is not only that we now need to correlate the records of all the courts which had criminal jurisdiction over a given area, the mammoth task spelled out by L.A. Knafla below, but the horrid prospect beckons of bringing in civil litigation as well.

The need to examine court records on a broad front is not only a challenge to historians interested in crime. Traditional analysis of non-criminal law has concentrated on the reported decision – reasonably enough since this has been, *prima facie,* where lawyers have gone to find their law. But when exploring change in law – especially the adaptation of old and the adoption of new actions in the fifteenth and early sixteenth centuries – we must not forget mesne process, or so the drift of recent research would suggest.[22] We have, in effect, to approach the law as the litigant did, with immediate concern for the utility and efficacy of the start of a suit, not its eventual hearing years away. The evidence is most complete for the action of *assumpsit,* where early decided cases are rare, in marked contrast to the number of suits commenced and abandoned. What plaintiffs were evidently concerned to do was to discover procedures which would compel defendants to settle, and the threat of an action was sufficient in a majority of cases; there was no need to fight the suit to judgement. Even what historians have often seen as a defect in the system – the possibility of suing in several courts at once – and the popular, though exaggerated reputation of the law for uncertainty, were both of benefit here, at least to the plaintiff. How uncertain the outcome if the defendant forced the plaintiff to make good his action, and how certain the bill for costs? And if this motivation could lie behind litigation, an important corollary follows. Once an action had been accepted by court officials and had proved its usefulness in bringing defendants to heel, the more it would be used, irrespective of the fact that it had never been tested in court. And if that action became a commonplace, the presumption would be raised that the remedy was sound in law or, at the least, was open to argument.[23] Indeed, if this 'new opinion' became talked about and favourably received at the inns of court, it could be that when an action eventually was tried, the court did little more than accept a *fait accompli.* On this construction it was the litigant who could generate real momentum for changes in the law to

[22]*Reports of Spelman,* ii, 256; M. Blatcher, *The Court of King's Bench, 1450-1550* (1978), pp. 111-37.

[23]Cf. the dicussion in *YB* Hil. 11 Hen. VII, p. 11 f. 15, quoted in E.W. Ives, 'The origins of the later year books', in *Legal History Studies* 1972, ed. Dafydd Jenkins (Cardiff, 1975), p. 139.

accommodate the needs of society; we are on the wrong tack if we concentrate exclusively on the alleged social bias of the profession and on the prejudices of judicial dicta. The law responded to the laws of supply and demand.

In the present state of our knowledge it is impossible to say how generally this hypothesis would apply to English law before the Reformation, still less to the changed law of the late sixteenth century and after. But it does raise a further issue of major importance for legal history. Clients beginning an action of *assumpsit* in the circumstances described were clearly not intending to fight a law-suit. Technically they can be classed as litigants, but what they believed themselves to be doing was something far nearer sending a final demand today. In other words, to understand the part played by law in society we need to ask what men thought they were doing when they appealed, as we think, to its procedures and authority. S.F.C. Milsom made a similar point some years ago in relation to the development of substantive law – the terms in which a society conceives of its law and the procedures which embody those conceptions, necessarily determine the issues which that law can cope with and shape the way in which those issues are understood – but the application is general.[24] It is clear, for example, that a majority of contested legal issues in the two centuries and more before the Civil War were settled by negotiation of some kind. Certain examples of this would effectively qualify as what, today, we would call formal arbitration, but it would be an anachronism to set negotiated settlements in this period within the ambit of the law, recognised by the courts and subject to their rules. Out-of-court settlements, both the few which could be now classed as arbitration and the great majority which could not, were in essence political. They were the means by which conflicts could be resolved in the interest of harmony within the community and a due recognition of status, prestige and obligation. In one sense out-of-court settlement was an appeal to an older authority, to a set of organic hierarchical and communal values. Such thinking even underlay the regular reference of cases to arbitration by the early courts of Chancery and Star Chamber and even the direct personal fiat of the king; decision was potentially dangerous, a seed for future trouble, accommodation was the better answer.

It is here, perhaps, that legal historians need to pay attention to anthropologists. To the latter, both litigation and negotiation (in all its varied forms) are modes of dispute settlement, each of which can be

---

[24] S.F.C. Milsom, 'Law and fact in legal development', in *University of Toronto Law Journal* 17 (1967), 1-19.

expected to carry its own set of values, assumptions and expectations.[25] It is, for example, possible to see that the motive in bringing a suit for defamation in an ecclesiastical court had often less to do with offended honour and the wish to disgrace the defamer than with a desire to restore relations with the offender on the basis of his public apology; the restoration of Christian charity was an objective which did strike a genuine response in the hearts of judges, litigants and witnesses alike.[26] Of course too much cannot be extrapolated from this. We do not yet know the position in other procedures and we know that plenty of individuals exhibited quite different motives, litigating trivial matters with a persistence and obduracy which defies simple explanation. But it is precisely the investigation of attitudes to disputes, combative as well as pacific, which is the challenge to the social historian interested in law.

When, in 1901, Maitland was invited, in place of the dying Lord Acton, to introduce a collection of *Essays on the Teaching of History,* he pointed to the increasing sophistication of the still-young discipline.

> History is deepening. We could not if we would be satisfied with the battles and the protocols, the alliances and the intrigues. Literature and art, religion and law, rents and prices, creeds and superstitions have burst the political barrier and are no longer to be expelled. The study of interactions and interdependencies is but just beginning, and no one can foresee the end.[27]

Eighty years later, the interactions and interdependencies of law and society are still only partly explored.

---

[25] Simon Roberts, 'Changing modes of dispute settlement: an anthropological perspective', in *Law and Human Relations,* Past and Present Society (1980).

[26] J.A. Sharpe, 'Litigation and human relations in early-modern England: ecclesiastical defamation suits at York', in *ibid.*

[27] F.W. Maitland, 'The teaching of History', in *Essays on the Teaching of History* (Cambridge, 1901), reprinted in *Collected Papers,* iii. 418.

THE LEGAL TREATISE AND LEGAL THEORY

A.W.B. Simpson

I

One of the curious features of the history of Roman Law up to the time of Justinian is the rarity of legal treatises which take the form of monographs, concerned with one branch or division of the law. Schultz, in *Roman Legal Science,* explained the lack of monographs in terms of the character of Roman legal science: 'A legal science which eschewed legal history, law reform, and legal philosophy, which laid stress mainly on case law and problems was only very mildly interested in system and abstraction, contained no place for a monographic literature of the modern type.' He further argued that failure to develop a monographic literature was one of the reasons why 'the stream of classical literature eventually ran dry'. Remarkable though it may be as the product of a feat of human organisation, the Digest itself is crudely arranged, and could only have been produced at the end of a long tradition of weakness in systematics. Even in the second history of Roman Law the monographic treatise appears late in the day, the study and exposition of the ancient texts being conditioned by their unsystematic arrangement until Jean Domat set himself the task of expounding the civil laws in their natural order. Roman legal science did, of course, produce the form of literature known as *Institutes,* the earliest example being Gaius's *Institutes.* The work was updated by Tribonian, Dorotheus and Theophilus and published as an educational text possessing legislative force in 533 A.D. In this version, or, as we would say, edition, the Roman literary form of *Institutiones* survived to influence legal literary culture in the mediaeval and modern period. But in the ancient world Gaius's work never generated monographic treatises taking the form of expanded expositions of its parts. If this had occurred, we should, presumably, never have been given the Digest.

Schultz's comments explaining the rarity of monographic treatises in Roman Law might well have been written of the common law; though no doubt one might wish to qualify them in some respects. Yet eventually it came about that our system did generate and sustain a treatise literature; it is further remarkable that in the United States the practice of writing treatises, having at one time been very strong indeed, has to-day more or less died out, and may die out with us too. In this paper I want to trace the development of the treatise tradition in the common law system, and develop an idea that was suggested by Schultz in relation to Roman Law. Schultz attempted to explain the literary activity of the ancient Roman lawyers by reference to the state of legal science, and though he does not in this context greatly develop this idea, he no doubt had in mind the fact that the forms of legal literature are closely related to lawyers' ideas of what it is, *qua* lawyers, they are doing, and what is the appropriate way for jurists, as jurists, to behave. More radically, I wish to suggest that certain literary forms are closely related to theories as to the nature of law itself, and that this is in particular true of the treatise.

By 'treatise' various forms of legal literature may be intended; what for present purposes I have in mind has been clearly identified by Plucknett in *Early English Legal Literature* (he uses the term text-book):

> The characteristic of the modern English text-book which concerns us at this moment is its method. It begins with a definition of its subject matter, and proceeds by logical and systematic stages to cover the whole field. The result is to present the law in a strictly deductive framework, with the implication that in the beginning there were principles, and that in the end those principles were found to cover a large multitude of cases deducible from them.

This description will sufficiently identify the type of literature I mean by the term treatise. Some subsidiary characteristics also need to be noted. The first is that the classical treatise is a monograph, purporting to deal only with a single branch of the law which is conceived of as possessing some quality of unity; treatises, unlike institutional works, are not comprehensive, though resembling institutional works in other respects. Thus Bracton, in my sense, is not a treatise, nor is Blackstone. The second is that the principled character of the treatise involves substantive principles, and excludes works whose structure is primarily determined by procedure. Hence Glanvil is not in my sense a treatise, whilst Stephen on *Pleading* is; indeed, the rise in the significance of substantive law may go hand in hand with the rise in the treatise. The third is that the boundary between a good treatise, a bad treatise, and something which is not worth regarding as a treatise at all is indefinite; the treatise is an ideal type, and in what follows I shall not be concerned to notice all works which might, arguably, be viewed as treatises of very poor quality.

II

For very considerable periods of its history the common law system produced hardly any treatises at all. In the mediaeval period the only one of any significance is Littleton's *Tenures.* So far as institutional works are concerned, there is only one which qualifies, and that is Britton, and it is conceivable that Britton's claim to Royal authority is imitative of the legislative force of Justinian's *Institutes*. The *Tenures,* whatever its merits, was hardly more than a tract, comprising approximately only 8,000 words of law French text in three books. Although my main concern is with a later period it is worth pausing to consider this remarkable literary anomaly, which has yet to receive full scholarly study. There is no sense in which Littleton merely systematises or digests cases, or is in any way based upon cases. The three books purport to provide the high theory which enables the reader to understand ' the arguments and the reasons of the law'. What is stated in the form of definitions, principles and distinctions is the author's understanding of the ' common learning' of the tiny coterie of lawyers whose views constituted the common law, and which was the presupposition of legal argument and debate. There are few references to actual cases, though many to hypothetical, and the author is quite uninterested in providing authority for his propositions, a fact which strikingly differentiates the *Tenures* from later treatises.

How the *Tenures* came to be written is mysterious, and there were no imitators. I suspect, but cannot show, that the books may have begun as lectures. The failure of Littleton to generate a tradition is perhaps explained by the very fact that the work was anomalous, and was unrelated to the educational exercises established in the later fifteenth century in the Inns. As to its intellectual basis, I shall say something later in this paper.

III

In the long period between the publication of the *Tenures* and the end of the seventeenth century there was a massive increase in the quantity and variety of legal literature available. The introduction of printing, coupled with the increase in the size of the legal profession, assisted this development, though for much of the period the printing of common law books was artificially restricted under the system of royal patents. But although attempts were made to write treatises, virtually nothing was achieved; the great books of the law in this period, the works of St. Germain, Fitzherbert, Rastell, Plowden, Dyer, Brooke, Coke, West, Rolle, Dodderidge, are not treatises. The typical form of literature was the collecting of statutes or cases (the two authoritative types of material). Parasitic upon these were systematising abridgements and indices, there were also formularies of various types, glosses on authoritative texts, and expositions of procedures. No doubt to these generalisations certain qualifications can be made. Hale I exclude, since his work was unfinished and long remained unpublished. Sir William Staunford's *Les Plees del Coron* (1557) and his *Exposition of the Kinges Prerogative* (1567) constitute treatises of a rudimentary sort, and the dedication of the latter makes the point that Staunford was quite consciously attempting to produce a new type of book, and thought that the route to producing such literature lay through a development out of the Abridgement, the established form of systematising literature.

Lawyers and their critics were, of course, fully aware of the disorderly and unmethodical appearance of the common law system. In so far as the law essentially was embodied in an oral tradition preserved and transmitted by those who practised in Westminster Hall, only long years of direct involvement could produce the belief that the system really was rationally coherent. One reaction to disorder was practical. From the fifteenth century onwards lawyers, sometimes for their own personal use and sometimes co-operatively, attempted to reduce the unwieldy mass of legal materials by digesting it under titles arranged, for the want of any better system, alphabetically. This generated the abridgements and common-place books, which remained a dominant form of legal literature until the nineteenth century; in a somewhat modified form the abridgement tradition has survived in such works as *Halsbury* in England and the *Corpus Iuris,* and *Corpus Iuris Secundum* in America. The systematising efforts of the compilers of abridgements made possible the production of a treatise literature based upon further analysis and subdivision of the material abridged. This was a process quite distinct from that which produced Littleton's *Tenures.* The *Tenures* is quite unrelated to any form of digest or abridgement of texts of cases; instead it states a systematic version of an oral tradition. William Staunford, as we have seen, saw clearly the route from abridgement to treatise. Less dramatic steps down this road could be, and indeed were taken. Once the material is sorted under titles, the next obvious move is to arrange the material within each title systematically by substance, rather than by a random, or chronological or position in the tray, or stream of consciousness sytem. This is not attempted in Statham (c. 1481) Fitzherbert (1514-16) or Brooke (1573). It is by Rolle (1668) and more elaborately by Viner (1741-53). Bacon's *Abridgement* (1736-66) goes further by directly expounding the law, and relegating the authorities to the notes. The process culminates either in the splitting up of the abridgement into separate monographs, or alternatively in the legal encyclopaedia, of which Halsbury's *Laws of England* (1907-17) is the classic English example, and the *Corpus Iuris* (1914-37) the American counterpart. An extraordinary feature of the evolution of the abridgement or digest form is the length of the process; it is worth noting, *en passant,* that in the civil law the process took even longer.

A striking example of an unsuccessful attempt to progress through the abridgement form to the treatise is William Sheppard's *Actions upon the Case for Deeds, Contracts, Assumpsits, Deceipts, Nuisances, Troves and Conversions, Delivery of Goods, and for other Malefeasance and Misfeasance,* which appeared in 1663. This is a substantial work of 387 pages (excluding the table of cases and index), and is dedicated to Lord Clarendon. The preface also indicates the way in which such a treatise is essentially evolved out of the abridgement tradition, and the text confirms this. Sheppard starts out boldly in an attempt to state, in a systematic way, the doctrine embodied not in oral tradition but in the multifarious published cases. His book begins at a high level of abstraction with a section entitled 'Of Actions in General'. There is a definition, followed by subdivisions. Twenty pages or so later, Sheppard's inability to arrange his material in a coherent manner has reduced the book to a disorderly abridgement of cases; by page 202 he has more or less given up. The rest of the book simply contains abbreviated reports of cases; the first 395 are described as; 'Some choice Cases for the illustration, and confirmation of all that is before said about Contracts and Assumpsits'. Sheppard's failure is explicable at one level simply by his lack of analytical skill; he was not clever enough at the job. But more generally it is noticeable that with the exception of Staunford and Hale the ablest lawyers who turned to writing in this period did not select the treatise form as a vehicle for exposition, presumably because of a recognition of its extreme difficulty, so Sheppard perhaps deserves some credit at least for bravery.

There was an alternative to this evolutionary process of modifying and refining the essentially crude structure of the earlier alphabetical abridgements. This was to make a heroic attempt to construct, by rational analysis, a comprehensive scheme for systematising the law. This feat was first attempted and achieved by Hale, and the resulting *Analysis of the Laws of England* made Blackstone's *Commentaries* possible. Hale's *Analysis* was by any conceivable standards an extraordinary achievement, and it is hardly surprising that it was unique.

IV

The practical approach to the untidy condition of the law then was to tidy it up, to systematise it. The alternative theoretical approach was to maintain that it was, in reality, already systematic, however improbable this claim might appear to the uninitiated. Here I must digress into jurisprudence.

The first major assault on Professor Herbert Hart's celebrated *The Concept of Law* (1961) was launched in 1967 in the *University of Chicago Law Review* by Professor Ronald Dworkin in an article entitled 'Is Law a system of Rules?' In this and subsequent writings and revisions Dworkin has boldly and somewhat improbably disinterred the belief in the existence and central significance of principles of law, lurking behind and making rational the apparently disorderly and arbitrary process of decision and adjudication. It is all as though the realists had never happened, and legal science still reigned. More recent and flamboyant expositions of this view have claimed that there is always, or almost always, a right answer to a legal question if one cares to dig, and there is now a growing and elaborate literature on the subject. This pays virtually no attention to the historical pedigree of the theory involved, which is (as are most things in jurisprudence) of extreme antiquity. It is not my concern in this paper to discuss the theory in its various forms analytically, but merely to relate it to the history of legal literature. So far as the civilian systems are concerned, there is an extensive literature, and as an amateur in that field I can only refer to Professor Stein's brilliant study, *Regulae Iuris.*

There are, however, indications that the late medieval common lawyers also accepted the idea that the common law was in part based upon what were called *maxims, grounds* or *principles.* This idea is found in an elaborate form in Fortescue's *De Laudibus* (c. 1470) where the *principia, maxima* or *universalia* of the common law are identified with the *regulae iuris* of the civilians. These maxims or principles were thought to possess certain special qualities. First, they were ultimate in that they could not be supported by any further arguments or logical demonstrations; hence it was idle to argue with anyone who doubted one, and equally idle to attempt to demonstrate a principle by arguments from authority. Secondly, they were self-evidently rational, or at least not contrary to reason. Thirdly, they had always been accepted, and thus they were timeless features of a timeless system. Fourthly, although only skilled lawyers could work out the detailed application of principles, yet their nature was such that even a layman could, by knowing the principles, acquire a general knowledge and understanding of the law which was deducible from them. With the belief in principles went a belief in there always being a right answer, and in the fifteenth and sixteenth centuries disagreement amongst the judges was regarded not as a reason for voting to resolve the dispute, but as a reason for continuing the debate until the right answer appeared; hence the interminable argument of great cases over periods of years.

The natural and sceptical reaction to the claim that the law is derived from principles is to ask for a statement or list of them, a request which was sometimes rather evasively handled. Thus in *Doctor and Student* the doctor is made to remark: 'I should like to hear some of these maxims'. The student obligingly replies: 'A large volume would not suffice to declare them fully, of which maxymes however in answer to your request I shall hereafter showe the part'. The large volume was not forthcoming. In the seventeenth century, when the somewhat similar and related claim for the existence of 'fundamental laws' was common, Edmund Walker in the course of discussions of Strafford's impeachment naively asked to be told what they were. Serjeant Maynard crushed him by saying that, 'if he did not know that, he had no business to sit in this House'. But no list was forthcoming. One is reminded of the modern jurisprudential theory of a rule of recognition, whose existence is asserted, but never made flesh; jurists never attempt to state specifically a particular rule of recognition. The theory of principles did rather better. Thus St. Germain did at least list twenty-five maxims, and in time the theory indeed produced a considerable literature. Stein himself argued that the earliest treatise, Littleton's *Tenures,* is an example:

> Thomas Littleton's *Tenures,* which was written between 1475 and 1481, a few years after Fortescue's treatise, was the first exposition of English land law based on principles instead of as a number of disconnected formulae concerning the procedure of real actions.

He points out that the author in a number of passages actually uses the terms principle and maxim to refer to basic propositions of law. It is difficult to be certain that the author was, as it were, self-consciously operating a legal theory in writing the *Tenures,* but I suspect that Stein is correct for a reason he does not mention; this is the virtually complete absence in the text of any citation of authority. It was quite central to the theory that principles or maxims neither needed authority nor support from argument, nor could any be provided. Coke put it thus: 'A maxime in law. A maxime is a proposition to be of all men confessed and granted without proofe, argument, or discourse. *Contra negantem principia non est disputandum.* ' Dr. Baker has also pointed out that the *Tenures* was called *les grounds de Master Littleton,* so that it was conceived of by contemporaries in the terms Stein has suggested.

But Littleton's *Tenures* neither belonged to nor founded a literary tradition, and the chief literary expression of the theory of principles produced a quite different form of literature which is now quite extinct. Just as the compilers of the Digest had lumped together in Title 50 *(De Diversis Regulis Iuris Antiqui)* a disorderly collection of *regulae iuris,* so common lawyers set about the task of making and publishing, and, inevitably commenting upon, collections of legal maxims. The best known early example of this form of literature is Bacon's collection of twenty five maxims. This was originally submitted to Queen Elizabeth I in 1597 to illustrate a general scheme to make the law more coherent and intelligible both to lawyers and to people generally. Bacon in fact had in mind a general scheme for restating English law, but he did not wish to alter the character of the system by codification, turning it, as he put it, into 'text-law'. A collection of maxims, together with a book of *Institutes,* and a book of *Terms of the Law* was to contribute to this operation principally at an educational level. The main body of the restatement was to consist of *Abridgements.*

After the publication of Bacon's *Maxims* in 1630, various other collections appeared – William Noy's *Treatise of the Principall Grounds and Maxims of the Lawes of this Kingdom* in 1641, Edmund Wingate's *Maximes of Reason* in 1658. Noy's was a small book, originally written in law French; it claimed to be 'A summary consideration of the whole law, divided into the laws of reason, custom, and statutes', these being the 'grounds' of the law of England, reason being the ground of the common law itself. In the section on the common law are listed a number of maxims under the sub-divisions Theology, Grammar, Logic, Philosophy, Political, Moral Rules, and Law Constructions. These are then illustrated and explained. Wingate is a much more considerable work of some 772 pages, setting out and commenting upon some 214 maxims. They include, interestingly enough, as number 147 'None shall take benefit or advantage of their own wrong', which, as you will recall, features prominently in Professor Dworkin's celebrated article 'Is Law a System of Rules?' This presumably derives from *Digest* 50.17 134.1 where the form is *Nemo ex suo delicto meliorem suam conditionem facere potest, a regula iuris* attributed to Ulpian. In the nineteenth century, the best known example is Broom's *Legal Maxims,* an enormously successful work which ran to ten editions between 1845 and, incredibly, 1939. In the third edition of 1858 Broom comments upon 105 maxims and lists 595, mainly in Latin, though a few are in law French; he arranged them under ten subject categories. Herbert Broom was a law teacher, and lectured as Reader to the Inns of Court in Common Law; he was a prolific author and his book was primarily intended for students, though he hoped it might be useful to barristers 'who may be desirous of applying a legal Maxim to the case before him'. His view of the place of maxims or principles is set out in the prefaces to his *Commentaries on the Common Law* (1856) and *Legal Maxims* (1845);

> In the Legal Science, perhaps more frequently than in any other, reference must be made to first principles. Indeed, a very limited acquaintanceship with the early Reports will show the importance which was attached to the acknowledged maxims of the law, in periods when civilisation and refinement had made comparatively little progress.

In simpler ages reference to these maxims 'so manifestly founded in reason, public convenience, and necessity, as to find a place in the code of every civilised nation' solved most problems; the complexity of modern life, though reducing their direct utility, has not deprived them of fundamental importance. Some are rather 'deductions of reasons' than 'Rules of Law', and can only therefore be *illustrated*. Broom here implies that specifically *legal* maxims require support from authority, by way of showing their reception, and 'by way of illustration, qualification or exception'.

It was possible for collections of maxims to be arranged not by an alphabetical scheme, but by some more rational substantive method, and thereby become a mechanism for the production either of a complete institutional scheme of arrangement, or of a scheme for ordering a particular branch of the law. In the seventeenth century, as Dr. Prest has shown, logical schemes for methodising the law (or any other body of learning) enjoyed a considerable vogue, and such schemes could be applied to the maxims of the law in an attempt to produce a systematic legal exposition. The most notable product of this movement was Finch's *Law,* posthumously published in 1627. Its arrangements influenced later institutional writers, particularly Thomas Wood, and in some degree perhaps Blackstone, but not, apparently, Hale. But although Finch's methodical scheme for expounding the 'body of our lawes' – what we would call substantive law – was workable and, until Hale produced a better one, the best on offer, his schematic division of maxims by source (though interesting jurisprudentially), was a dead end, and could never have formed the basis for either an institutional or a monographic exposition of the law. The last significant collection to methodise maxims was Edmund Wingate's *Maximes of Reason* (1658); later collectors of maxims, such as the author of *The Grounds and Rudiments of Law and Equity,* returned to an alphabetical scheme.

Though Broom continued to be edited until 1924, and although maxims still feature in legal exposition, argument and justification, they are now regarded as slightly comical, and the form of literature directly related to them is dead. It is noticeable too that in modern theoretical works they are hardly, if at all, mentioned as 'sources of law'. I doubt whether the revival, in a new guise, of the theory associated with them will generate new collections of legal principles for Dworkin's judge Hercules to rely upon. The decline of this form of literature is partly explained by the rise of the treatise, which expounded the law in a different and more coherent way than was possible by any rearranged scheme of maxims. Three other factors may have been significant. Firstly, it came to be thought improper to invent maxims; one could only collect them like zoological specimens. By their nature they ought to be as established and antique as possible. Hence, the collector was inhibited from attempting more elegant and satisfactory exposition of the law; he was in a sense condemned to unoriginality, though he could gloss his texts. Second, maxims had to be in another language, normally Latin; the maxims of equity form an exception here. A text built upon Latin tags could not continue to generate respect once the dominance of the traditional classical education declined; stylistically, the use of Latin maxims, once thought elegant, is now a subject for jokes. Third, the tradition enshrined in collections of maxims was that the common law formed a coherent whole; this view has given way to the view that only individual branches of the law are coherent, and even this view is now doubted. Maxims have for a variety of reasons come to appear archaic.

V

Plucknett regarded the treatise as essentially a product of the nineteenth century, and suggested that the great name in its history would, when that history came to be written, be that of Joseph Story, whose first treatise, one of nine, appeared in 1832. Story chose the law of bailments as the first branch of the law to expound. It is not without significance that this was a subject which had been chosen by an earlier and celebrated treatise writer, the great literary scholar Sir William Jones, whose *Essay on the Law of Bailments* had been published half a century earlier in 1781. Although it was in the nineteenth century that the treatise became the dominant form of legal literature, it is in the eighteenth that it first became established.

The great publishing event of the eighteenth century was of course the appearance of Blackstone's *Commentaries* in 1765-9, preceded by the *Analysis of the Laws of England* in 1757. The Commentaries originated in lectures delivered in Oxford from 1753 onwards. After 1758 these were delivered by Blackstone as Vinerian professor, the endowment being derived in part from the other great legal publication of the century, Charles Viner's twenty-three volume abridgement (1741-57). Blackstone was an institutional work, but its success must have considerably encouraged the production of monographic writing in a literary style; certainly before it appeared there was little indeed of any substance published. Apart from embryonic works such as Ballow and Nelson we are left with only two pre-Blackstonian treatise writers – Hawkins and Gilbert. Sergeant William Hawkins (1673-1746) was a Cambridge graduate and an Inner Temple man, and his *Treatise of the Pleas of the Crown*, whose first volume deals with the substantive law, was published in 1716-21 and ran through seven editions in the eighteenth century, and one in the nineteenth. Hawkins was, of course, able to utilise as a quarry earlier work, particularly Coke's *Third Institute*. This in part explains the provenance of the work; it belongs to a tradition started by Staunford and continued by Pulton and Coke. But the principal obstacle to institutional or treatise writing is the daunting problem of methodically arranging essentially disorderly material; given a usable scheme, all that is needed is hard work, together of course with analytical and literary skills. Hawkins, like Blackstone after him, relied on a scheme devised by Sir Mathew Hale; in a real sense both works were posthumous products of Hale's analytical genius. The motivation of Hawkins is explained in his preface; he set out 'to vindicate the Justice and Reasonableness of the Laws concerning criminal Matters, and to reduce them into as clear a Method, and explain them in as familiar a Manner, as the Nature of the Thing will bear.' The 'method' was in reality Hale's work, not Hawkins'.

The position of Sir Geoffrey Gilbert (1674-1726) in the history of the treatise is far more intriguing and problematical, for although a fair amount is known about his writings they have not been made the subject of a modern study, as they deserve. A very considerable corpus of monographic writing is attributed to him, all of it appearing after his death. Apart from two collections of reports, monographs on no fewer than sixteen distinct branches of the law appeared in print between 1730 and 1763 dealing with the following subjects: Devises (1730), Tenures (1730), Uses and Trusts (1734), Dower (1734), Common Pleas (1737), Court of Exchequer (1738) Debt (1740), the Constitution (1740), Ejectment (1741), Evidence (1754), Court of Chancery (1756), Equity (1756), Distress and Replevin (1757), Rents (1758), Executions (1763), Kings Bench (1763). In addition,

22

considerable parts of Mathew Bacon's five volume *New Abridgement of the Law* up to the title *Simony* (published between 1736 and 1766) were lifted from manuscripts of Gilbert, and in the fifth edition of that work by Sir Henry Gwillim in 1798 a treatise by Gilbert on Remainders was published from one of Francis Hargrave's manuscripts and a manuscript treatise on both formal and informal contracts (including mortgages) survives. Some of Gilbert's works appeared in more than one version, and some appeared in disguise.

> It was the hard fate of the excellent writings of the late Chief Baron Gilbert to lose their author, before they had received his last corrections and improvements, and in that unfinished state to be thrust into the world, without even the common care of an ordinary editor.

Further investigation might well locate other works by Gilbert or derivation from his writings; I suspect that *A General Abridgement of Cases in Equity* (1732) may be an example. In the absence of a scholarly study of Gilbert's life and work it may be premature to form a view as to how or why he came to write so much; so far as I know there is no direct evidence on the question. However, it is at least probable that Gilbert had been engaged upon a comprehensive encyclopaedia of the law, and that the treatises are, as it were, segments of a work of this character developed out of the abridgement tradition.

Blackstone himself was, as I have said, an institutional writer, not a writer of monographs, and he wrote not primarily for lawyers but for what are now called intelligent laymen, a concept which includes law students who are, by definition, laymen. Now Blackstone, it must be remembered, was essentially a civilian and an academic; his disappointed ambition was to become professor of civil law at Oxford. His principal contact with legal practice dates from after the publication of the *Commentaries,* not before, and had he not become Vinerian professor and published the *Commentaries* I think it is safe to say that nobody would ever have heard of him as a common lawyer. Placed in the context of common law writing, the *Commentaries* appear to belong to no tradition; nothing remotely resembling them had appeared in the English language before. It must however be remembered that in the eighteenth century quite a number of very substantial legal works, presumably intended for intelligent laymen rather than specialists, were published in English and appear to have been well received. These strangely forgotten works belong to the civil and natural law tradition, though one such work, Thomas Wood's *An Institute of the Law of England,* or, *the Laws of England in their Natural Order, according to Common Use* (1722) took as its subject matter the common law. Some were translations of continental jurists – Jean Domat (1704-22), Baron Pufendorf (1710-29), Jean Burlamaqui (1748, 1752, 1784). Others were home produced – Thomas Wood (1704), John Ayliffe (1734), John Taylor (eight editions between 1754 and 1828), Thomas Rutherford (1754). At this time a familiarity with the principles of civil and natural law (not very clearly distinguishable) was regarded as a desirable part of general education for gentlemen. Hence scholarly, substantial legal works, written in stylish prose, and available in handsome editions were apparently widely read (or at least purchased) in eighteenth-century England before Blackstone published his *Commentaries*. But apart from Wood's *Institutes*, an uninspired work, nothing comparable had emerged from the common law world since Bracton, five centuries earlier. Blackstone, disappointed in his ambitions as a civil lawyer, became Vinerian Professor in 1758. He set himself the task of doing for the common law what had already been done for the civil, and vindicating his new charge as a rational system 'built upon the soundest foundations, and approved by the experience of ages'. Indeed, whilst extolling the virtues of the civil law he sounded a note of caution:

> we must not carry our veneration so far as to sacrifice our Alfred and Edward to the names of Theodosius and Justinian. . . if an Englishman must be ignorant of either the one or the other, he had better be a stranger to the Roman than the English institutions.

A spirit of nationalistic self-satisfaction permeates the *Commentaries*, and it is striking that once English law had been expounded in the language of the scholar and the gentleman, as civil law had previously been, legal writing generally took on a *literary* character it had previously wholly lacked. The publication and success of Blackstone must have encouraged this development, as it must have encouraged the writing of more detailed studies of branches of the law which had been treated in outline by the master. Furthermore, the discursive literary style of the *Commentaries*, which sharply differentiated such a work from glosses on lists of maxims, must have furthered the idea that this was the better way to expound the principled science of the law.

In the later eighteenth century there were published a number of significant monographs; the two earliest were described as 'essays' – Charles Fearne's *Essay on the Learning of Contingent Remainders and Executory Devises* (1772) and Sir William Jones's *Essay on the Law of Bailments* (1781). Both works were of an elegant but esoteric character. Charles Butler spoke of Fearne's *Essay* in much the same way as Coke spoke of Littleton, though with more realism: 'No work, perhaps, on any branch of science, affords a more beautiful instance of analysis: but it is not immediately perceivable by any person, to whom both the subject and the work are not familar'. Jones's *Essay* was more self-consciously based upon a system which Sir William thought could be applied to any branch of the whole science of the law:

> Should the *method* used in this little tract be approved, I may
> possibly not want inclination, if I do not want leisure, to discuss
> in the same form *every* branch of *English* law, *civil* and *criminal*,
> *private* and *publick;* after which it will be easy to mould into
> distinct works, the three principal divisions, on the *analytical*,
> the *historical*, and the *synthetical* parts.

Fearne and Jones were followed by a number of treatise writers of varying attainments, the most important being Park, Bayley, Kyd and Powell. Of these John Joseph Powell (*c.* 1755-1800), was perhaps the most important and successful treatise writer of the later eighteenth century, writing major works on Mortgages (1785), Powers (1787), Devises (1788) and Contracts (1790), as well as producing a collection of conveyancing precedents. He also edited Fearne (1795), and is thought to have been his pupil. Of Powell, little is known. He had been admitted to the Middle Temple in 1775 and called in 1780, and what impelled him towards legal writing is not known. His books, which were clearly vary successful, expressed the standard theory of the time – law was a science, founded upon principle, and the aim of the treatise writer was, as he put it in his book on contracts, to 'discover the general rules and principles of natural and civil equity' upon which the decisions of the Courts were based. He explained that 'all reasoning must be founded on first principles. The science of the law derives its principles either from that artificial system which was incidental to the introduction of feuds, or from the science of morals.' This was the classic credo of the treatise writers.

VI

In nineteenth-century England the legal treatise came to be the typical form of creative legal literature. Many of the authors of the nineteenth-century treatises are still, in name at least, familiar to all English lawyers, either because their works have lived on in 'editions', or because their treatises are still consulted. Everyone knows of Woodfall on *Landlord and Tenant* (1802), Sugden's *Vendors and Purchases* (1805), Chitty on *Contract* (1826), Stephen on *Pleading* (1827), Lewin on *Trusts* (1837), Jarman on *Wills* (1841-4), Williams on *Real Property* (1845), Blackburn on *Sale* (1845), Williams on

Personal Property (1848), Taylor on *Evidence* (1848), Mayne on *Damages* (1856), Fry on *Specific Performance* (1858), Lindley on *Partnership* (1860), Benjamin on *Sale* (1868), Pollock on *Contract* (1876), Anson on *Contract* (1879), Pollock on *Tort* (1887), not to mention the most successful, and possibly the worst, of them all, Archbold's *Criminal Pleading and Evidence* (1822), which remains the essential Do-It-Yourself manual for the Crown Court practitioner. The authors of the nineteenth century were men of varied background. Some few, like Archbold, were professional legal writers; others, like Chitty, were practitioners who were also involved in the provision of legal education. Some wrote to advertise themselves, or simply to make ends meet. More curious explanations exist as to why some lawyers turned to authorship. Leake was apparently encouraged to write through deafness, which ruined his practice. Woodfall, it is said, broke his leg. In the later nineteenth century the tradition of treatise writing by academics began with Pollock and Anson, though it is only in very recent times that academics have tended to predominate. This is hardly surprising; in England, university-based legal education has only existed on any considerable scale since the second world war. So far as the form of the treatise is concerned, the most interesting development, though it came to nothing, belongs essentially to the history of the codification movement. It took the form of writing treatises in the form of codes, the code being the logical next step in the process of systematisation beyond the discursive treatise. This was attempted by Stephen, Chalmers and Pollock, and imitated by others.

The treatise writers of the nineteenth century, in so far as they self-consciously embraced a theory of law, inherited and claimed to express the belief that private law essentially consisted in a latent scheme of principles, whose working could be seen in and illustrated by the decisions of the courts, where they were developed and applied. These principles the text writer set out to expound in a rational and coherent method, as was appropriate to a science. Though the legal theory associated with the treatise tradition is still expressed to this day, there has been, I suspect, a significant decline in the belief that these principles (or at least many of them) are of universal validity; hence, the link between the treatise and the belief in natural law has become attenuated almost to vanishing point. To writers who claimed to be formulating universal rational principles, the lack of personal authority was not particularly significant; it was what they wrote, not the fact that they wrote it, which mattered. With the decline in this spirit the treatise writer's formal status inevitably declines, since what he says appears to matter only in so far as it can be supported by judicial authority, or is accepted as correct by the judiciary. He, who

has no authority, relies on authority and not on reason. This approach
is typified by Chalmers, who, in a preface to his *Digest*, written in
1878, explained that a proposition of law in a Digest (as contrasted
with an authoritative code) 'merely amounted to a verifiable hypothesis
as to what the law is' and the verification he had in mind was by cases.
This is the spirit of positivism.

VII

In America the history of the legal treatise took a rather different
course. The first significant expository work was Zephaniah
Swift's *System of the Laws of Connecticut* (1795-6), and it was Swift
who was the first American treatise writer. Nathan Dane's
Abridgement, published in eight volumes between 1823 and 1824,
was the first attempt to offer American lawyers an alternative to the
English abridgements (particularly Bacon's *Abridgement)* on which
they had previously had to rely, and the publication of Kent's
Commentaries between 1826 and 1830 provided an indigenous
alternative to Blackstone which was hugely successful. In 1829,
Joseph Story, who had been appointed Justice of the Supreme Court
in 1811, became the first holder of the chair endowed by Nathan Dane
at Harvard, and from 1832 until 1845 he published his remarkable
series of treatises – on *Bailments* (1832) *the Constitution* (1833),
Conflicts (1834), *Equity* (1835), *Equity Pleading* (1838), *Agency*
(1839), *Partnership* (1841), *Bills of Exchange* (1843), *Promissory
Notes* (1845). Had his health not broken down (he died in that year,
partly through overwork), further treatises would have followed.
Thereafter in America the treatise writing tradition was firmly
established, and such works were produced on an extraordinary scale.
From Story's time onwards, the production of treatises was associated
with organised, systematic legal education; this was of course
developed much earlier in America than in England, and on a much
more impressive scale. This does not mean that the treatise writer
was, typically, a cloistered academic, since the law schools until
Langdell's time employed experienced practitioners as professors.
But the writing of treatises became an appropriate and prestigious
activity of law professors.

The establishment of the treatise-writing tradition in American
took place in a climate of thought very different from that which
obtained in England. The treatises dealt of course with the common
law. But there had, after all, been an American revolution, and there
was a certain incongruity in the continued use and further reception of
a disorderly body of law which was essentially English, and many

aspects of which were regarded as highly objectionable. There was also a strongly established dislike and distrust of lawyers as a professional class, and the evolution of a legal profession was in any event a recent innovation, and one which was by no means universally welcomed. The early American legal writers were, in a sense, on the defensive, and for this reason they were anxious to demonstrate that the enterprise upon which they were engaged, the exposition of the American common law, was a respectable one. Obviously, it would not do for them to present the common law as English judge-made law which Americans for some bizarre reason should continue to respect in spite of the revolution. They wrote in a nationalistic spirit, and inevitably stressed the American character of the law which they expounded, and the degree to which English common law had been rejected or modified in American. On the other hand, the amount of indigenous material available to them was extremely limited, and they therefore made extensive use of English materials, materials which could not be presented as possessing any authoritative character in America. The theory of law which was appropriate to their writings was essentially that of the rationalistic natural lawyers. Law was a science, based upon rational principles, and the function of the jurist was to expound these principles in a systematic manner; in his search for them he might appropriately use any juridical material which came to hand, both as a source of illumination, and as illustrative material. Story in particular wrote in this eclectic spirit, and quotes in his preface to his treatise on *Agency* Sir William Jones's assertion that 'What is good sense in one age must be good sense, all circumstances remaining, in another; and pure unsophisticated reason is the same in Italy and in England, in the mind of a Papinian or a Blackstone.' Jones was indeed something of a favourite, since he had in his *Essay* pointed the way to a style of treatise writing which suited American conditions. In this spirit it was possible to ransack not only the English and American sources, but also the civilians and natural lawyers for the best law, an enterprise which had the additional advantage of demonstrating the author's scholarly abilities, and contributing thereby to the prestige of the author and the task on which he was engaged. And so the treatises poured out, culminating in the vast works of Williston, Corbin and Scott.

Yet in American today the treatise is more or less dead as a form of legal literature; it will probably turn out that William Prosser was the last prestigious American treatise writer. I should like to close with some speculations as to why this has come about. From the very beginning the treatise in America had to contend with the fact that American law was administered in a considerable number of different jurisdictions, each state potentially possessing its own common law, a potentiality which came to be fully realised. This jurisdictional fact was obviously an obstacle to the exposition of a universal common law by the text writers, but not perhaps a fatal obstacle; they could still aim to present a rational scheme of private law and hope that it would, by its very intellectual force, be received in the various State jurisdictions. The problem presented by the multiplicity of juris- dictions was aggravated by another phenomenon – the rising bulk of legal material, particularly law reports, and this in its turn went hand in hand with an increased significance attached to reported decisions. As more and more cases became available, they were bound to be used. Even in the early nineteenth century, when the problem in reality hardly existed, the sheer quantity of legal books was a continual source of alarm and complaint. All this threatened the treatise tradition; how could the systematic writer reconcile his presentation of the law as a coherent set of principles with the shambles accumulating in the law libraries?

One possible reaction is associated with Christopher Columbus Langdell. Langdell did not invent the idea of legal science, which had been a commonplace of legal thought long before his time, nor did he invent the case-book. He has, however, two achievements to his credit or discredit which are relevant to the history of the treatise. His version of legal science was one in which, although the principles of the law were to be found in cases,

> the cases which are useful and necessary for this purpose at the
> present day bear an exceedingly small proportion to all that have
> been reported. The vast majority are useless, and worse than
> useless, for the purposes of systematic study.

This theory enabled the treatise writer to purvey a sort of higher or better law in much the same spirit as that in which the medieval civilians presented the better law of the Digest; it licenses the systematiser to cope ruthlessly with bulk and diversity. Langdell's other achievement was, of course, the case method of instruction, and this generated a need for a type of literature which generations of American academics have spent their energies producing – the case- book, or today the collection of cases and materials. Lectures can readily be turned into treatises; case-books cannot. But although after Langdell's time the production of case-books and the writing of law review articles (it was during his Deanship that the *Harvard Law Review* was founded) came to absorb a very considerable output of creative energy, the great treatises, what one might call the ultimate legal treatises, are products of this century – multi-volume works like

Wigmore, Williston, Scott and Corbin. So the decline of the treatise cannot be blamed upon Langdell.

What appears to me to have deprived the treatise of its intellectual respectability was the realist movement which, however inchoate it may have been, has profoundly affected the attitude towards law of the products of American law schools. Lawrence Friedman, the recent author of the first general history of American law, and himself a graduate of a leading and not notably *avant garde* law school, thus describes the activities of the draftsmen of the American Restatement with unconcealed derision:

> They took fields of living law, scalded their flesh, drained off their blood, and reduced them to bones. The bones were arrangements of principles and rules (the black letter law), followed by a somewhat barren commentary. . . . . The chief draftsmen, men like Samuel Williston and Austin W. Scott of Harvard. . . . . were authors of massive treatises in the strict, Langdell mold. They expended their enormous talents on an enterprise which, today, seems singularly fruitless. Incredibly, the work of restating (and re-restating) is still going on.

This view of the enterprise of methodising the law is plainly quite incompatible with the flourishing of a treatise tradition which sets a special value upon the very enterprise which Friedman thinks is singularly fruitless. In taking this line, Friedman (whom I only quote by way of example) merely reflects a view which is now perfectly widespread. Now the school of thought which adopts a somewhat cynical approach to the assertion that the common law consists in a body of principles, and which ridicules the claim that common law adjudication is anything but arbitrary, has a long history in both England and America. There is nothing new in the iconoclasm of the American realists in their iconoclastic moods: Jeremy Bentham said much the same a century or more earlier. What is new is the reception of this notion among lawyers, and in this sense the great contribution of this movement to legal theory has been the recognition that it is possible to have lawyers, and flourishing lawyers, without law in the sense in which law has been traditionally understood. Whatever the merits or demerits of this arrangement, it finds no place for the legal treatise.[1]

---

[1] This paper is an abridged version of a fuller study of the history of the legal treatise, and is here presented in essentially the form in which it was delivered at the Conference, without supporting notes; a fuller annotated version is available in the University of Chicago Law Review for 1981.

REMEDIES FOR CHATTELS

J.L. Barton

The doubts which were expressed in the Middle Ages upon the question whether a *praecipe quod reddat* for chattels would lie against the third hand have sometimes been assumed to reflect a Germanic idea that a man should seek his trust where he placed it. Be this as it may, by the early fourteenth century the view of the common lawyers seems rather to have been that there is a distinction between a simple detention of another's goods and a wrongful detention. A detention will be wrongful if the defendant have contracted to restore the goods to the plaintiff, and do not. It will be wrongful if the goods were wrongfully taken. It will not be wrongful if the defendant have the goods by the delivery of the person who had the custody. Thus, it is not enough to allege merely that the goods are mine, and that they have come to the hands of the defendant.[1]

As a reporter points out in Michaelmas Term of 6 Edward II, the law is otherwise if the chattel in demand be a deed evidencing my title to freehold land.[2] This is a chattel of a very special kind. The reporters of the early fourteenth century do not seem wholly certain whether a writ for title-deeds be properly *detinue*, or a distinct form of action *de cartis reddendis*.

It is this limitation upon the scope of the action for wrongful detention which accounts for the longevity of the *actio de re adirata:* the finder is no trespasser.[3] When the appeal of larceny still lay against any possessor, this action was merely a civil form of the appeal, and Bracton seems to assume that if the possessor deny the claim, the owner's only course is to count against him a second time, adding words of felony, and thus appeal him.[4] This would be a dangerous course, once the possessor was no longer required to show how he had come by the goods, but might plead the general issue and put himself on the country. If the jury found that the goods were the appellor's, but that the appellee did not take them, but found them, the appeal failed and the goods were forfeited to the King.[5] It is not wholly clear how this difficulty was met. An obscure note in the year-

[1] *YB* Trin. 16 Edw. II, 490.

[2] *Year Books of Edward II,* xiii, SS 34 (1918), 167 (headnote). Compare *Year Books of Edward II,* iii, SS 20 (1905), 123

[3] *YB,* Trin. 46 Edw. III, pl.1 f.15.

[4] Bracton, f.150b.

[5] Inter North., 3 Edw. III, Corone 367.

book of 21 & 22 Edward I states that a plaintiff who demands a thing as *endiré* may be required to make his law, his own hand the twelfth, *ke la chose ly fut endirée*.[6] It is unusual to give the proof to the plaintiff rather than to the defendant, but the reporter may have been thinking of the defendant who claims nothing in the goods, but puts the plaintiff to proof of his title. In one of the two forms of count for this action in the *Novae Narrationes*, the plaintiff is made to allege that he formally offered to prove his title before the bailiffs and men of the vill.[7]

The action for wrongful detention seems to have been substituted for the *actio de re adirata* less because of any deficiencies of the older remedy than because, once it had been settled that no action would lie against the executor in any case in which the testator might have waged his law, the common lawyers were obliged to hold either that the bailor had no remedy for the goods after the death of his bailee, or that the executors of the bailee might be charged not as executors, but because they had the goods: they chose the latter alternative.[8] It could still be argued as late as 1370 that though *detinue* will lie 'for the mischief' against any possessor after the death of the bailee, in his life it lies against him alone.[9] By this date, however, the general view was that *detinue* might be deemed an action founded upon property, and in 1371 we find it used in place of the *actio de re adirata*, against a defendant who has seized the plaintiff's ass as an estray and, according to the plaintiff, has refused to restore him upon tender of a reasonable sum for his keep.[10] The count upon a trover first appears in the last years of the century.[11]

The change created problems. It was a moot question whether one executor of a bailee might be sued without his co-executors, on the ground that he was being sued as possessor and not as executor.[12] The difficulty was finally avoided by holding that the possession of one executor is the possession of all.[13] It seems never to have been finally

[6]*Year Books of Edward I*, Rolls Series (1863-79), ii. 467.

[7]*Novae Narrationes*, SS 80 (1963), 329.

[8]*Year Books of Edward III*, Rolls Series (1883-1911), x 511; *YB* Trin. 29 Edw. III, 38

[9]*Ibid.*, Mich. 43 Edw.III, at f.29a, *per* Belknap, sjt.

[10]Compare the first objection to the plaintiff's count Trin. 1 Edw. II, in *Year Books of Edward II*, i, SS.17 (1903), 29 and in *YB* Hil. 39 Edw.III, f.6. *Ibid*, Pas. 44 Edw. III, pl.30 f.14.

[11]*Year Book 13 Richard II*, Ames Foundation (1929), Mich., p.56.

[12]Pas.31 Edw.III, Briefe 341; *YB* Hil.39 Edw.III, 5.

[13]*Ibid.*, Mich. 41 Edw.III, pl.35 f.30.

settled whether one executor of a bailee who appeared alone at the grand distress might be required to answer without his companions by 9 Edward III, st. 1, c. 3, or whether the case were outside the statute because he was being sued for a wrong which he had himself committed, not for a duty of his testator's.[14] It could be argued that the bailee of goods which were not his bailor's property had charged himself twice over by his own folly, to his bailor upon the bailment, and to the owner upon a trover.[15] This seems to have been an opinion to be professed rather than applied. There is no reported case in which such a bailee actually was charged twice over, and in 1460-61, when it was finally necessary to decide the point, Prisot C.J. held that the rival plaintiffs should interplead, since it would be unreasonable for the defendant to be twice charged when there was no default in him.[16]

The difficulty is a significant one, however. In becoming an action based upon property, *detinue* had not ceased to be an action based upon contract. The plaintiff who sues upon a bailment, as distinct from a trover, does not allege any property in himself, though counsel anxious to oust the defendant of his law may argue that *detinue* does not lie for goods which have been 'wasted', and that account is therefore the proper remedy.[17] It is submitted, therefore, that Brian C.J.'s observation in 1479, that where the goods have been altered but the property has not been changed the bailor may have *detinue*, and that he has taken it for clear law that a plaintiff who can recover the thing shall never have an action on the case, has been misunderstood.[18] A rather shocked reporter points out in a note that if this be law, the bailor will be without remedy for damage to his goods, save where he recovers all in damages because the goods are completely destroyed. The action on the case was the ordinary remedy for misbehaviour by the bailee, whether he had damaged the goods, or misused them, or merely used them in a manner not authorised by the bailment.[19] Hence Brian C.J. argued in 1473 that it would lie merely against the original bailee, and not against a sub-bailee from him, but his brethren

[14]*Ibid.*, Hil.11 Hen.IV, pl.20 f.45; Hil. 13 Hen.IV pl.2 f.12; Hil.14 Hen.IV, Pl.30 f.23, pl.37 f.27; Pas. 2 Hen.V, pl.29 f.6; Mich.21 Hen.VI, pl.1 f.1; Mich.7 Edw.IV, pl.23 f.20.

[15]*Ibid.*, Trin.9 Hen.VI, pl.9 f.17; Hil.9 Hen.VI, pl.4 f.58; Mich.19 Hen.VI, pl.6 f.3.

[16]*Ibid.*, Hil.39 Hen.VI, pl.3 f.22.

[17]*Ibid.*, Mich.22 Edw.IV, pl.10 f.29, at f.30 a *per* Brian C.J. *Ibid.*, 20 Hen. VI pl. 2 f.16.

[18]*Ibid.*, Hil.18 Edw.IV, pl.5 f.23.

[19]*Ibid.*, Pas. 12 Edw.IV, pl.20 f.8, *per* Brian C.J.; Hil.21 Edw.IV, pl.9 f.75, at f.76b, *per* Nele and Pigot, sjts.; Hil.21 Edw.IV, pl.24 f.79.

were against him on this point.[20] It does not seem to have been thought material in this case that the plaintiff had an action of *detinue* pending for the same goods.[21] The difficulty in the principal case was that the plaintiff had alleged that the defendant had broken up the plate confided to him, and had converted it to his own use. The phrase is an old one. In the civil law, the *tutor* who converted his pupil's money to his own use was charged with interest at the maximum legal rate.[22] Since the canonists tended to argue by analogy from the tutor to the executor it is not surprising that in the common law the executor who converts the goods of his testator to his own use is answerable to creditors *de bonis propriis*.[23] So, if a defendant in trespass *de bonis asportatis* justified for distress damage feasant, it was a good replication that he had converted the goods to his own use.[24] It would have been imprudent, to use no stronger language, for a defendant who had made away with the goods to plead a plea which would estop him from denying thereafter that he had them, and that he was bound to restore them upon payment of amends. It would seem that any bailee who keeps the goods for his own purposes, rather than from simple malice towards his bailor, may be said without impropriety to convert them to his own use. The bailor who complains that his goods have been converted is clearly renouncing his property and hoping to recover all in damages. It is this, it is submitted, which explains the violence of Brian C.J.'s reaction. If case will lie for conversion, there will be little room left for *detinue*. It is not easy, however, to offer a reason why the action should not be competent. Case lies against a bailee for misconduct, and a bailee who makes away with the goods certainly misconducts himself. That a bailor could not have an action on the case if he might maintain *detinue* was certainly new law, and that a bailor whose property was divested could not maintain *detinue* was, if not a completely novel suggestion, one not hitherto countenanced by authority. *Detinue* had lain before 1479 for goods which could no longer be restored, and where the goods had been lost by the bailee's misbehaviour it was concurrent with the action on the case.[25] Thus in 1473, the Common Pleas had to consider whether it were a good plea in case against a bailee by whose neglect a horse had died that the

[20]*Ibid.*, Mich.12 Edw.IV, pl.9 f.13.

[21]*Ibid.*, Mich.12 Edw.IV, pl.2 f.11.

[22]Digest 26.7.7.4.; Codex 5.56.1.

[23]*YB* Mich.11 Hen.VI, pl.9 f.16; Pas. 11 Hen.VI, pl.28 f.35; Mich.34 Hen.VI, pl.42 f.22; Mich.9 Edw.IV pl.27 f.47.

[24]*Ibid.*, Mich.28 Hen.VI, pl.24 f.25.

[25]*Ibid.*, Mich.5 Edw.III, pl.24 f.38, at ff.39b-40a, *per* Herle J.; Trin.3 Hen.VI, Judgment 5.

34

plaintiff had previously brought an action of *detinue* for the same horse, in which the defendant had made his law.[26] We do not have their decision, but it was not suggested in the argument that if one of these actions were well brought, the other must have been ill brought. Brian C.J. did not wish to permit bailors to oust bailees of their law by using case as a substitute for *detinue*. In 1505 Thomas Frowyk, the next noteworthy Chief Justice of the Common Pleas, held that it was no objection to an action on the case that a formed action would have lain on the same facts, provided that the action on the case were brought for a different wrong, and though his brethren were not prepared to agree that it would lie for the non-delivery of goods sold, they seem to have held that it would lie for their conversion, provided that property had passed.[27] In the King's Bench in the same year, Fineux C.J. held that in an action of trespass for breaking bulk and converting the goods abstracted, the conversion was the only material allegation, and the breaking bulk was not issuable.[28] With both the Chief Justices in favour of the new action, its success was assured.

It is submitted, therefore, that it is beside the point to seek for an original 'conversion' which would have left the plaintiff without remedy by action of *detinue*. The argument that conversion originally meant a *specificatio* – the extinction of property in goods by their transformation into some new thing – depends upon the assumption that *specificatio* was recognised by the common law.[29] The common lawyers did admit that the property in chattels might be extinguished if they were converted from personalty to realty by incorporation into another's freehold, but no other change in their character was material so long as it was possible to identify them.[30] Since, at the end of the fifteenth century, it was for some time uncertain whether the common lawyers were not going to receive the distinction between *fructus naturales* and *fructus industriales,* there is every reason to think that the civilian doctrine of *specificatio* was consciously rejected.[31]

[26] *Ibid.*, Mich.12 Edw.IV, pl.10 f.13.

[27] *Ibid.*, Hil.20 Hen.VII, pl.18 f.8. See also Robert Keilwey, *Reports d'Ascuns Cases* (1688), ff.69b, 77a, and for the declaration, A.K.R.Kiralfy, *A Source Book of English Law* (1957), p.150.

[28] YB Mich.20 Hen.VII, pl.13 f.4. For a fuller account of the case see J.H.Baker, *The Reports of Sir John Spelman,* ii, SS 94 (1978), 249.

[29] A.W.B.Simpson, 'The introduction of the action on the case for conversion', in *LQR* 75 (1959), 364.

[30] YB Mich.35 Hen.VI, pl.3 f.2, *per* Prisot C.J.; Hil.5 Hen.VII, pl.6 f.15; Mich.12 Hen.VIII, pl.2 f.9 and see Baker, *The Reports of Sir John Spelman,* ii.212.

[31] YB 37 Hen.VI, pl.22 f.35; Pas.12 Edw.IV, pl.10 f.4, at f.5a; Trin.14 Edw.IV, pl.4 f.6; Trin.15 Edw.IV, pl.11 f.31; Mich.2 Hen.VII, pl.4 f.1; Pas.5 Hen.VII, pl.9 f.16; Trin.12 Hen.VII, pl.4 f.25. Compare gl. *non habendam,* Digest 6.1.35.Pr.

It has also been suggested that the common form of declaration in trover was adopted because the finder, as distinct from the bailee, ceased to be answerable in *detinue* if he no longer had the goods.[32] This would have been the case, had *detinue sur trover* been a civilian *actio in rem*. It does not appear that it ever was. Even a determined supporter of the view that the bailee's executors are charged merely on their own possession and not in any respect upon the bailment was not prepared to draw the conclusion that executors who had taken possession of goods bailed to their testator might get rid of them with impunity, and Brian C.J. held that a finder is chargeable in *detinue* in the same manner as a bailee at will.[33] Fitzherbert's *dictum* in 1536, that a finder who has bailed the goods over is no longer answerable in *detinue*, was adopted on one occasion by Wray C.J., but seems never to have been universally accepted.[34] Thus Brooke suggests that the finder is not liable if he accidentally lose the goods, but he will be if he has 'impaired' them or bailed them over, and in *Vandrink and Archer's Case* it seems to have been assumed that the law was the same in trover.[35] We may suspect that the doctrine that the finder who no longer has possession is answerable in case but not in *detinue* developed after the action on the case for conversion, and that its attraction was that it made it possible to argue that this action was not in truth any exception to the 'rule against double remedies'.

For the same reason, it is submitted that the usual sixteenth-century allegation, that the defendant has sold the goods to persons unknown and converted the proceeds to his own use, owed its popularity less to a felt need to show that there was no identifiable defendant against whom the plaintiff might have *detinue* than to a ruling in 1510 that sale of the goods is a misdemeanour for which case will lie.[36] The allegation that the buyers were unknown made it unnecessary for the plaintiff to set out their names in the declaration. Since conversion was the gist of the action, the defendant who had not converted the goods might give this in evidence under the general issue.[37] It is therefore uncertain whether, in the early period, the plaintiff were bound to prove the conversion alleged in his declaration,

[32] S.F.C. Milsom, *Historical Foundations of the Common Law* (1969), pp.326 ff.

[33] *YB* Mich.11 Hen.IV, pl.20 f.45, at f.47a, *per* Hill J.; Mich.12 Edw.IV, pl.2 f.11.

[34] *Ibid.*, Pas.27 Hen.VIII, pl.35 f.13; Anon. (1557), William Leonard, *Reports* (1658-75), iv.189.

[35] Detinue de Biens 40; (1590), Leonard, *Reports*, i.221.

[36] Milsom, *Historical Foundations*, pp.325-6; Anon., Keilwey, *Reports*, f.160a.

[37] 3 Mich. 1 & 33 Hen.VIII, Robert Brooke, *La Graunde Abridgement* (1573), 'Accion sur le Case', 109; 4 Edw.VI, *ibid.*, 'Accion sur le Case', 113.

or whether proof of any conversion would be sufficient. It was not until 1577 that it was actually decided that a traverse of the sale to persons unknown is no plea, since it is the conversion and not the sale that is the cause of the action, but the rule may be earlier.[38] In 1550, a defendant pleaded that the goods were pledged with him for a debt still unpaid, for which he detained them as well he might, and traversed the conversion. According to Brooke, some held the plea good, and others held that he should have pleaded the general issue and given the special matter in evidence for the detainer.[39] Whatever the theory may be, it would seem that a defendant who has refused to restore another's goods is liable to find himself in difficulties if he have no explanation to offer.

We may suspect that the true nature of a conversion was already becoming a mystery of the law. By the end of the century, it was arguable that a refusal to restore goods upon demand was a conversion in itself. This was the opinion of Gawdy J. in *Easton v Newman: detinue* and trover were alternative remedies for the same wrong, as *detinue* and case were alternative remedies for loss by negligent keeping, and debt and case for the non-delivery of goods sold.[40] It was an opinion which did not commend itself to all of his brethren. In the view of Sir Edward Coke, a refusal to restore the plaintiff his goods was evidence from which the jury might infer that the defendant had converted them, but this was not an inference which might be drawn by the court.[41] Alternatively, the phenomena might be saved by invoking a *dictum* of Prisot C.J. in 1455.[42] If my bailee lose goods, I may have *detinue* against the finder, for I might have had *detinue* against the bailee. If I lose my own goods, the finder does no wrong in finding them, and I have no action until he has refused to redeliver them to me, when my remedy is trespass. Littleton at once contradicted him – a refusal to restore could not convert a finder into a trespasser – and we are told that no one answered Littleton's objection.

[38] Anon., Leonard, *Reports,* ii.13. In *Lord Mounteagle v. Countess of Worcester* (1555) there was a similar traverse, which was held bad on the ground that the defendant has concluded with a verification instead of to the country, so that the substantial question was not decided: James Dyer, *Reports of Cases* (1794), 121a; William Bendlowes, *Les Reports . . . des divers Resolutions* (1661), 41; Edmund Anderson, *Les Reports . . . des Mults Principals Cases* (1664), i.20.

[39] 4 Edw.VI, Brooke, *Abridgement,* 'Accion sur le Case', 113.

[40] (1595) George Croke, *The Reports*: Elizabeth (1661), 495; John Gouldesborough, *Reports of. . . Choice Cases* (1653), 152; Francis Moore, *Cases Collect and Report* (1663), 460.

[41] *Isaac v Clark* (1614), Edward Bulstrode, *The Reports* (1688), ii.313; Henry Rolle, *Les Reports* (1675-6), i.131.

[42] *YB* Trin.33 Hen.VI, pl.12 f.26.

However, a trespass will divest the property in goods if the victim of the trespass so choose, and Brian C.J., zealous as ever to maintain the boundaries between actions, had once denied that the victim was entitled to that election which had traditionally been allowed him.[43] If the finder's refusal to restore the goods divests the owner's property, he cannot maintain *detinue,* which is a reason both for holding the refusal a conversion and for allowing the owner to maintain trover. This seems to have been the view of Fenner J. in *Easton v Newman,* and Coke said that it was the ground of the decision.[44] On this view, however, the bailee who refused to restore goods did not convert them. This seems to be the significance of the rather obscure argument in arrest of judgment in *Gumbleton v Grafton,* that the plaintiff had not alleged that he had lost the goods, and that the conversion did not take away the property, but he might have *detinue.*[45] This was a rather desperate objection to urge after a verdict finding the conversion, for it could succeed only on the assumption that no action for the conversion of goods could lie in any circumstances against a bailee, and Moore does not notice it, but the court, in overruling it, observed that the conversion did take away the property. This distinction survived the doctrine that a conversion of goods makes the party converting them a trespasser *ab initio,* which was decisively rejected in *Isaac v Clark,* but Dodderidge J. in that case was of opinion that though the plaintiff was entitled to recover, he could not sue for conversion, but should have brought a special action on the case which was the bailor's proper remedy where the privity of bailment was determined by the misconduct of the bailee.[46] Rolle states that Croke J. agreed with Dodderidge, but according to Bulstrode, Croke held that a denial by a bailee might not only destroy the privity of bailment, but might amount to a conversion, provided that there were a pertinacity and contumacy in the manner of the denial. Rolle, in his *Abridgment,* treats the case as deciding that a denial by a bailee is merely evidence of a conversion, but the emphatic assertions of Coke C.J. and Haughton J. that no denial can ever be more than evidence seem to have led some judges in the later years of the century to take

---

[43] *Ibid.,* Pas.19 Hen.VI, pl.5 f.65. On this see J.B. Ames, 'The disseisin of chattels', in *Lectures in Legal History* (Cambridge Mass., 1913), p. 1616 and P. Bordwell, 'Property in chattels', in *Harvard Law Review* 29 (1916), 374, 351; *YB* Mich.6 Hen.VII, pl.4 f.7, at ff.8b-9; Pas.10 Hen.VII, pl.13 f.27. Contrast *ibid.* Mich.2 Edw.IV, pl.8 f.16.

[44] See above at n.47; *Isaac v Clark* (1614), Rolle, *Reports,* i.131, citing a manuscript report.

[45] (1600) Croke, *Reports,* 781; Moore, *Cases,* 623.

[46] (1614) Rolle, *Reports,* i. 59, 126; Bulstrode, *Reports,* ii.306; Moore, *Cases,* 841: John Godbolt, *Reports* (1653), 210.

38

the view that where trover is brought against a bailee a denial is not even sufficient evidence.[47]

It has been suggested that the roots of this doctrine go back a long way; if an appeal of larceny, or an *actio de re adirata* which was merely an appeal without words of felony, would lie against the medieval finder who would not return the goods, we must take it that the finder who would not return the goods was already deemed a trespasser *ab initio*.[48] It is submitted, however, that this is an anachronistic argument. The doctrine is relatively recent, and is a testimony to the continuing influence of the opinion that if an action on the case is to lie for what is in substance a wrongful detention of the goods of another, it is necessary for the credit of the law to maintain that it is in truth brought for something other than wrongful detention: an opinion whose influence is by no means at an end.

[47] Henry Rolle, *Un Abridgement des Plusieurs Cases* (1668), i.5; *Walker's Case* (1647), William Clayton, *Reports* (1651), 127. Compare the *dicta* in *Holdsworth's Case* (1638) and in *Strafford* v. *Pell* (1656), *ibid.*, 57, 151.

[48] J.B.Ames, 'Trespass de bonis asportatis', in *Lectures in Legal History,* p.61.

THE CARRIER IN LEGAL HISTORY

J.N. Adams

In *The Carrier's Liability* Fletcher argued that the doctrine of freedom of contract played an important part in the development of the law relating to the carrier's notices.[1] That law in turn was the foundation on which the adhesion contract developed. I would like to argue that in the development of the law up to *Parker* v *SER* the doctrine of freedom of contract was of slight, if any, importance.[2] It is in the twentieth, rather than in the nineteenth, century that the doctrine of freedom of contract in this context seems to have had the most influence. I believe that the legal history of the nineteenth century, like that of any other century, can be understood only by detailed analysis. Furthermore I do not believe that the development of any body of legal doctrine stands in a crude casual relationship to the development of prevailing ideology.

The origin of the Carriers' Notices

I believe that the circumstances which led to the widespread use of notices were roughly twofold. The change from pack-mule to waggon was necessitated by the larger cargoes which needed to be shipped as the economy grew. Secondly there was an increase in small valuable cargoes such as bank notes.[4] The emergence of large carriers firms provided defendants who were actually worth suing. There is evidence that one man carriers businesses were highly unstable, but in the litigation after c.1800, the same large firms repeatedly appear as defendants.[5] The expansion in the turnpike network favoured the transition of the larger carriers into national carriers; however, the public highway system remained appalling up to the *Highways Act of*

[1] E.G.M. Fletcher, *The Carrier's Liability* (1932).

[2] (1877) 2 C P D 416.

[3] For rather a different view see P. Atiyah *From Principles to Pragmatism* (Oxford, 1978).

[4] See generally P.S.Bagwell *The Transport Revolution from 1770* (1974). It is to be remembered however that until the 1850s the majority of goods were nevertheless dispatched by water *(ibid)*.

[5] For example examination of the Hull Directory for 1838 reveals that there were 125 firms, but only twenty-four of these had been in existence twelve years earlier *(ibid)*; the names most frequently met with are Waterhouse, Horne, Gray, Willan and Pickford (the origins of the latter firm can be traced to 1649: see J. Copeland *Roads and their Traffic* (David & Charles, Newton Abbot, 1968).

1835 and must have increased the carriers' losses through damage and delay.[6]

The actual legal development which led to the notices was the emergence of the carriers insurers' liability, on which I largely follow Fletcher.[7] He under-estimates the importance of *Southcote's Case* however: it was the probable legal justification for the notices, for it tended to be cited quite indiscriminately.[8] I believe that the origin of the notices themselves may well have been an opinion of Lord Kenyon. This is suggested by Horne's evidence to the 1825 Committee, and Dunning, the Solicitor-General for whom Kenyon devilled, appeared for the defendant in *Gibbon v Paynton*.[9] The fact that the notices varied, does not preclude their origin in a single opinion.[10] The practical reason for recognising the notices was simply that the carrier having become insurer, it was felt to be not unreasonable that insurance should be paid for as such.[11]

Preoccupation with the influence of freedom of contract, prevents the right question being asked about the development of the carriers' notices, which is 'why did the carriers' written terms come to be preferred to the ordinary common law terms?' The reason for this I

[6] The first turnpike was established along part of the Great North Road in 1663. After 1700 many were established. By the mid- 1830s, 1,116 trusts managing 22,000 miles of road were in existence. (See Bagwell, *Transport Revolution);* the *Highways Act 1555* had set up a system of maintenance which was both local and amateur. During winter months at any rate, many roads were unfit for wheeled transport of any kind. Parliament's attempts to ameliorate the situation (for example by regulating the size of waggon wheels and number of horses (see e.g. 22 Car. 2 c.12, 5 Geo. 1 c.12)), caused great hardship to carriers. These rules are given as a reason for the publication of *The Carrier's Guide and Companion* (1760); the only extant copy I have managed to trace is in the University of Pennsylvania Library. It appears to be the first monograph relating to carriers.

[7] n. 1 above.

[8] See e.g. *Symons v Darknall* (1628) Palmer 523 – goods damaged by negligence.

[9] J. Campbell, *Lives of the Chief Justices; (1769)* 4 Burr. 2298. *The Report of the Committee on the Regulation of Charges for Conveyance and Porterage* B.P.P. 1825. At the end of the Report Horne, a leading carrier, lays before the Committee some observations on the provisions necessary for the relief of carriers. He observed that until Lord Ellenborough the carrier's notice was good, and that it was dictated by Lord Kenyon himself. Both the form of the notice and the way it was published suggest that the practice might have been recent. The absence of any information on the subject in the *Carrier's Guide and Companion* (n.6 above) may also suggest that the practice started after 1760

[10] H. Jeremy *Law of Carriers* (1815), p. 45 observes that they had in general each adopted a particular form of notice. Sometimes notices varied even between offices of the same firm – e.g. *Gouger v Jolly* (1816) Holt 317.

[11] See Fletcher *Carrier's Liability,* p. 39. While this appears to have been the view of the courts, it was not necessarily the view of the carriers' customers – see W. Phillips, *Strictures on the Unfounded and Illegal Claims of the Carriers* (1800).

have already suggested.[12]The existence of the theoretical alternative
of common law terms of carriage when combined with the increasing
emphasis on the requirement that the notice should be proved to have
been 'brought home' to the plaintiff, provides I believe the real
explanation as to why the courts were apparently prepared to sanction
a widening of the carriers' exemption from liability, for if the notice
was shown to have been 'brought home' the implication was that the
plaintiff had preferred those terms to the common law ones. On the
vexed question as to whether the notices operated originally in
contract, or by limitation of profession, I have come on the whole to
the view that they were contractual. Certainly there seems to have
been no doctrine that a unilateral act on the part of the carrier
sufficed.[13] The first monograph on carriers, by Jeremy, certainly held
the view that they were contractual.[14] The view that they operated by
limitation of profession seems to gain currency from Erle J.'s
judgement in *McManus v L & Y Ry.*[15] In *Smith v Horne* Burrough J.
argued that a notice, if it constituted a special contract, would have had
to be shown on the record.[16] He overlooked a distinction, however: if
the particular notice operated only in limitation of damages to the
usual £5, it did not need to be set out in the declaration since without it
the declaration contained an allegation of the entire act or duty to be
done by the carrier in virtue of the consideration.[17] If, on the other
hand, the declaration of the value of the goods and payment according
to that amount formed part of the consideration for, and a condition of,
the carriage, proof of such notice would bar the action.[18] Before the
Hilary Rules 1834, neither form needed to be specially pleaded.

I have found no case prior to the *Carriers Act 1830* in which the
notices were held apt to exclude liability for negligence, even ordinary
negligence, if proved.[19] The problem seems to have been essentially
one of proof. Not only did the plaintiff have the onus of proving

[12]J.N. Adams, The Standardisation of Commercial Contracts or the Contractualisation of Standard Forms, in *Anglo-Am. L.R.* 7 (1978), 136.

[13]See A. Leslie, *Law of Transport by Railway* (2nd edn), p. 23.

[14]Jeremy, p. 41. See also the evidence of Horne cited in n. 9 above, in which the expresses the same view.

[15](1859) 4 H & N 327, 329. Perhaps the view derives from a misreading of *Southcote's Case* (1601) 46 Rep 836, 84a.

[16](1818) 8 Taunt 144. He also said that the doctrine of notice was never known until *Forward v Pittard* (1785) 1 T R 27, which he had argued, a quite mistaken view.

[17]*Clarke v Gray* (1805) 6 East 563.

[18]*Latham v Rutley* (1823) 2 B & C 20; E. Chitty, *Pleadings* (1831) 2, 356 n.a.

[19]In his evidence before the 1825 Committee (n. 9 above) Horne stated that the charge for carriage was based on the assumption that the carriers were not liable *except* they were negligent.

negligence, but it also had to be shown that the negligence had caused the loss.[20] Jones on *Carriers* says that the carrier's obligation after a special acceptance is to use as much diligence as a private bailee for hire, but no more.[21] He will not be liable for slight negligence. For this proposition Jones cites *Nicholson v Willan,*[22] where a parcel had been accepted to go by mail, but was booked for another coach. In point of fact there was no proof that it had gone by either, and it may well have gone by the mail. There was no proof of misfeasance, only of slight negligence in booking, and that not necessarily relevant to the loss. If this view that the carrier after a special acceptance remained liable for negligence is correct, what are we to make of *Leeson v Holt?*[23]

Fletcher wrote: 'Historically this case may be said to mark the acceptance by the judiciary of the carrier's right to exclude his liability for events for which he was morally answerable'.[24] I believe that this view is quite erroneous. The notice given by the carrier was that all packages of looking-glass, plate-glass, household furniture, toys etc. were to be entirely at the owner's risk as to damage, breakage etc. Lord Ellenborough said:

> If this action had been brought twenty years ago, the defendant would have been liable, since by the common law a carrier is liable in all cases except two, where the loss is occasioned by the act of God, or of the King's enemies using an overwhelming force, which persons with ordinary means of resistance cannot guard against. It was found, that common law imposed upon carriers a liability of ruinous extent, and in consequence, qualifications and limitions of that liability have been introduced from time to time, till as in the present case, they seem to have excluded all responsibility whatsoever, so that under the terms of the present notice if a servant of the carrier's had in the most wilful and wanton manner destroyed the furniture entrusted to them, the principals would not have been liable. If the parties in the present case have so contracted, the plaintiff must abide by the agreement, and he must be taken to have so contracted if he chooses to send his goods to be carried after notice of the conditions.

[20] *Nicholson v Willan* (1804) 5 East 507; *Harris v Packwood* (1810) 3 Taunt 264.

[21] G.F. Jones, *Treatise on the Law Governing the Rights and Liabilities of Common Carriers* (1827); p. 29 (a more analytic book than Jeremy).

[22] n. 20 above.

[23] (1816) 1 Stark 186.

[24] Fletcher, *Carrier's Liability,* p. 185. He attributed this to the growing influence of freedom of contract. But, as I have pointed out, that doctrine does not logically entail that one party's printed terms shall prevail over the common law terms.

Apart from its interest as an anticipation of the *Carriers Act 1830*, the case does not in reality appear to have been a significant one. Its only interest for contemporaries was apparently the 'bringing home' point. The plaintiff was given the verdict because although evidence of publication in the *Gazette* was held admissible, it was not proved that the plaintiff was in the habit of reading it. The case is not cited at all by Jones, and appears only in Hammond's *Digest* for this bringing home point.[25]

What then are we to make of it? I have been unable to trace any case subsequent to it in which a similar clause was used. The carriers generally seem to have stuck to their £5 notices. Whilst there may be some significance in the form of this notice, it does not appear to be the forerunner of a trend. Probably the thinking of the draftsman, who may have been the carrier himself, was simply that it was well established that a notice could be published requiring the value of goods above £5 to be declared otherwise the carrier would not be liable. Why not instead of such a blanket term, which may miss many bothersome cargoes valued under £5, list the troublesome goods. That is advantageous both to the carrier, and to the public who have non-risky goods valued above £5 carried at carriers risk. It may well be that for the classes of goods covered by the notice, the draftsman assumed that the effect would be the same as a £5 notice of the type which required the value of goods above £5 to be declared, and if not the carrier would not be answerable for them. As I have argued, these were ineffective to exclude negligence liability if the plaintiff could prove it. It is quite probable that the draftsman of the *Leeson v Holt* notice assumed that it would have the same effect. Lord Ellenborough may well have gone further therefore than the draftsman intended. Whilst this may be significant, it is to be borne in mind that his remarks were entirely obiter. They may simply have been off-the-cuff reaction to the novel form of the notice. It might well be true that if the parties had contracted that the carrier's servants might destroy the goods wantonly, then the plaintiff must abide by the agreement. It is quite another thing to say that the court would have *held* that they had so contracted. All the cases suggest that they would not. This case itself suggests that there would be considerable difficulty proving such a notice had been 'brought home'. The fact that the case was ignored by contemporaries and especially by Jones, scarcely supports

---

[25] Hammond, Digest, 1, 417. The only other citation I have traced is in Harrison's *Digest* for the same point. Comyn, who asserts that the carriers' notices protect against the consequences of personal neglect cites only *Nicholson v Willan* (1804) 5 East 507, and *Harris v Packwood* (1810) 3 Taunt 264 both of which cases are dealt with in the text above.

the view that it was a legal turning point. The ability of the carrier to exclude negligence liability was a product of the *Carriers Act 1830.*

Exclusion of liability for negligence

The *Carriers Act* was passed because the carriers needed protection.[26] If they were insurers, they ought to be paid as such.[27] Section 1 of the Act listed goods whose value if above £10 had to be declared. If the value was above that sum but not declared, it was held in *Hinton v Dibbin* that the carrier was not even liable for gross negligence.[28] This was a perfectly reasonable construction of the Act; for the exemption from liability in s.1 and in the long title was apparently absolute and furthermore s.8 provided that nothing in the Act should protect the carrier from the felonious acts of his servants, suggesting that he was not liable for anything less than this (while the servant was expressly stated to be liable for negligence).

Hinton v Dibbin is a case of central importance in that it established clearly for the first time that a carrier could be excused liability for negligence. The next step was to hold that the same exclusion of liability could be achieved by act of the parties themselves. This development occurred in *Wylde v Pickford.*[29] In order to understand this case it is necessary to dwell a little on technicalities of pleading (it was after all argued before Baron Parke). The first count of the declaration contained the usual statement of delivery to the carrier and failure to take proper care of the goods (which had disappeared between London and Athlone). The plea to this count stated that the defendants were common carriers and had given notice that they would not be responsible for loss of, or damage to, certain goods, that they received the goods on the terms of that notice and the goods (which were not of a sort listed in s.1 *Carriers Act)* were not at the time of delivery insured according to their value paid for. The plaintiffs demurred. It was held that the action being founded on breach of duty *ex contractu,* the defendants accepted the goods only on the terms of the notice, the allegation in the

---

[26] See the 1825 Report n. 9 above. The petition of the carriers to the House of Commons originally put forward a bill raising the limit of liability from £5 to £20. The Act was more advantageous to the carriers however. It fixed the amount at £10.

[27] See n. 11 above.

[28] (1842) 2 QB 646.

[29] (1842) 4 Price 31.

plea of a special contract was sufficient and a special averment of the plaintiff's consent was unnecessary.[30]

Willis for the plaintiff argued that this plea did not contain a sufficient statement of a special contract in that it did not state that the plaintiff accepted the terms of the notice. Against this Martin argued that the notice did not operate as a special contract, but as a limitation of the carrier's liability at common law, saving gross negligence.[31] Willis, replying to this argument, asked the obvious question: how could a party by his own act free himself from liability? He pointed out that the *Carriers Act* was applicable to the latter part of the journey over land and either the notice was effective as a special contract under s.6, or it was void under s.4 as a public notice.

Parke B. held that the carrier was competent to limit his liability because he was entitled by common law to insist on the full price of carriage. If such price was not paid, he was entitled to insist on his own terms. These terms operated by way of a special contract. To the objection that it was not alleged that the plaintiff had consented to the terms of any such contract he pointed out that the plaintiff was in a difficulty: he could not enforce the defendant's obligation as common carriers, because he was not willing to pay for the price of carriage beforehand, and if he sued therefore on a bailment on special terms, it could only be on the defendant's special terms. In the event, the plaintiff however succeeded on the count of conversion through misdelivery.

This reasoning must be borne in mind if we are to understand the subsequent cases. These cases at first sight seem to confirm that freedom of contract had been given full rein.[32] Closer examination suggests otherwise however. A crucial point, is that all these cases involved cargoes which, while outside the letter of the *Carriers Act,* nevertheless fell within its spirit. They all involved railways, and it would appear that the railways confined the use of such special contracts to livestock and similar cargoes.[33] There were other important factors however.

[30] See *Dickon v Clifton* (1764) 2 Wils 319; *Govett v Radnidge* (1802) 3 East 62; *Ansell v Waterhouse* (1817) 6 M & S 385; *Bretherton v Wood* (1821) 3 B & B 54. Jeremy, *Law of Carriers,* p. 117.

[31] In support of this he cited *Gibbon v Paynton* (1769) 4 Burr 2298; *Harris v Packwood* (1810) 3 Taunt 264; *Marsh v Horne* (1826) 5 B & C 322.

[32] See for example the judgements of Parker and Martin BB in *Carr v Lancs. & Yorks. Ry.* (1852) 7 Ex. 707.

[33] See W. Hodges, *Law Relating to Railways* (1847), Ch. II. Shelford, *Law of Railways* (1845) and E. Walford, *Law of Railways* (1845) are two earlier books on the law of railways. They are not so substantial and learned as Hodges, but are interesting

The first of these was the undeveloped state of the law of agency. In *Walker v York and NMR* the fish merchants at Scarborough were served with a notice which inter alia provided that the railway company would not be responsible for the delivery of fish in any certain or reasonable time, nor in time for any particular market etc.[34] They were very angry and many tore up the notices and said they would not be bound. The plaintiff, who was among them, denied having been served, or that he had ever consented to be bound. He said to the station master 'What is the use of sending that old fellow to serve these notices? They are of no use'. The jury were directed that if they were satisfied that the plaintiff was served with a notice, they might infer as a fact that the goods were sent under the terms of a special contract, unless the plaintiff had unambiguously dissented from its terms. Lord Campbell C.J. approving the judge's direction suggested that not only should the plaintiff have signified his disapproval, but the defendants should have acquiesced in it, and in this case there could be no such acquiescence for there was no one at Scarborough having authority to receive the goods on any other terms, and the paper had expressly said this. Wightman J. and Coleridge J. similarly stressed the absence of authority of the railway servants to vary the terms, even if the plaintiff had objected.

A further factor was the new emphasis on pleading engendered by the Hilary Rules of 1834.[34] We have already seen that a notice of the type which disclaimed the carrier's liability for loss of goods above £5 in value needed to be stated in the declaration, otherwise if proved by the defendant, the declaration would be bad for variance.[36] We have also seen that this would not absolve the carrier from the duty to take reasonable care, or at any rate it would not absolve him from the consequences of gross negligence. The solution for the plaintiff was simply therefore to add a count to the declaration pleading the notice.[37] The Hilary Rules however prohibited the pleading of more than one count on the same cause of action.[38] Moreover the forms of the notice were now arguably appropriate to exclude liability for negligence.

for the light they shed on the development of these special contracts. Shelford for example considered that under such special contracts the railway remained liable to exercise ordinary care. He also thought that a notice amounted to a special contract. Neither view of course was tenable at that time.

[34] (1853) 2 E & B 750.

[35] R. Gen. Hil. T. 4 W reg. 5 founded on 3 & 4 W. 4 c. 42. s.1, 23.

[36] *Latham v Rutley* (1823) 2 B & C 20.

[37] See E. Chitty, *Pleading* (1831) 2, 356 n.a.

[38] The 6th edn of Chitty (1836) contains the same note as the 5th relating to the old £5 notices. The problem referred to here must not have occurred to the author at that time.

The dilemma in which this placed the plaintiff can be seen in the important cases of *Shaw v York & NMR, Austin v Manchester, Sheffield and Lincs. Railway, Chippendale v Lancs & Yorks Railway, GNR v Morville, Carr v Lancs and Yorks Railway.* [39]

In Shaw's case, the notice was indentical to that in *Palmer v Grand Junction Railway.* [40] Alderson B. at the trial directed that it did not exempt the defendants from the duty to use ordinary care, or an adequate carriage. On argument for a new trial, the plaintiff's counsel as usual cited *Bodenham v Bennett, Birkett v Willan, Sleat v Fagg, Wylde v Pickford* and Story on *Bailments* as well as *Lyon v Mells* in support of this proposition. [41] The argument for the railway company was presented by Knowles, Joseph Addison and Barstow. It was to the effect that the count, which charged the defendants as common carriers, varied from the proof, which was that the defendants did not carry as common carriers, but under a special contract. They suggested that it might be that the defendant notwithstanding the terms might be liable for negligence, but that was a different liability from that declared on. Lord Denman C.J. in a very short judgement accepted this argument without citing further authority.

Austin v Manchester, Sheffield & Lincs Railway turned on a similar point of pleading. Patterson J. cited Parke B. in *Wylde v Pickford,* where he stated that the normal mode was to aver that the goods were delivered by the plaintiffs to the defendant and had been received by the defendant to be kept or carried in a particular way. Patterson J thought that had the declaration stated that the contract was for carrying with a certain limitation, it would have been good. Coleridge and Wightman JJs agreed. Erle J expressed the view that the effect of the contract would have been to exclude negligence liability, and referred to the fact that the carriage was at a cheaper rate.

In Chippendale's case counsel for the plaintiffs tried to argue that *Austin's* and *Shaw's* cases merely turned on points of pleading and

[39](1849) 13 Q. B. 347; (1851) 16 Q.B. 600; (1851) 21 L J Q B 22; (1852) 21 L J Q B 319; (1852) 7 Ex 707.

[40](1841) 8 M & W 372 – the earliest case involving a special contract. The clause in question read 'This ticket is issued subject to the owners undertaking all risks of conveyance whatsoever, as the Company will not be responsible for any injury or damage (however caused) occurring to horses or carriages travelling upon the Grand Junction line'. The Grand Junction railway, it is interesting to note, in cooperation with Chaplin and Horne achieved a monopoly which Pickfords challenged in *Pickford v Grand Junction Ry.* (1841) 8 M & W 372. See also *Carriers Case in Reference to the Railways* (1841). One of the problems at this period was that the carriers could actually undercut the railways.

[41](1817) 4 Price 31; (1819) 2 Br, Ald 356; (1822) S B & Ald 342; n. 36 above; 2nd. ed. s 264; (1804) 5 East 437.

that *Lyon v Mells, Garnett v Willan* and the statement in Storey was still good law.[42] Coleridge and Erle JJs. however, held that the wording was appropriate to exclude negligence liability. Erle J was at pains to point out, however, that he thought the limitation reasonable, the contract being for the carriage of livestock. *GNR v Morville* and *Carr v Lancs. & Yorks Ry,* were similar decisions.

Walker's case, and the others, led to great public disquiet, the outcome of which was the *Railway and Canal Traffic Regulation Bill.*[43] Although it was argued on the part of the railways that a member of the public might require them to carry as common carriers, this was of little consolation (even if they were common carriers of the goods in question) to a person requiring transport to know that he might sue if he rejected the company's terms, and they refused carriage.[44] In the event, the bill was passed and the *Railway and Canal Traffic Act 1854* is a further landmark in the development of the law relating to standard form contracts.

This Act made the railways liable for loss in respect of carriage of goods.[45] Contracting out was allowed, but the contract had to be signed by the consignor, and as finally constructed, the terms had to be reasonable.[45] The burden of showing this rested on the railway company.[47].

Parker reasserts the old law:

After 1851, the parties to an action became competent as witnesses.[48] This presented an obvious problem for 'meeting of minds' theorists: what if a plaintiff denied knowledge of the written terms (as he was likely to do)? This problem is manifest in the decision in *Henderson v Stevenson.*[49] That case might be seen as a sympton of the late nineteenth-century tendency to tidy up doctrine, a tendency apparent in Beale's somewhat bizarre desire to hold that tickets (whose

[42](1821) 5 B & A 53; n. 41 above.

[43] See *Peek v N. Staffs Ry* (1862) 10 H L C 473.

[44] See House of Lords debate 26 May 1854.

[45] It was originally proposed that it should also apply to passenger carriage, but in the event it only applied to goods.

[46] *Peek v N. Staffs Ry* n. 43 above.

[47] *Peek* n. 43 above.

[48] 14 & 15 Vic. c.99.

[49] (1875) 2 Sc App 470.

49

juridical status as he rightly pointed out had not received much attention) were a new species of negotiable instrument.[50]

In the event, *Parker v SER,* a case of deposit and therefore outside the 1854 Act, and involving a £10 notice, reasserted the old law. Bramwell B. in that case stressed that implied understanding that the terms were reasonable. That was stressed in the cases which led up to the *Railway and Canal Traffic Act* which we considered above. Freedom of contract as a doctrine preventing the courts from considering the reasonableness of terms I suggest is a twentieth-century development, rather than a nineteenth.[51] Fletcher's account of the influence of the doctrine on the development of the carriers' notices, must be substantially revised.

[50](1887) 1 H L R 17.

[51] It is not to be forgotten that the 1854 Act was at first construed on the basis that if the consignor had signed a special contract, the terms for that reason must be reasonable – *Beal v S. Devon. Ry* (1860) 29 L J Ex 441. This view did not survive – *Simons v G. W.R.* (1856), 26 L J C P 25; *McManus v Lancs & Yorks Ry.* (1859) 29 L J Ex 353; *Rooth v NER.* (1867) 36 L J Ex 83; *Peek v N. Staffs Ry.* (1860) E B. & E 986. Something like the *Beal v S Devon Ry* thinking seems to underline the twentieth-century cases. Victorian judges were wiser!

'SIN OF ALL SORTS SWARMETH': CRIMINAL LITIGATION IN AN ENGLISH COUNTY IN THE EARLY SEVENTEENTH CENTURY

Louis A. Knafla

All men do see, and good men do behold it with grief of mind, that
sin of all sorts swarmeth and that evildoers go on with all licence
and impunity. If the cause be searched for it shall never be found
in the want of laws, for sin in this age and light of the gospel is not
only detected by the mouth of the preacher but also prohibited by
the authority of the prince... What shall we do with laws without
manners? And what shall we get by complaining of faults if they
be not cut off by severity of punishment? The cause of this evil,
no doubt, is originally in the mischievous minds of the offenders
themselves, but yet secondarily and not finally in the remiss
dealing of those persons that are put in trust with the execution of
such laws as we have.[1]

These words, coming from the pen of a man who was a part-time
resident of Greenwich for more than forty years, a justice of the peace
for the county of Kent for nearly two decades, and who otherwise
became renowned for his work as a bencher of Lincoln's Inn, deputy
in the Alienation Office, Keeper of Records in the Rolls Chapel and
Tower of London, and Master of Chancery, cannot be taken lightly as
a sketch of crime and its administration in Kent in the early
seventeenth century. William Lambarde was a scholar of Anglo-
Saxon and ancient antiquities who carried out research and wrote
the first history of Kent, compiled manuals for the instruction of
parish officers and JPs, and composed a book on the history and
jurisdiction of the central and local courts of law. He was, moreover, a
man who had an ear close to the ground and the people of his native
county. A successful gentleman farmer, he was as much at home with
the technical aspects of arable farming and animal husbandry as he
was with the law.[2]

Lambarde believed that a country was only as strong as its
governors, and as the desire of its people to work for justice. Devoutly
religious, he held that good people obeyed the law while the evil ones

[1] *William Lambarde and Local Government*, ed. Conyers Read (Ithaca, 1962), pp.
68-9.

[2] Biographies include Wilbur Dunkel, *William Lambarde, Elizabethan Jurist 1536-
1601* (New Brunswick, 1965); and, especially, R.M. Warnicke, *William Lambarde
Elizabethan Antiquary 1536-1601* (Chichester, 1973), where his work as JP is
assessed at pp. 54-73, 103-16.

committed felonies and misdemeanours in disturbance of the peace. He exhorted jurors, in long sermons delivered as 'charges', to encourage the reporting of crimes committed, and to present and indict the offenders.[3] And as a judge he applied the law strictly and harshly to those who were convicted.[4] Nonetheless, Lambarde was also a humble man who believed in equal justice for rich and poor alike. Thus he worked to relieve the poor of their miseries while he applied the law sternly to protect the property rights of the landed gentry of whom he was a member. He contributed generously to the unemployed, endowed the first hospital for the poor, and assisted in the creation of the first house of correction for the rehabilitation of criminals. An English county could have perhaps no better commentator on crime and the administration of criminal law than Kent thus has. One of the purposes of this essay is to inquire into the extent to which Lambarde's belief 'that sin of all sorts swarmeth and that evil doers go on with all licence and impunity' is historically tenable as a summary of the problems facing criminal administration in the early seventeenth century.

This view was widely held. Numerous Elizabethan and Jacobean judges and writers enlarged upon it in considerable detail.[5] Moreover scholars today accept the notion that crime was increasing in the late years of the sixteenth and the early years of the seventeenth centuries. Preliminary studies of local societies and courts lend some factual basis to this notion.[6] One scholar, however, has attempted to go beyond the range of literary evidence and the sampling of court records to test the frequency of recorded crime over a long sequence of the records themselves: namely, the assize indictment files for the Home Counties.[7] While realising that 'statistics provide only the

[3] Read, *Lambarde,* pp. 67-149.

[4] Kent Record Office [KRO] Q/SRg, the Gaol Delivery Roll. His attendance was not frequent. See also his earlier *Ephemeris* edited by Read in *Lambarde,* pp. 15-52.

[5] The best general guide is J.S. Cockburn, 'The nature and incidence of crime in England 1559-1625: A preliminary survey', in *Crime in England 1550-1800,* ed. J.S. Cockburn (1977), pp. 49-71. An interesting analysis of the literary evidence is T.C. Curtis and F.M. Hale, 'English thinking about crime, 1530-1620', in *Crime and Justice in Europe and Canada,* ed. L.A. Knafla (Waterloo, 1981), pp. 111-26.

[6] Joel Samaha, *Law and Order in Historical Perspective: The Case of Elizabethan Essex* (1974), chap. I, app. I; Peter Clark, *English Provincial Society from the Reformation to the Revolution* (Hassocks, 1977), pp. 235-51; J.A. Sharpe, 'Crime and delinquency in an Essex parish 1600-1640', in Cockburn, *Crime,* pp. 90-104; and M.J. Ingram, 'Communities and courts: Law and disorder in early-seventeenth-century Wiltshire', in *ibid.,* pp. 110-34.

[7] J.S. Cockburn, *Calendar of Assize Records,* HMSO, 1975 to the present. Published volumes to date are *Sussex Indictments – Elizabeth I* and *James I* (1975), *Hertfordshire Indictments – Elizabeth I* and *James I* (1975), *Essex Indictments – Elizabeth I* and *James I* (1979), and *Kent Indictments – Elizabeth I* (1980). The

52

most fragile guide to criminality', James Cockburn nevertheless concludes tentatively that they 'support the contemporary notion that crime was increasing during Elizabeth's reign'. They also indicate that offences against property dominated criminal proceedings at law, and that the offences of larceny, burglary or robbery comprised approximately 73 per cent of all indictments in the five Home Counties including Kent.[8] A second purpose of this essay is to examine this question of the structure of crime from the perspective of all secular criminal litigation in a single English county in the early seventeenth century.

A structure of crime for early seventeenth-century Kent can be derived from a study of the litigation recorded in the regional and local secular courts which had criminal jurisdiction. The research base for this has been prepared in the course of work on a publication for the Public Record Office entitled *Kent at Law, 1602*.[9] This publication will provide a full calendar of all legal records in 1602 (bringing the matters entered to their conclusion), with separate volumes for the local secular courts; the bill, or equity and prerogative courts; the common law courts; and the ecclesiastical courts.

The evidence summarised below has been taken from the records for the courts of assize, county and borough quarter sessions, borough assembly and mayorial courts, the Cinque Ports, port-moot, hornblower, fair, hundred courts and courts leet for the first three calendar years of the seventeenth century, 1600-2. All references to annual figures represent the yearly average for each of these years. Since modern commentators estimate that the surge of crime rates in Elizabethan England came to a peak in the late 1590s, and began a gradual decline in 1605-10, the years selected for this essay may represent the high plateau for recorded crime in the era.

The Kent assize indictment files for Elizabeth's reign have just been calendared by Professor Cockburn, and he has allowed me to use them for this study. My examination of the typescript for 1600-2, which has been verified by my own calendar of these proceedings for 1602, reveals the following annual figures based on indictments for

remaining four volumes are in the press. I would like to thank Professor Cockburn for his helpful criticisms and comments in the preparation of this essay.

[8]Cockburn, 'Incidence of crime', pp. 52-5, 65-70. See more generally J. Hall, *Theft, Law and Society* (Indianapolis, 2nd ed. 1952), Part I.

[9]To be published by HMSO. I would like to thank Dr. Roy Hunnisett for his generous help and wise counsel in assisting my work in these records. I am also grateful to the staff of the Kent County Archives at Maidstone, and to the Canada Council for a research grant.

principals and accessories: eighty-four indictments, of which 73 per cent were for crimes against property, 21 per cent crimes against persons, and 6 per cent crimes against the peace.[10] The offence of grand larceny comprised 61 per cent of the crimes against property. The indictments averaged seven per population of 10,000, the population of Kent being calculated conservatively as approximately 130,000 in 1600.

These figures compare favourably in the structure of recorded, if not total, crime for the Home Counties in the early seventeenth century. My calculations for Essex, Sussex and Hertfordshire for the same years indicate the percent of property crimes as approximately 75 per cent, 77 per cent, and 79 per cent respectively. Making a reasonable allowance for error, the 73 per cent for Kent places crimes against property at the same level as those of its neighbouring rural counties. With regard to total crime, the average number of indictments per 10,000 for Essex, Sussex and Hertfordshire were twenty, twenty-one, and forty-four in comparison to seven for Kent.[11] While the figure for Hertfordshire may be peculiar due to problems in estimating its population and particular local and demographic concerns, the assize indictments reveal that at this level of jurisdiction recorded crime was apparently less in Kent than in the neighbouring counties.

Finally, many historians – and especially sociologists and criminologists – regard crimes against the person which are felonies as most indicative of the extent of violence in society.[12] The figures for homicide, murder and manslaughter which fall into this category are easily calculated. In this instance the figures for the three Home Counties specified are 0.7, 1.4, and 1.6 per 10,000 respectively. The figure for Kent is 0.7, reflecting the lower level of its sister rural county on the southern coast, Sussex. In concluding the assize data, the structure of personal, property, and public oriented crime in Kent was similar to that of the other Home Counties, but the frequency of recorded crime was at a lower level than its rural neighbours.

The type and extent of recorded crime changes significantly when one moves from a court concerned solely with indictable criminal

[10] PRO, ASSI 35/44/5-6.

[11] Cockburn, *Sussex Indictments – Elizabeth I*, pp. 371-418; *Hertfordshire Indictments – Elizabeth I*, pp. 148-75; and *Essex Indictments – Elizabeth I*, pp. 489-550.

[12] For example, G. Geis and H.A. Bloch, *Man, Crime and Society* (New York, 2nd ed. 1970); R. Quinney, *The Social Reality of Crime* (Boston, 1970); and Leon Radzinowicz, *Ideology and Crime* (New York, 1966). For this particular period see Samaha, *Law and Order*, pp. 17-24, 114-39.

offences to courts such as those of quarter, borough and town sessions which heard a wide range of indictable and non-indictable criminal and semi-criminal offences. However, before any analysis of criminal litigation can be made, a profile of criminal offences in their broadest and most all-inclusive nature must be established. The job is not an easy one. Contemporaries had little interest in categorising types of crime into personal or property, and felonies and misdemeanours. Neither Ferdinando Pulton, William Lambarde, or Sir Edward Coke used such distinctions.[13] And few modern scholars agree in their historical conceptions of such categories.[14]

The problems in formulating a structure of criminal offences are numerous. These include a lack of study of contemporary attitudes towards crime, a hazy knowledge of the apprehension-committal-arbitration system, the scarcity of pre-trial materials, the completeness, or otherwise, of court records, and the limitations of the records themselves. Hence the evidence presented here is no more than an attempt to recreate the scope and content of criminal litigation. The unit of evidence for examination includes all references to 'suspects' whether they are principals or accessories, for indictable and non-indictable criminal or semi-criminal acts. No secular court possessing a significant amount of criminal jurisdiction in the county is excluded And every action containing a measure of wrong-doing that is injurious to persons, property, the state or community as an offence tried and punished by statute, local ordinance, common law or local precedent by capital or corporeal punishment, fine or imprisonment is defined as criminous. The intent is to present a structure of criminal offences that bears a relatively close relationship to the extant records of the secular courts.[15] The result is, hopefully, a workable definition that is as broad as possible in order to allow the reader to determine for himself what he wishes to define as criminous, and what weight or importance he wishes to attribute to the various kinds of criminal offences.

---

[13] Sir William Staunford, *Les Plees del Coron* (1557); Ferdinando Pulton, *De Pace Regis et Regni* (1604); William Lambarde, *Eirenarcha* (1581); and Sir Edward Coke, *Second Part of the Institutes of the Lawes of England* (1642). William Hawkins, *A Treatise of the Pleas of the Crown* (1716-21), was the first author to devise a structure for the subject.

[14] Sir J.F. Stephen, *A History of the Criminal Law of England* (1883), vols. 2-3; Sir W.S. Holdsworth, *A History of English Law* (1924), 4.492-521; Leon Radzinowicz, *A History of English Criminal Law and its Administration* (1948), vol. 1; and Cockburn, 'Incidence of crime'.

[15] This is similar in some ways to the approach of Ingram, 'Communities and courts'. I would like to thank Professor John Beattie and Professor James Cockburn for their suggestions on this section.

55

The five general categories that have been constructed to include from the records all of the criminally related offences are: crimes against property; crimes against persons; crimes against the peace; religious and moral offences; and public nuisances.[16] Property crimes include, on the capital side, grand larceny, robbery, burglary, abduction and arson; and for non-capital, petty larceny, forgery, embezzlement, illegal entry and enclosure, and damage stemming therefrom, poaching, and offences against the game laws. Personal crimes include, for capital offences, homicides, witchcraft, infanticide, and rape; and for non-capital, assault, scandalous words, perjury, and misdemeanours.[17] The third major category – crimes against the peace – comprises treason, riot, sedition, seditious words, disorderly and unlicensed alehouses, vagrancy, offences against gun control legislation, offences against the coin, negligent escape, and corrupt officials.[18] The fourth category of moral and religious offences includes recusancy, bastardy, buggery, sodomy, gambling, tippling and swearing.[19] Finally one has the less serious category of public nuisances. Often called trespasses, they were actions against rules and regulations for the public good such as operating overloaded carts, the failure to repair bridges, highways, mills and sewers, extending buildings into the streets, and making dunghills and dumping sullage in streets and churches.

Two additional categories might have been fashioned from the offences listed above. One is sexual offences, but they are not sufficiently clear or frequently prosecuted to make the distinction separately viable for the period, and thus are included in crimes against the person and moral offences. Another possible category is suggested by the interesting but murky field of recognisances. While the records used to date are not specific in their contents, fines were

[16] Certain problems such as the distinction between trespass and misdemeanour, and crime and tort, have been avoided in this brief discussion.

[17] Several caveats should be noted. First, a few offences such as slander, riot, and witchcraft could be felonies or misdemeanours depending upon the facts. Second, some offences were misdemeanours for the first and/or second offences, and felonies for subsequent occasions. These are some of several limitations to the grouping of offences for quantitative analysis. It can only serve as a general yardstick for understanding larger problems.

[18] Vagrancy is the most difficult offence to detect in the records. See A.L. Beier, 'Vagrants and the social order in Elizabethan England', *Past and Present* 64 (1974), 12-26; and P. Slack, 'Vagrants and vagrancy in England, 1598-1664', *EcHR* 27 (1974), 374-6.

[19] The problem of recusancy was a major one for the Privy Council and the administration of justice. It dominates, for example, *The Lord Coke His Speech and Charge* (1607), especially ff. D-G2v. Sexual offences, however, were infrequently reported.

levied frequently for persons who, having been bound over, failed to either maintain good behaviour, keep the peace, or appear to give evidence in a trial.[20] Some of these offences may belong in either crimes against the peace, moral offences, or public nuisances. But lacking further evidence, it is still too early in our research to include them as offences in criminal litigation as defined in this essay. It should be noted, however, that it is possible for many of the individuals named to have been presented before a court and discharged with the taking of a recognisance as a form of temporary or even final judicial resolution.[21]

With these categories established, one can set out the evidence from various courts to assess how their records reflect the structure of criminal litigation in Kent in the early seventeenth century. First of all the profile of recorded crime from the assize files for 1600-2 differs from that of the period overall. Suspects for property crimes and crimes against the peace remain similar at 74 per cent and 8 per cent of indictments respectively, while those for personal crimes drop to 15 per cent and moral offences are added for 3 per cent. Grand larceny remains the largest single offence at 45 per cent while murder was the largest personal offence. These figures are also similar for earlier and later years with the exception of crimes against the peace, which increase in the 1590s at the expense of personal offences.[22] Nonetheless the general structure of recorded crime as revealed by the indictments of the assize circuit is similar for either set of categories. Property offences predominate, and grand and petty larceny comprise the lion's share of recorded crime before that court.

The court of quarter sessions for the county of Kent met not four, but five times a year: twice at Canterbury, and three times at Maidstone, the county seat. Headed by a number of prominent landed gentlemen, the court was extremely active. The sheer volume of its depositions and other judicial papers bears testimony to an institution that was both assiduous in its administration of the law and painstaking in its attention to detail.[23] As a result the number of suspects for criminal causes tried there was nearly three times that

---

[20]I would like to thank Dr. Tim Curtis for the opportunity to read his interesting unpublished paper on 'Binding over'.

[21]For example, KRO Q*SR1/6-7, 13; SR3/3, 9-11, 14-15.

[22]PRO ASSI 35/44/1-6.

[23]The quarter sessions records are in themselves quite extensive. They include in addition to the sessions records for this period the sessions papers (QM/SB 424-6), constables rolls (QM/S/SRO), indictments (QM/SI 1600-1602), inquisitions (QM/SIq/16/21), draft minutes (QM/SM 14-20), certificates (QM/SO 2-4), and writs (SM/SP 10-12).

dealt with at assizes in and for Kent, and the structure of offences that appeared on the record was significantly different.

The average number of criminal suspects recorded per annum in the period by the county quarter sessions was 221. Crimes against the peace comprised 40 per cent of the total, personal crimes 24 per cent, public nuisances 18 per cent, and property and morals offences 9 per cent each.[24] The most numerous forms of crimes against the peace consisted of rioting – often associated with violating the game or poaching laws, disorderly alehouses with their drunken clientele, and vagrancy. Most personal offences were assault causing 'the blood to flow'. The negligence or failure of officials to carry out their responsibilities was a prominent public nuisance, and the refusal to repair bridges and washed-out highways was a frequent nuisance to a county whose roads serviced considerable trade for the London and continental markets. If one were to add the large number of recognisances taken for good behaviour (sometimes sixty per annum), the majority of which were defaulted, the profile of crime revealed by the county quarter sessions places offences against the peace and order of the community more frequent than all property and personal crimes combined.

Thirdly, we come to the local courts for boroughs, towns, markets, marshes and hundreds. The number of courts for which a relatively complete record is extant for a three-year period in the late sixteenth and early seventeenth centuries is thirty-seven, stemming from fifteen localities or jurisdictions.[25] Because the research was undertaken only after an exhaustive examination of all local court records from the period 1570-1630 in order to find the year in which the major part of the records was extant, only a few of these courts lack records for 1600-2. The process of assessing these records for this essay has been a very complex one. Those with a record for 1600-2 have been calculated specifically. Those whose records are extant from an earlier or later date in the era have been reckoned at their average annual figures for a three-year period. The intent has been to err on the side of caution.

The total number of suspects in these local courts for criminal offences was 898 per annum, which is more than four times that of the county quarter sessions, and three times that of assizes and quarter sessions together. These figures exclude a number of other local

[24] KRO SR1-3.

[25] The localities or jurisdictions were Dover, Faversham, Folkstone, Fordwich, Gravesend, Hythe, Lydd, Maidstone, New Romney, Queenborough, Rochester, Romney Marsh, Sandwich, Canterbury and Tenterden.

courts which may have possessed a measure of criminal jurisdiction but whose records are not fully extant for any period in the era. Crimes against property were 4 per cent of the offences, personal crimes 22 per cent, crimes against the peace 16 per cent, moral offences 26 per cent, and public nuisances 29 per cent. In comparison to the county quarter sessions, the more traditional categories of property and personal crimes were similar in their proportions of recorded crime. The most significant changes were in the very large decline of crimes against the peace, and the large increase in moral offences and public nuisances.

Taking the statistics of all four varieties of court together, it is clear that crime in Kent in the early seventeenth century was spread much more widely among the kinds of criminal offences than one would imagine, and this conclusion is due largely to the range of courts whose records of criminal litigation have been included in this profile. The assize circuit court contributed 7 per cent of the total number of criminal suspects for the county, quarter sessions 20 per cent, and the other local courts 73 per cent. Property crimes were the smallest category, comprising 10 per cent of the criminal causes. Crimes against the person were 22 per cent, and crimes against the peace 20 per cent. Moral offences comprised 22 per cent and public nuisances 25 per cent. The overall crime rate amounts to 92 per 10,000 of population. When one realises that a number of possible suspects have been left out, and that an indeterminate number of manorial courts which exercised minimal criminal jurisdiction are excluded, the conclusion of this statistical exercise is that the extent of both serious and property-oriented crime is geometrically in inverse proportion to what much of the historical and legal press have interpreted in the past. What is important in this regard, however, is not any precise importance to the figures themselves, but the general profile of recorded crime in the broadest sense which emerges from them.

It has often been said that studies of society and the law based on statistics lack an awareness of the life of the law. Rather than fall prey completely to that charge, I would like to switch from what we might call quantitative to qualitative evidence. What were the local judges, jurors, attorneys and litigants concerned with? The record shows an unmistakable preoccupation with a range of everyday subjects reflective of a society much more closely in touch with the human body, human passions, staying alive and getting ahead than we are in a post-industrial and technological world. There is an overwhelming concern for knocking heads, stealing sheep, running livestock over other people's land, stealing useful goods and utensils, slandering officials, merchants and gentlemen, harbouring vagrants and other criminals, over-indulging and rioting in alehouses, fornicating out of wedlock, extending privies into the streets, throwing dung and garbage in the highways, pissing in the churches, and other acts of alleged criminality. A nagging question, however, continually confronts the reader: what does it all mean?

In perhaps the most elegant overview of criminal actions at common law in the early modern period John Baker writes: 'A true understanding of a legal system, as of chess or cricket, is only to be had from experience of the variety of action and result which can occur within the rules. The rules do not prescribe who will win, and (at least in a legal system) they are not always followed; but they do explain what the participants are up to.'[26] These words force the question of what *were* the participants before the courts up to. The following illustrations from the depositions and records of county and borough courts provide an impressionistic analysis of the variety of action that suspects incurred. They also capture the essence of crime and criminal litigation in Kent in the early seventeenth century.

Property offences were important in Kent, and they involved a wide range of people in both urban and rural areas. They were not usually, however, crimes of utter necessity. The following informations taken in January 1601 are a case in point. Thomas Rode of Goudhurst, scythe-smith, claimed that he had four scythes stolen from his shop by Henry Peirson of Horsmonden, labourer. Rode also claimed to have lost many other scythes earlier, and suspected that they were stolen by Peirson 'or some of his confederates'.[27] Abraham White of Warden, husbandman, stated that he bought two scythes from Peirson for 4s 6d. So did other labourers.[28] The evidence appears to support the theft of goods for resale by one labourer to others.

A similar but more nefarious offence was that of sheep, cow and cattle stealing. In a series of fascinating depositions from the New Romney court, Thomas Pinkaman of Great Chart, carpenter, was traced across the southern parts of Kent to the Sussex border and back again, in between working as a carpenter for a Mr. Etherick.[29] The

[26] J.H. Baker, 'Criminal courts and procedure at common law 1550-1800', in *Crime in England*, p. 15. See his other major essay on 'The refinement of English criminal jurisprudence 1500-1848', in Knafla, *Crime and Justice*. I would also like to thank Dr. Baker for his useful comments.

[27] KRO/QM/SB 404, 3 January 1601.

[28] *Ibid*., SB 405.

[29] New Romney [NR] JQ f 1/2/49-53.

following small episode is typical of Pinkaman's activities. On Thursday 10 June 1602 he went with William Carpenter to Goodman Snode's place where they played at the tables. In the afternoon they went to Thomas Daucken's house with James Harrison and another man where they stayed until 2.00 or 3.00 p.m. Then Pinkaman and Daucken went to Snode's again, where they ate and drank some more, and Pinkaman went home. At midnight Edward Maxselle called on Pinkaman to go to Romney, and once there they went to Snave's place. About one hour before the sun rose they were at Snave's Green, and 'ther a red goord cowe did com' from the churchyard 'that did fytt them'. But they lost her. They then slept for about a half hour in a field of wheat, and went to Giles King's house in Ivychurch where they ate and drank. Pinkaman then went to Mr. Simon's house where he drank a little, and departed to Mr. Etherick's house 'to woorke'.[30] Pinkaman appears to have maintained this pace for weeks. Despite the great amount of detailed evidence that was accumulated he was not brought to trial in this period. The evidence indicates, however, that he and others must have been very adept both at theft and evading the arms of the law. Both the Kent-Sussex weald and marshland areas were popular haunts for such activities, and the lack of law enforcement officials and centres in those parts made possible a thriving thieves' paradise.

Crimes against the person were largely assault, and the prosecutions against assault causing the blood to flow were frequent. The county quarter sessions minutes and examinations record numerous instances, and they are not merely the result of domestic quarrels or a vagrant's exuberance. For example, Francis Coram, weaver, aged thirty, met Richard Maister, aged twenty-six, and Richard Hunt, aged twenty-nine, at a Mr. Hunt's victualling house in Appledore. While the examinations of all three men differ,[31] the facts seem to be as follows. Maister and Hunt drank two or three pots of beer in the early afternoon. They called Coram over to join them, and they drank some more. Coram left, and they continued drinking until sundown. At that time Maister and Hunt left to visit in Brookland. Either Coram was asked to join them for the journey, or he followed them. About half the way along Coram asked to borrow 12d. They fell out and, according to Coram, Maister swore that Coram should give him 12d, and 'did streeke his staffe out of his hand and both the said Maister and Hunte did fall to beattinge of him haveinge nothinge to defend himselfe

Maister havinge a bill and Hunte a mole staffe untill such tyme as they compelled this examynant to delliver the money, which he did.'[32]

Similar assaults are found among all social classes of people in the boroughs and smaller towns.[33] Even the clergy were involved. In testimony given at Maidstone sessions, George Hawkes of Ightham, yeoman, on the advice of his parson Henry Seliare, 'did violentlie take' the body of Katherine Fulwood 'beinge verie great with child', carried her into a lane not far from the beacon, and with considerable force 'did verie cruellie and uniustlie against lawe, nature and humanitie whipp and beate the said Katherine'.[34] Several knights and gentlemen were called to apprehend him, and he was bound over to good behaviour. The act of forcefuly taking the law into one's own hands was not infrequent in this period. But if local officials had difficulty in securing the obedience of their people, their own attitudes and actions did not always inspire confidence. This is clearly apparent when one looks at the category of crimes against the peace.

John Church, miller, who was born in Ripon, Yorkshire, and aged twenty-six, had been in Appledore, Kent, for about a year when he had first a dispute with James Harbor, miller, with whom he worked, and then libelled the mayor and jurats of New Romney. He said 'that hee would make the highest the lowest', and that 'hee would knock downe the signe of Robert Symons of this towne, vitler, to the grounde'. He denied this, as well as calling Mr. Smyth a traitor. He was also accused of saying 'that hee woulde cause all Kent to bee plucked out by the eares'. Another witness, however, testified that he did not call the mayor a traitor, but only 'lord major, which hee sayeth hee thought hee ought those tearmes to use'.[35] Slandering a town's officials, however, was no worse an offence than the officials' sons desecrating God's house. Teenagers – even privileged ones – could be just as rebellious as experienced millers and weavers. The following examination of John Watson and others for trespass and riot in a parish church provides an interesting example.

John Watson 'confessed that hee threwe three hassocks (*trusshes*) at them that threwe at him', namely: Robert Clarke, Simon Harwood, and 'the rest hee knows not'. John Morley and John Watson said that

[32] KRO/QM/SB 430, 28 March 1602.

[33] For example, the Queenborough Court of Law Days, KRO/Qf/JMs/3; the Faversham Sessions of the Peace, KRO/FA/JQs 40; and New Romney Hundred Court, KRO/JQ f 1/1/60.

[34] KRO/QM/SB 426/19, 438, 13 April 1602.

[35] KRO/QM/SB 448, 27 July 1602.

a butcher boy spoke to Morley as follows: 'take heede such a one hath a beastley things viz man's dunge in his hand lest hee rubb it about your mouth'. Inquiring who it was, they said it was 'a long man', John Clark the younger. William Tylman declared that it was believed that William, Walter Benbowe's boy, stole a bundle of sticks and Coltone's boy pinched another. He confessed 'that hee threw three hassocks at them that threwe at him but knoweth not who they may be'. Stephen Mylener confessed 'that he threw two hassocks at the candle which the boyes had sett vp in the chancell and more hee threwe not'. Henry Eades confessed that because Clarke and he stood 'by the ringers together, Henry Mynge pissed vpon the sayd Clarke'. Clarke responded that 'hee did no manner of harme in the churche, and as for the pissing out of the pulpette hee the sayd Clarke sayeth that hee heard twoo or three saye that William, Mr. Thurbarne's man, did it'. He culd not remember who said it, but thinks it was Willison. 'Henry Mynge confesseth that hee pissed in Wymon's man's shooes. Jonas Kenwood confesseth that hee threwe the hassock which Watson threwe at him: and no more.'[36] Most of these teenagers were the sons of New Romney jurats and town officials. They represented a continuation of that pattern of local dissent between the members of the governing class that dominated the history of the borough from at least the 1580s.[37]

Moral offences were in some senses an extension of crimes against the peace. Some of the rulers of this society were becoming very concerned to expose and prevent fornication, bastardy and bigamy, which comprised frequent moral offences. Like recusancy and vagrancy, these offences were regarded as evils that worked against the peace, order and godliness of an agrarian society. Thus when Richard Punchyn got tired of his first wife he forged a death certificate for her and married a second time. With that success under his belt, he forged his second wife's death certificate and married a third time. Caught, and confessing to his crimes, he was imprisoned in Canterbury Castle. When he was eventually delivered from the prison by the justices, he was sent 'to be imployed in her Majesties service in Ireland'.[38] Punchyn followed an increasing flow of Kent convicts to the Irish wars at the turn of the century.

[36] KRO/NR/JQ f 1/2/62, 26 November 1602.

[37] The *APC* and *CSP Dom.*, 1584-1601. Mr. Thorold Tromrud, of the University of Toronto, who is doing a doctoral dissertation on the poor in late sixteenth and seventeenth-century Kent, is writing an article on this subject. Similar major disputes occurred in Canterbury, Faversham, and Sandwich. The context is narrated effectively by Clark, *English Provincial Society*, pp. 221-68.

[38] KRO/QM/SB 409, 12 January 1602.

Simple fornication and bastardy were prosecuted with equal zeal in some communities, as the examples of Barbara Heeler and Elizabeth Bingham reveal. Barbara Heeler, a young woman of Boughton, was drinking with Austin King in the Spread Eagle. After spending some time with their hosts, 'they removed to a beed chamber behynde the stocke'. When King and Heeler called for more beer, the hosts 'warmed it and carried it to them', and one customer went outside, and tried to look in. Finding the latch drawn, the windows shut, and the curtains pulled, he tried to force open a window but was unsuccessful. Leaving the house, his master said to him 'there wilbe good doeings annone'.[39] Later, Elizabeth Lager, a servant at the house, said that she saw Heeler with King earlier 'in a lofte over the haule alone togeither', and that at another time Heeler went into the woods with him.[40]

Although bastardy was a much graver offence, the examinations for this moral crime were no more thorough than those for fornication. Elizabeth Bingham, servant of George Dawson, declared that Anthony Rodes, servant of Mr. Stafford, 'hath gotten her with chyld and that noe other but he hath gotten the same'. He told her that 'yf she wold suffer him to have to doe with her, that then he wold marry her and she sayeth that uppon that promise he hath often had to doe with her'. The first time was the evening of the Sunday before or after Michaelmas [29 Sept.] 'in the fyld at the other syde of the streete behynd the barne of Mr. John Thurbarne'. They had come together by Mr Dawson's back gate and Rodes asked her to walk a little way with him. Then he went to the barn and told her to go to the field and that he would come to her. Before then he 'did also al that tyme promise to mary her' several times, and she says that 'she had a ring of his in her custody' together with other things. Examined before the other parties, Elizabeth Bingham said that 'no other had to doe with her and that it was uppon his promise to marry her', and that she was a wife before her landlord, a Mr. Thurlos, came to her. She also denied in front of Rodes that Thurlos 'had to doe with her about the tyme of the night of the place before mencioned'. Elizabeth explained that Rodes, after going to the devil with Mr. Stafford, 'did often resort to her . . . and was very acquyted [acquainted] with her and often used her [sexually]'.[41] Fornication, and especially bastardy, were prosecuted more consistently by the justices of evangelical communities like New Romney than by the county justices of the peace.

[39] KRO/QM/SB 408, 10 January 1602.
[40] *Ibid*. 408/2.
[41] KRO/NR/JQ f 1/2/14, 5 April 1602.

Finally we come to public nuisances. While not as serious as moral offences, they were nonetheless crimes or semi-crimes which offended the propertied and monied interests. Many local courts had large lists of public nuisances which were presented by grand juries, and convicted and fined by the judges.[42] The failure to repair dykes could lead to the flooding of large tracts of land.[43] And the failure to repair a wooden bridge that fell into a river near Yalding brought 'great damage of her majesties subiectes' and prevented travel and commerce from Biddenden to Sutton Valence.[44] Equally burdensome, or perhaps bothersome, was William Hogben of Elham, husbandman, who allowed the excrement from his cattle to run down into the highway called Shettlefield, where it putrified. Posting a bond and being tried by a jury, he was judged not guilty.[45] Numerous instances such as these reflected the relationships between entrepreneurs and landowners, landowners and tenants, and local officials and the 'agrarian proletariat'. These relationships involved problems which, in failing to be resolved, were passed on as in other avenues of life to the mill of litigation.[46]

There were, of course, many other kinds of criminal causes litigated in the local secular courts which ranged from a serious to semi-criminal nature depending on the facts. These included alehouse-keepers who harboured vagrants, deserted soldiers, and convicted criminals; masters who verbally and physically abused and injured their apprentices, and apprentices who stole from their masters the clothes and tools which were owed to them. Enclosures were rebuilt to enforce the departure of people who had settled on land unaware of fences which previous owners had failed to maintain; rivers and gutters were diverted to provide water for arable and pasture farming, and dykes holding out the sea were breached by persons who hauled away a few too many stones for their own use. Few areas of life in Kent were unaffected by crime and its litigation.[47]

[42] Such as the Faversham Law Days, KRO/Fa/JV/86/1; the Maidstone Burghmote Court, KRO/Ma/410A; the Queenborough Law Days, KRO/Qb/JMs3; and the Petty Lathe of the Level of Romney Marsh, KRO/S/Rm/SO1. It should be mentioned that local judges had great discretion in these nuisances or 'trespasses'.

[43] KRO/QM/SB 428, c. 1602.

[44] KRO/QM/SB 435, 30 October 1602. For earlier problems see KRO/SR 1/13.

[45] KRO/Q/SR 3/33, 12 January 1602.

[46] See, for example, the relationships and problems discussed by W.G. Hoskins, *The Age of Plunder* (1976).

[47] See also the interesting collection of materials for Kent – *Kentish Sources VI: Crime and Punishment*, ed. Elizabeth Melling (Maidstone, 1969); and A.L. Beier, 'Social problems in Elizabethan London', *Journal of Interdisciplinary History* 9 (1978), 203-21. I would also like to thank Dr. Beier, and the social history seminar at the University of Lancaster, for their helpful comments on an earlier version of this paper.

The pattern of criminal litigation is also revealing of contemporary attitudes and practices. Everywhere, from the largest boroughs to the smaller towns, disputes were litigated monotonously, often on a weekly basis.[48] A cause would at times stretch over months, with one party appearing, another making a pleading or answer, the other asking for a copy; one requesting an adjournment for more consultation, the other demanding to be put upon the country; the jury is called but it does not appear, writs are issued to distrain the jurors, and when they come the parties ask for another day in hopes of an agreement. Most of the causes would be settled and agreed upon eventually without a judgment. Judges saw no necessity to push for a speedy end of the matter so long as there was a ray of hope for a private agreement. Parties would often be represented by local attornies, the court by its sergeant-at-mace. Only after the parties and their attornies could reach no agreement would trial by jury take place.[49] Jurors, however, were being assembled across the county weekly for such trials, regardless of how many were required. Thus the statements of pamphleteers in the 1640s, that trial by jury was the birthright of all Englishmen, were not expressions in reminiscence of a golden age of the past, but statements based on the reality of trial by jury in the local courts of county, borough, town, hundred and marsh which had become part of a living memory.[50]

Let us now return to where we began. If Kentish society was mischievous and highly litigious in the early seventeenth century, if property-oriented offences did not predominate criminal proceedings broadly based, and if judges and jurors were relatively faithful in their duties, what are we left with? In a sense, we are left to study what Lambarde himself charged his jurors to look for.

> It is you that can see, if you will, the roots and first springs of all these evils that infest and trouble the country, and in you therefore chiefly it lieth to cut them off in the tender herb and before that they do grow to dangerous ripeness. For, if you would find out the disorders of alehouses, which for the most part be but nurseries of naughtiness, then neither should idle rogues and vagabonds find such relief and harborow as they have, neither should wanton youths have so ready means to feed their pleasures and fulfill their lusts, whereby, besides infinite other

[48] The best examples are the Gravesend Court Book, GR/JB 1; the Dover Hundred Court Book, KRO (uncatalogued); and the Romney Marsh Borough Court Book, KRO/RM/JR2.

[49] The best discussion is S.E. Prall, *The Agitation for Law Reform during the Puritan Revolution 1640-1660* (The Hague, 1966), pp. 54-67.

[50] The wider implications of changes in process for the shaping of the criminal law are discussed by Baker, 'Refinement of jurisprudence', in Knafla, *Crime and Justice.*

mischiefs, they nowadays do burden all the country with their misbegotten bastards. If you would complain of unlawful gaming in the day, of untimely walking in the night, and of unseemly appareling all the year, you should hew and cut in sunder the first steps, as it were, of those stairs which do lead up to pickery, theft, and robbing. . . The same might be said almost of all other offenses, the which of small seeds at the first wax in time to be great weeds by your too long sufferance and forbearing.[51]

Thus felonies cannot be studied without misdemeanours, and property crimes must be examined with personal, religious and moral ones. 'Sin of all sorts swarmeth' and 'evildoers go on with all license and impunity' because the resort to law has come to embrace the kaleidoscope of life. The suspects of recorded crime are large in number, but convictions are more difficult to obtain because somehow society must get on with the job of feeding, clothing, nurturing and salvaging the plight of its people. In the end criminal litigation in this era will not make sense until the whole fabric and structure of 'crime' from nuisances to felonies are studied within the social, economic, religious, cultural, and demographic context from which it arose.

Frederick William Maitland, in writing 'Why the History of English Law is not written', stated that legal records are our only major source for the history of the medieval era, and that for legal history to become intelligible it must come to grips with the more pervasive and fundamental questions of everyday life.[52] It seems to me that these statements apply as much to the early modern as they do to the medieval era. Maitland also wrote, in 'The Shallows and Silences of Real Life', that English historians, in failing to deal with the more vulgar affairs of the commonplace, in failing 'to show what the laws made in Parliament, the liberties asserted in Parliament, really meant to the mass of the people', were failing in their profession. The real task, he said, of plodding through the thousands of manuscripts which lay unconsulted, was tough and laborious. Some day, he hoped, it would be otherwise, and the history of any period would place the local courts and officials, with the people who owed suit there, in the very foreground. Then, he concluded, legal history would become more than a mere caricature.[53]

The task of reconstructing the past is as important to the study of crime as it is to the history of the law. A few brave historians have

[51] Read, *Lambarde*, pp. 70-1.

[52] *The Collected Papers of Frederick William Maitland*, ed. H.A.L. Fisher (Cambridge, 1911), i. 485-6.

[53] *Ibid.*, i. 468-9.

67

already begun the job that Holdsworth called for more than half a century ago.[54] But any attempt to sketch the structure of crime, and to interpret the administration of criminal justice must rethink the problem of defining crime, determine what particular crimes meant and just how important they were, and discover what the courts actually did. In the meantime studies such as this one represent the beginning, more than the end, of our knowledge and thought of crime and criminal litigation in the early modern era.

[54] Alan Macfarlane, in discussing the history of crime, said: 'It is only by combining the records of all the courts and of other local documents that we can gain some idea of what these patterns mean'. *Reconstructing Historical Communities* (Cambridge, 1977), p. 185; see also pp. 49-66, 114-35, 182-8.

EQUITABLE RESORTS BEFORE 1450

J.B. Post

For the practical purposes of most lawyers, and many legal historians, it has generally been enough to say that equity was a body of principles – perhaps, more accurately, a body of procedures and attitudes – applied by the English side of the court of Chancery.[1] The pre-natal development of these principles has been explored in various civilian and prerogative directions, and we can see how Chancery drew upon a mixture of administrative procedures, common law fundamentals, and civilian constructions, in order to produce its own version of common sense.[2] Yet the earlier we examine Chancery's equitable jurisdiction, the less satisfactory it seems that we should identify the emergence of this type of jurisdiction with the emergence of this court. If we begin to consider the patterns of litigation in the late fourteenth and early fifteenth centuries, when the equity side of Chancery first became a record-keeping court to any effective degree, we can watch the procedures and the records adopting the measured and ever more popular tread of bill and answer, replication and rejoinder; but we are not witnessing the development of a new type of court or a new type of justice – rather, it is the emergence to formality (and, more gradually, to pre-eminence) of a tribunal whose uniqueness lay in its central bureaucratic power and not in the quality of justice it dispensed.

It is of course perfectly fair to say that Chancery's equity was 'supplementary law'; it was a commonplace of petitions in Chancery to assert, often with reason, that the common law made no provision for a particular predicament, or that, if it did, the prerogative powers of the chancellor were needed to prevent the defeasance of the common law by common force or trickery.[3] The classic and in some ways the simplest instance of this supplementary law was the matter of uses,

---

[1] F.W. Maitland, *Equity: also The Forms of Action at Common Law,* ed. A.H. Chaytor and W.J. Whittaker (Cambridge, 1909), *Equity,* lecture I; cf. J.L. Barton, 'Equity in the medieval common law', in *Equity in The World's Legal Systems,* ed. R.A. Newman (1973), p. 139.

[2] Maitland, *Equity,* lectures I-II; Barton, 'Equity', pp. 139-55; *Select Cases in Chancery, A.D. 1364 to 1471,* ed. W.P. Baildon, SS 10 (1896).

[3] Maitland, *Equity,* pp. 18-20; see in general M.E. Avery, 'The history of the equitable jurisdiction of Chancery before 1460', in *BIHR* 42 (1969), 129-44, and 'An evaluation of the effectiveness of the court of Chancery under the Lancastrian kings', in *LQR* 86 (1970), 84-97.

where the legal title of the feoffees after the principal's death conflicted with their moral obligation to follow his wishes for the disposition of his lands. The victory of the trust over the crown's feudal dues was won in the fourteenth century – in 1401 Prince Hal declared that it was 'expressly against law' to ignore the oral conditions of an enfeoffment – but it could not be won at common law, and Chancery's trade increased accordingly.[4] To some extent this development was a matter of policy; patterns of litigation, patterns of documentary survival, and above all contemporary comment suggest that John Waltham, as master of the rolls from 1381 to 1386, used what Blackstone called 'a strained interpretation of the . . . . statute of Westminster II' to devise ways of enforcing equitable rights.[5] By such means (introduced, in all probability, less to expand Chancery's share of litigation than to meet increasing demands with increased resources) Chancery evolved as the purveyor of a more flexible justice supplementary to the common law.

Yet this development of a distinctive area of law should not lead us to suppose, hindsightedly, that Chancery's equity side grew around this feature alone; it is much more important to regard the medieval Chancery as a supplementary jurisdiction than as a jurisdiction of supplementary law. Maitland wrote of the early fourteenth century that 'no hard line is drawn between the true petition of right which shall be answered by a *fiat justitia* and all other petitions. 'Right' and 'grace' shade off into each other by insensible degrees, and there is a wide field for governmental discretion'.[6] Chancery was the normal agent of this discretion; increasingly from the thirteenth century onwards, the chancellor was expected to implement, or to make an administrative judgment upon, policy or detail in cases which had been referred to the king or the king in council for decision.[7] It is, indeed, difficult to distinguish 'council' jurisdiction from 'chancery' in judicial or quasi-judicial cases, since the perpetual cross-reference from one to the other seems to have reflected only the scale of the cases and not their legal standing, and the royal administration tended

---

[4]*Anglo-Norman Letters and Petitions from All Souls MS. 182*, ed. M.D. Legge, Anglo-Norman Text Soc. 3 (1941), p. 297 no 231 (all documentary quotations are rendered into modern English). See J.L. Barton, 'The medieval use', in *LQR* 81 (1965), 562-77.

[5]W. Blackstone, *Commentaries on the Laws of England* (1769), 3.51; Barton, 'Equity', pp. 145-6.

[6]*Memoranda de Parliamento*, ed. F.W. Maitland, Rolls Series (1893), p. lxviii.

[7]J.F. Baldwin, *The King's Council in England during the Middle Ages* (Oxford, 1913), ch. X; *Select Cases before the King's Council 1243-1482*, ed. I.S. Leadam and J.F. Baldwin, SS 35 (1918).

to treat the two as an integral court of law.[8] But governmental discretion was by no means the only reason why cases were brought in Chancery. The number of petitions to this jurisdiction which were dismissed with the words 'sue at common law' gives the misleading impression that Chancery wished, and was generally expected, to deal only in supplementary law. In fact Chancery was willing to consider, and judge, cases which were perfectly well within the cognisance of the existing courts.[9] Chancery's record-keeping was often limited to brief annotations on the parties' submissions, and, unless there are examinations or memoranda, it conceals the extent to which cases were considered before being rejected or acted upon. In 1358 a petitioner with an essentially common-law problem submitted a petition to the king; it seems that he was disappointed, but not out of hand – 'the king', noted a clerk, 'handed the petition to . . . . his chancellor, ordering him to call upon the treasurer, justices, and others of the king's council, and others whom this business touches, and let them know the contents of the petition. . . .'[10] Forty years later a petition was dismissed to the common law; what actually happened was that the chancellor patiently heard all the evidence on both sides, realised that the suit was over title to land and vexatious at that, and publicly told the plaintiff to 'hold her noise'.[11] More telling, perhaps, than isolated instances are the complaints of the commons – not upheld by the crown – that Chancery was becoming too frequently involved in matters of land tenure and other common-law business which lay outside its province; these complaints followed hard upon Waltham's expansion of Chancery's procedures, and the increasing volume of case papers surviving from his time onwards evinces no reluctance to deal with matters which were actionable at common law.[12]

Chancery's substantial judicial function, throughout the fourteenth century and far into the fifteenth, was to accept a degree of authority, unfettered by the formalities of common law, in cases submitted to it. Such cases might have remedies at common law, or they might not;

[8]'Courts, councils, and arbitrators in the Ladbroke manor dispute, 1382-1400', ed. J.B. Post, in *Medieval Legal Records edited in memory of C.A.F. Meekings*, ed. R.F. Hunnisett and J.B. Post (1978), p. 296 n.48; cf. Baldwin, *King's Council*, pp. 254-61, for the development of different bureaucratic procedures, and A.D. Hargreaves, 'Equity and the Latin side of Chancery', in *LQR* 68 (1952), 481-99, for arguments of stronger contrasts.

[9]Hargreaves, 'Equity and the Latin side', 481-99.

[10]C 44/35, no 20.

[11]'Courts, councils, and arbitrators', p. 320 no 100.

[12]*Rot. Parl.* 3.267 no 33 [1389]; 323 no 52 [1394];cf. 446 no 162 [1399]; Avery, 'Equitable jurisdiction of Chancery', especially 130-4.

they might involve conspiracy, or fraud, or malfeasance, but they might equally involve title, or detinue, or covenant. What mattered to litigants – or at least to the plaintiffs – was the advantage of Chancery's legal freedom and administrative power. The chancellor would not knowingly give a judgment at variance with the proprieties of common law, but he could summon and examine witnesses at his discretion, order the production of documents or the impounding of goods as he thought fit, in the course of making a decision which was not bound to follow known paths only; moreover he could, if policy, justice, or fees induced him to do so, push through these processes at a speed which gave the victor a rapid vindication and the loser a briefer uncertainty, but which could never be matched in Common Pleas or at assizes.[13] It is therefore all the more important to realise that Chancery was not unique; in quality and manner it was merely the broadest and most potent of the many equitable jurisdictions which were familiar to the medieval litigant but whose memory, in default of records, scarcely survives.

The origins of equitable jurisdictions were probably the same as the origins of common law jurisdictions, but developing in a society where recognised and relatively inflexible legal and procedural structures already existed. Long before lawmen put pen to parchment, disputes within a community were resolved for private satisfaction and public quiet by the expedient of deference – a cause was put by one or both parties to a common superior executive. Hence the jurisdiction of lord or community in the manor, the hundred, the county, and the network of traditions and authorities which crystallised as the common law of the realm. Against the background of this developed and circumscribed system the less formal resorts would have grown in much the same way. The common submission to judgment, or imposition of judgment, at common law tended (save in the courts administered centrally) to be based upon ties of a limited nature, normally tenure or residence: the jurisdiction of a manor extended primarily to its tenants, that of a hundred to its suitors, that of a lord to his enfeoffed retainers, that of a market to its licensed traders. Other resorts came to be needed, not only because of a desire for less formal and quicker procedures, but because different sorts of relationship involved deference to different types of authority; employees, colleagues, and partners, for example, did not necessarily have conventional links. Thus the spontaneous adjudication of executives between those submitting to their authority – feed retainers to seigneurial employers, magnates to the king in council – developed in complexity as relationships and litigation

[13] The procedures and their advantages are described by Avery, 'Chancery under the Lancastrian kings'.

became more ramified and subtle, as the use of these equitable jurisdictions became more common, and as the need for recognition at common law became apparent.

In order to explore the range of these jurisdictions, let us suppose that, at some stage in the middle of the fourteenth century (although for most purposes a century either way would be immaterial), Stephen and William are at odds, and they, or one of them, or perhaps their friends and neighbours, wish the dispute to end. They are both free men, with sufficient resources to consider litigation, but they do not want to sue at common law, whose expenses and delays, and perhaps limitations of available actions, are not encouraging. The precise nature of the dispute need not worry us, and was probably foggy enough at the time. There may be a definable bone of contention – a debt unpaid, an assault unrecompensed – or there may be a catalogue of troubles, in which Stephen's bailiff broke William's fences, and William burned Stephen's muniments. There may be a chronic feud, involving lively remembrance of Stephen's father as a fraudulent executor, or William's father as a piratical merchant. Obviously, the more varied the causes, the less satisfactory any one established court – archdeaconry, or assizes, or admiralty – is likely to be. What do the parties do?

Their first resort, if the matters are not of great substance and thus are likely to be resolved by a modest settlement one way or another, might be submission to the decision of a common friend or acquaintance. Inevitably such transactions went unrecorded, but in a litigious society they were probably not quite without procedures and protocol, and many of the suits which were abandoned without trace in common-law courts must have been settled by the intervention of a third party. In our less closely integrated communities of today, few minor disputes are put systematically to third parties, but in closeknit local groups it was accepted. In the better-documented sixteenth and seventeenth centuries it is possible to see disputes referred to local individuals qualified by rank, popularity, or mere age to bring harmony out of conflict; one Cotswold village worthy who died in 1684 is celebrated on his memorial in the parish church for his function as a local mediator.[14] We can hardly doubt that men with moral authority served similar functions at earlier dates.

---

[14]M.J. Ingram, 'Communities and courts: law and disorder in early seventeenth-century Wiltshire', in *Crime in England 1550-1800*, ed. J.S. Cockburn (1977), pp. 125-7; 'He was endued with wisdom great / and made up difference when debate / 'twixt friends and neighbours; he was one / that soon made up their union': Daglingworth, Glos, brass to Giles Hancock.

Despite the lack of evidence, this last assumption does not rest wholly upon extrapolation from later periods, and guesswork from first principles. It is also a ready inference from the peacemaking functions attributable to the guilds. Now the guilds were very far from homogeneous. In London the great livery companies operated trading and industrial monopolies at national and sometimes international levels. In major towns such as Coventry an amalgamated guild, though nominally religious, could constitute the highly organised social face of local government.[15] In a smaller community there might be a parish guild dedicated to nothing more ambitious than the maintenance of altar lights, and an occasional feast.[16] But from the mid-fourteenth century, when many of the religious guilds were established and the trade guilds begin to leave records, there are indications that, among the many social activities which these varied bodies sought to provide for their members, mediation in disputes was prominent. 'For rest, unity, and peace', as the London Mercers put it, and 'for a more convenient remedy, and more profitable, than process and rigour of the law', many guilds included among their ordinances regulations for the settlement of quarrels.[17] The regulations were not necessarily very demanding, but they did offer a framework for simple third-party mediation. To take one example from a small parish: 'If any brother or sister offend another in word or deed, let him not implead him until the alderman, dean, and brothers have tried to make concord.'[18] Or again: 'If any men of the company be wrath, they shall take two men of the brothers to accord them, and if they may not accord them they pay a penny to the light and pursue to the common law wheresoever they will.'[19] Admittedly the penalties for non-observance – usually a few pence for alms, or wax for the altar light – were seldom likely to worry anyone disputing an heiress, or a manor, but those who framed the ordinances clearly hoped that the friendly offices of neighbours and colleagues could produce fair, though not necessarily formal, settlement (one parish used the word 'reasonable') in disputes which would otherwise be sued at common law.[20] Some local authorities can be

[15] See the editors' introductions by M.D. Harris (vol 1) and G. Templeman (vol 2) to *The Records of the Guild of Holy Trinity, St Mary, St John the Baptist and St Katherine of Coventry,* Dugdale Soc, 13, 19 (1935, 1944).

[16] See in general H.F. Westlake, *The Parish Gilds of Mediaeval England* (1919).

[17] Mercers' Hall, Book of Ordinances c.1465, no xl; for the original ordinance of 1347 see the Warden's Account Book 1347, 1391-1464. (References to the Mercers' records were kindly supplied by Jean Imray). Westlake, *Parish Gilds,* appendix.

[18] C 47/44, no 310 [Outwell, 1389].

[19] C 47/45, no 360 [Cranborne, 1387].

[20] C 47/41, no 193 [St Austin, Watling Street].

74

detected in closely similar arrangements: the burgesses of Beverley were forbidden to go to law without first submitting discords to their fellows, while the mayor and sheriff of Bristol held informal sessions at regular intervals, to obviate litigation, thus providing what a resident described in 1479 as 'the greatest preservation of peace and good rule... that can be imagined'.[21] The evidence for any of these arrangements in action is scarce, but we do know that the London mercers sometimes used their guild procedures in commercial disputes, while the Trinity guild of Coventry is mentioned as the third party in two land disputes – once in 1384, when the guild master was invoked as a negotiator, and once in 1404, when it acted as custodian of an award.[22] There is thus good reason to suppose that our Stephen and William might have considered submitting their differences to the informal moral authority of the elders of their community, especially if either or both of them belonged to an organisation under whose auspices that authority could be exercised.

If, however, Stephen or William feels that the issues at stake, or their social repercussions, merit more weighty, though still legally informal, treatment, they may agree to a loveday. The term 'loveday' (*dies amoris, jour d'amour*) was used widely from the thirteenth century onwards, and in circumstances which varied 'from the vicar's pacification of scolding women to treaty-making on the borders'.[23] In legal contexts usage was narrower. In local courts, notably the hundred, leave for a loveday was sought by and granted to the parties in lieu of joining issue, sometimes happening with such regularity that mesne process in the local court was clearly being used as a lawyer's letter would be today, as an earnest of general intention rather than as a commitment to litigation.[24] Here the intention of the court, as with the far more common but less specific *licencia concordandi*, was to allow litigants to settle matters between themselves; the phrase clearly alludes to a day (presumed to be before the next court) on which the parties would choose to meet and come to terms.[25] But

[21] HMC, *Report on Manuscripts of Beverley Corporation*, p. 43 [1354]; *English Gilds*, ed. T. Smith, L. T. Smith, and L. Brentano. Early Eng Text Soc [original series] 40 (reissued 1924), p. 426.

[22] Mercers' Hall, Acts of Court; *Catesby v Bagot*, over Bubbenhall mill: E 41/394, m.3 schedule 4d. *Zouche v Damet*: HMC, *Fifteenth Report*, appendix XI, p. 142.

[23] J. W. Bennett, 'The mediaeval loveday', in *Speculum* 33 (1958), 361; the article analyses extensively usages of the term. See also M. T. Clanchy, 'Law and love in the middle ages', pp. 6-8, in *Law and Human Relations*, Past and Present Soc., 1980.

[24] 'Three courts of the hundred of Penwith, 1333', ed. G. D. G. Hall, in *Medieval Legal Records*, p. 179 n. A; *The Rolls of Highworth Hundred 1275-1287*, ed. B. Farr, Wilts Rec. Soc., 21, 22 (1965-6), e.g. pp. 22, 32, 35.

[25] Bennett, 'Mediaeval loveday', 354-5.

lovedays were not used solely to terminate current litigation; they could also be agreed by the parties in the first instance, and the scattered references to occasions like these suggest something slightly different from the mediation of third parties, and more elaborate than simple negotiation. The notable feature of these lovedays is that the parties were represented – either additionally, or in their absence – by their friends or lawyers, without necessarily having a neutral party present. Thus two litigants in 1384, who could not even agree on the way to sue a final settlement, at least agreed to a loveday at which three representatives of each should consider the matter; in fact the loveday was a failure, but the representatives arranged a further loveday at which the immediate cause of dispute was concorded.[26] That was a case of trespass, but very similar arrangements can be found in cases of title to land. At the level of minor disputes, between men of modest substance, lovedays may have involved only neighbours, or (if many principals were involved) a proportion from each side; more consequential cases were treated accordingly. Thus in 1411 a squire and a franklin enlisted an esquire and two knights each to settle a feud, while the lordly but unmannerly lovedays in *Tirwhit* v *Roos* were organised by the chief justice of king's bench and recorded on the parliament rolls.[27] It is thus open to our two disputants to agree on the social or professional level at which their differences should be treated, and to commit their affairs to appropriate representatives. The negotiations will be oral, and the conclusions will not be binding at common law, but the weight of professional judgment or county opinion will probably be behind any settlement which is reached.

If none of these expedients seems attractive, Stephen or William may feel it worth while to appeal to the authority of a magnate. This will invoke a third party, but at a level which will justify the briefing of agents, if not of counsel, and the resultant procedures will be suitably elaborate.[28] From the twelfth century onwards we can see that lords gathered around themselves bodies of advisers, probably originating as meetings of major tenants, but gradually coming to include professional lawyers and administrators; some would be the lord's own staff, others being paid annuities to lend their political or professional expertise to the conduct of the lord's business. By the middle of the fourteenth century these bodies had crystallised into

[26] *Catesby* v *Bagot:* E 41/394, m.3 schedules 4d and 6d.

[27] *Meryng* v *Tuxford:* KB 27/614, Rex mm. 9 and 12 [ex inf. Edward Powell]; *Rot. Parl:* 3.650-2.

[28] This and the following paragraph are based on 'Courts, councils, and arbitrators', 295-7, and sources cited there.

permanent and recognised institutions essential to every magnate; their main functions lay in the fields of estate management, politics, and litigation, but a consistent incidental duty was the settlement of disputes.[29] Throughout the fourteenth century we find mention of this judicial capacity, either in the reference of cases to seignorial councils or in the citation of their judgments; the council of the earldom of Cornwall dealt with estate disputes in the last quarter of the thirteenth century, and Edward II as prince of Wales treated his council as a private court of law.[30] By the end of the fourteenth century we have plenty of evidence, though scattered, for the way in which such councils went about their business.

Let us suppose that one of our litigants – Stephen – decides to appeal to the authority of an earl with whom he served in the French wars. He will begin by writing a petition to the earl, setting out his case against William; the petition will be in much the same style and format as a bill to the chancellor or the king. The earl will then appoint a day for his council to hear the case, and will instruct William to appear as well. The effectiveness of the whole procedure depends on the acquiescence of William. If he is a retainer or a tenant of the earl, he will doubtless come as a matter of obedience, reluctant or otherwise; if he has no such relationship, his attendance will depend either on the earl's wider political or personal sanctions, or on William's acceptance of the earl's moral authority. If William and Stephen both attend on the appointed day, they may well feel that the occasion calls for lawyers, perhaps apprentices or serjeants at law; after all, any magnate worth his salt will have a judge or two on his council, or serjeants of the first rank, and litigants therefore need adequate representatives. At the meeting the council will assess the written submissions and documentary evidences of each party; if necessary it will examine witnesses summoned in advance. It will hear comments or set speeches by counsel. It will then make some sort of decision along lines which again smack heavily of Chancery and the king's council. The matter may be referred to an official or a subcommittee – just like council business referred to the chancellor – for further consideration; the petition may be dismissed; Stephen may be told to sue at common law; or he may get a decision in his favour, with rulings on damages or restitution. This last judgment will only work if both

---

[29] R.I. Jack, 'Entail and descent: the Hastings inheritance, 1370-1436', in *BIHR* 38 (1965), 10, for William Beauchamp's council in 1390. More generally, see J.R. Maddicott, *Law and Lordship: Royal Justices and Retainers in Thirteenth- and Fourteenth-Century England,* Past and Present Supplement 4 (1978).

[30] N. Denholm-Young, *The Country Gentry in the Fourteenth Century* (1969), pp. 128-9.

parties are under the earl's discipline in some enforceable way, but the meeting would probably never have taken place unless there was a good chance that its outcome would be accepted. Yet the possibility of challenge remains, for the judgment of a seignorial council is not a bar to action at common law.

None of these forms of settlement, at any level, was recognised in law; in 1268 even the king, in ruling on a case submitted to him as lord, pointed out that his award did not prejudice subsequent litigation.[31] If some or all of the matters in dispute between Stephen and William are actionable at common law, the only means of reaching a binding equitable judgement is by arbitrement and award.[32] This means that Stephen and William will enter into mutual bonds, submitting themselves, on pain of an agreed sum, to abide by the award of named arbitrators. The variations on the procedures were many. Sometimes the bonds were simple recognisances for debt, which were lodged with a neutral party or with the arbitrators; when the award was made, they were given to the successful party, who could then sue for debt if the award was not accepted by his opponent. The submission to arbitrement could be oral, provided that it was made in solemn form. In 1366, when the defendant in *Audley* v. *Audley* ignored the award of the king in council, it was held that his submission to the arbitrement had been made before the chancellor, the treasurer, and the council, and should therefore be taken as binding.[33] In 1401 three parties submitted to arbitration under an oath made before the earl of Salisbury and the mayor of Salisbury, among others.[34] At a less exalted level, a manorial court was competent to witness that such a submission had taken place before it.[35] Most conveniently, however, the submission and other particulars would be contained in the bonds. In the early fifteenth century, for example, the complex case of *Ferrers* v. *Erdswick* was the subject of mutual bonds of 500m., containing the conditions: the parties should go to a certain meadow on a certain day, each with up to fifty supporters (four knights, twenty gentlemen, and the rest varlets), and appoint two knights and a squire each as arbitrators; in the event of disagreement between the arbitrators, Richard earl of Warwick was to act as umpire, and, if either party failed to observe the award, the bonds were to be

[31]*CalChR*, 2.92 *(St Denis v Valencia).*

[32]'Courts, councils, and arbitrators', 294-5 and references.

[33]*CCR 1364-8*, pp. 237-9.

[34]*Anglo-Norman Letters*, pp. 391-2 no 327; cf. pp. 124-5 no 74.

[35]Essex Record Office, D/DU 102/12 m.2 and 57 m.12d (*ex info* Marjorie McIntosh).

delivered to the other.[36] Like all legal agreements, arbitrements were liable to evasion and collusion, but it is clear that in the common law courts, when arbitrement was pleaded in bar, that such a plea was itself good. If, therefore, our two litigants choose to submit to this form of arbitration – whether using local friends or the justices of both benches – they will, barring accidents, make a legally binding end to their differences.

Against this background, then, Chancery's equitable jurisdiction in the fourteenth and early fifteenth centuries looks less distinctive. Its decisions are no stronger than those of any other tribunal outside the common law – in 1387, indeed, two Chancery litigants put themselves on the chancellor's arbitrement, recognising that any award made merely by virtue of his office would remain legally informal.[37] If Stephen or William petitions the king or the chancellor, with a view to a hearing in Chancery, he is not invoking some kind of justice which Chancery alone dispenses. There are, certainly, types of case, notably administrative malfeasance, which are statutorily the chancellor's business; there are other areas in which Chancery will, in the course of the fifteenth century, move towards a monopoly of litigation. The real distinction of Chancery, however, lies not in its justice but in its administrative powers. Its decisions are made with freedoms and restrictions which are familiar in many institutions, of varying formality and at every level; it administers those decisions with all the force of the central department of state.

This conclusion suggests that two familiar arguments in particular need revision. Firstly, the wide range of cases tackled by Chancery, and the general freedom of equitable decisions from any constraints of established procedures, indicate that the links between canon law and Chancery's equity were tenuous. Of course, the influence of canonists, as Chancery clerks or as chancellors, upon procedures and judgments must have been substantial, just as the influence of canonists as common-law justices in the thirteenth century must have been; but this does not mean that civilian doctrines played any larger part than the general doctrines of the common law in formulating the judgments of the court. There is nothing in the records to suggest that litigants resorted to Chancery to get civilian treatment; it is far more likely that they sought the natural justice and common sense which at lower levels would have been meted by mediators unversed in either law. Secondly, the development of Chancery's activities does not support

[36] Common Pleas, De Banco Roll, calendared in Wm Salt Arch. Soc. *Historical Collections*, (original series) 17, pp. 51-2 (*ex inf.* Edward Powell).

[37] *Domingo v Prophet:* C 44/37B, unnumbered memorandum and examinations.

the idea of a response to the demands of an expanding commercial clientele. Such a response, if based on the presentation of cases in legally difficult fields, would surely have occurred in the thirteenth century rather than towards the end of the fourteenth; and when Chancery proceedings become observable in bulk, they are not primarily about covenant, debt, and service as agent (which are still the basic fodder of hundred courts, piepowder, and other traditional jurisdictions, well into the second half of the fifteenth century), but about real property, chattels, and offences against the person. The use made of Chancery by its litigants is the clearest indication that its attraction lay not in the legal characteristics of its judgments but in the administrative characteristics of its procedures.

THE DEVELOPMENT OF EQUITABLE JURISDICTIONS, 1450-1550

J.A. Guy

This paper serves two functions. It offers a progress report on recent scholarly investigations of English equitable jurisdictions in the period 1450-1550, and concludes with a *caveat* and a suggestion for still further research. Limitations of space require that my remarks must be confined primarily to the equitable jurisdiction of the court of Chancery.

Until 1974, scholars believed that the key development of Chancery occurred in the reign of Henry VI (1422-61), resulting from the chancellor's decision to protect uses. For the purposes of definition, 'uses' were created when the ownership of land was transferred from the original owner to two or more trustees, who became morally bound to discharge such obligations regarding profits and eventual ownership of the land as were enshrined in the deed of trust.[1] A simple form was when a landowner enfeoffed a group of friends to his own 'use', and after his death to that of his heir upon whom a freehold estate was to be settled by reconveyance. The feoffor could thus conserve the heir's assets by avoiding such feudal incidents as *primer seisin,* relief and wardship. Uses were also contrived to execute the wishes of feoffors after their deaths, achieving in effect the devising of land by will which feudal law forbade. A settlor would enfeoff his friends to his own use during his life, and thereafter 'to the use of the performance of his last will' as declared either then or later. Provision could be made for his widow or another before the ultimate beneficiary entered, and it was possible for a man who settled on himself with remainders over to leave a reversionary interest in his feoffees, their heirs and successors, obliging them to make final disposal of the land according to his expressed wishes. All this caused a good deal of confusion, but the real drawback was that the courts of common law offered slender protection against feoffees who defaulted on their agreements. Common law would protect the right of the feoffor or his heir to re-enter a property if such a condition had been declared at the time of the enfeoffment. But the interests of other beneficiaries enjoyed no legal sanction. It was the chancellor, following after 1450 the example of the ecclesiastical courts, who began the slow but steady process by which other interests became guaranteed on the ground of conscience.

---

[1] For the best modern discussion, see E. W. Ives, 'The genesis of the statute of uses', in *EHR* 82 (1967), 673-99.

According to Miss M. E. Avery, the equitable jurisdiction of Chancery was a direct response by an instrument of central government to social pressure from fifteenth-century landowners who found the restrictions of common law increasingly irksome. These men wanted to dispose of their lands freely after their deaths, to evade feudal taxes, and to insulate themselves against forfeitures to the Crown in case of dynastic attainders. Miss Avery demonstrated that Henry VI's chancellors after John Kemp (1450-54) complied by defending on a large scale the interests of the *cestui-que-use*, another triumph for private rights which mirrored the monarchy's weaknesses in an age of bastard feudalism and the Wars of the Roses. Less satisfactorily, she bolstered her account with statistics aimed at proving Chancery's rise as an established court of equity before Edward IV's accession, systematically counting all those cases which had come to Chancery from Essex and Kent before 1460. She found that, although 28 per cent of her cases involved uses by 1426, hardly any concerned the interests of beneficiaries other than the feoffor or the heir at that date. But by 1450, almost 65 per cent of the counted cases concerned equitable interests founded on uses, and this figure had risen to a staggering 90 per cent by 1460.[2]

In 1974, however, Dr Nicholas Pronay published an important revisionist essay. Pronay used similar materials and case-counting techniques, but discovered a quite different terrain, one thick with potholes for the notion that Chancery's equitable jurisdiction was consolidated before 1461. By examining materials over a broader chronological base, Pronay argued effectively that Chancery's new jurisdiction was settled during the Yorkist period, not the Lancastrian. After 1461, the number of suits filed per annum in Chancery quickly doubled from a hitherto steady 126 to 243, and from 1475-85 doubled again to 553 cases a year. Thereafter, numbers grew more slowly: 571 suits per annum during the period 1485-1500; and 605 per annum from 1500 to 1515. The Yorkist expansion also had an institutional impact, because it was in Edward IV's reign that Chancery began to change its personnel and routine into recognizably established forms. For instance, a previously clerical personnel was now steadily replaced by a professional staff of civil lawyers from the universities.[3] Regarding the significance of uses in Chancery's development, Pronay refuted the position adopted by Miss Avery. Throughout the

[2] M. E. Avery, 'The history of the equitable jurisdiction of Chancery before 1460', in *BIHR* 42 (1969), 129-44.

[3] N. Pronay, 'The chancellor, the Chancery, and the Council at the end of the fifteenth century', in *British Government and Administration*, ed. H. Hearder and H. R. Loyn (Cardiff, 1974), pp. 87-103.

fifteenth century, he observed, most Chancery cases came from the towns and mercantile community. Miss Avery had studied two rural areas, Essex and Kent; thus the predominance of uses in her analysis reflected a biased method of selection. For example, Essex and Kent provided 25 of the cases from one bundle of documents she had analysed. But the total number of cases in that bundle was 333, of which more than half came from the towns. In another of Miss Avery's bundles, Essex produced six cases and Kent 14, but London on its own accounted for 52 cases, almost all of which were mercantile. Furthermore, Kent turned out to be a most unsatisfactory county for statistical purposes. The erection of a use there was an easy way of extending Kentish notions of partible inheritance to possessions acquired by Kentishmen outside Kent, and was an equally easy way of defending Kentish eldest sons from the fragmentation of familial estates otherwise subject to partible inheritance. At best, then, Miss Avery had simply shown that uses were a principal reason for Kentishmen applying to Chancery.[4]

Dr Pronay next constructed his own systematic statistics. These were derived from an analysis of a complete bundle of Chancery proceedings (C 1) filed between 1474 and 1483, some 206 cases. Of these, a striking majority came from towns and the mercantile community. It was discovered that a mere 11 per cent of cases concerned detention of deeds or uses, and only 6 per cent were equitable cases on uses. From these and other data, the conclusion seemed inescapable that Chancery business quadrupled during the Yorkist period because the court was admitting a wide jurisdiction in commercial equity. If this was in fact so, the true origins of the court of Chancery as known to the Tudors must plainly be found in its response to the needs of the Yorkist mercantile community.[5] Nevertheless, the matter cannot be settled conclusively. We still do not know how many of the new commercial cases were actually *equitable*, and Dr Pronay sheds little light on the point. The scale of the problem is perhaps best put in perspective by a statistic which neither Miss Avery nor Dr Pronay mentions. Two-thirds of all cases in the present Chancery proceedings at the Public Record Office offer no documentation other than the bill of complaint, and thus few means of finding out what is really going on. We shall return to this point. Respectfully acknowledging the major significance of Dr Pronay's research, we may also question whether he has satisfactorily proved his claim that Chancery's business quadrupled in the Yorkist period.

[4]Pronay, pp. 92-4.
[5]Pronay, pp. 89-90.

As he himself informed Miss Avery, many fifteenth-century Chancery proceedings were oral. We do not know how many oral petitions or petitions constructed as a brief note rather than a formal bill of complaint were dealt with. We are in danger of confusing the number of written petitions with the actual volume of Chancery's business. Manifestly, this excellent argument boomerangs on its inventor.[6]

We move next to the period of Wolsey's ascendancy (1515-29), studied in his doctoral dissertation by Dr Franz Metzger. Here the late-medieval system of equitable arbitration is distinguished from the modern system of equitable jurisdiction, and Wolsey is characterized as a consistent and distinguished practitioner of the earlier style. More important to the present discussion, a thorough analysis is given of 7,476 Chancery cases filed during these fourteen years. This shows that 46 per cent of cases on the equity side of Chancery now concerned detention of deeds or uses, and only 20 per cent of cases were from the towns and commercial community.[7] In other words, there had been a marked reversal of emphasis since the reign of Edward IV, something not previously noticed. The towns provided almost all the mercantile suits of Wolsey's day, and 16 per cent of all Wolsey's cases came from the City of London, 73 per cent of which concerned either bonds or debts. Yet here, too, there had been a pronounced adjustment since the period 1474-83, when 25 per cent of all extant cases came from London. The questions thus are: (1) had there been a boom in cases of detention of deeds and uses between 1480 and 1529, a boom which, if proved, was as major a phase in the development of Chancery as the Yorkist expansion of commercial suits?; and (2) had there been a swing to the country between 1483 and 1529? I can add that Dr Metzger's monumental analysis of Chancery's work under Wolsey is firmly supported by my own statistics for Sir Thomas More's thousand days in that court (1529-32). Of More's 1,122 suits, I classified 47 per cent as real property suits and 15 per cent as mercantile cases.[8]

---

[6] A destructive critic might ask whether *any* counting of fifteenth-century Chancery cases really does much more than add artistic colour to large and otherwise bald assertions. Confidence in the case-counting technique is not increased by a later statement of Dr Pronay's that under Wolsey, Chancery's annual rate of growth accelerated to 770 cases per annum from a previous 605. On Dr Franz Metzger's figures (see below), the annual total for Wolsey should be no higher than 534 – a discrepancy between two case-counters of 44 per cent.

[7] F. Metzger, 'Das Englische Kanzleigericht unter Kardinal Wolsey, 1515-1529' (Erlangen Ph.D., 1976), statistical appendices. I am most grateful to Dr. Metzger for sending me a print-out of his analysis, and to Professor G.R. Elton for lending me his personal copy of Dr Metzger's thesis.

[8] J. A. Guy, 'Thomas More as successor to Wolsey', in *Thought: Fordham University Quarterly* 52 (1977), 275-92.

At present all we can do to answer the questions is to follow Dr Metzger's observation that 78 per cent of Chancery's proprietal cases under Wolsey came from outside London, and note his tentative statistic that only 6 per cent of all cases in Chancery at this date seem to turn in argument on the equity of uses, as opposed to 44 per cent of cases which necessarily make reference to a use and its historical consequences for those involved. On this particular point, wholly equitable cases on uses appear under Wolsey to be where they had been in 1474-83, pegged at 6 per cent, whereas detention of deeds cases, most of which were in fact probably cases of disputed title which might have been tried in Common Pleas, had risen by 1529 from five per cent to 40 per cent of all cases in Chancery. We are thus back to a suggestion made by Dr E. W. Ives in 1968, re-emphasized statistically by Dr Marjorie Blatcher in 1978, that what is at stake is a massive influx of general property business into Chancery between 1450 and 1550, an influx at the direct expense of the common law courts, especially Common Pleas.[9] This shift towards Chancery and other courts of equitable jurisdiction, notably Star Chamber, Requests and the court of Duchy Chamber, was not specifically encouraged by successive lord chancellors after 1450, a rule to which Wolsey perhaps became an exception, but was consequent upon the advice given to litigants by common lawyers, who saw real advantages for their clients in Chancery's procedure, with its facilities for arbitration and extra-legal compromise, and its relatively impressive armoury of enforcement potential. Furthermore, the shift towards Chancery and the conciliar courts became sufficiently pronounced by Sir Thomas More's time to generate an atmosphere of keen debate within the legal profession, a debate in which the controversial issue was not the rise of equitable jurisdictions *per se*, but of parallel jurisdictions at common law and equity, especially in real property suits.[10] The point of controversy in the 1530s was that the development of a 'rival' forum for litigation based on Chancery and the rest raised disturbing questions about competing jurisdictions, both at common law and equity, and between individual courts within the equitable arena. Unregulated competition between parallel royal jurisdictions raised, as it seemed for the first time in English History, the truly awful prospect of perpetual litigation, especially in real property suits.[11]

[9] E. W. Ives, 'The common lawyers in pre-Reformation England', in *TRHS*, 5th series, 18 (1968), 165-70; M. Blatcher, *The Court of King's Bench, 1450-1550* (1978), pp. 167-71.

[10] This matter is fully discussed in my book *The Public Career of Sir Thomas More* (New Haven and Brighton, 1980), chs. 2-5.

[11] Cf. C. M. Gray, 'The boundaries of the equitable function', in *AmJLH* 20 (1976), 192-226.

Accordingly, almost everyone agreed that whatever Chancery was allowed to do it must not be permitted to rock the foundations of common law, irrespective of the equities of individual cases or however indefensible in conscience existing maxims of law were as rational principles.

There is not space to expatiate on this theme, merely to note that the problem of parallel jurisdictions marked the point of confluence between Chancery's severest critics and Christopher St German, equity's most learned defender in the sixteenth century. According to St German, it was not the existence of Chancery, which was in most cases salutary, but the element of overlap which would introduce the arbitrariness and uncertainty into English law claimed against Chancery by the critics. It was thus undesirable that Chancery should intervene indiscriminately to remedy legal loopholes. A number of hard cases existed where equitable relief had to be left to the private consciences of the parties. As St German wrote in his *Little Treatise Concerning Writs of Subpoena*:

> When a man that hath right cannot come to his right at the common law but that this should follow an inconvenience or a contradiction in the court, for eschewing whereof the common law will give him no remedy, and then if he should have a *subpoena* the same inconvenience or contradiction would follow in the Chancery, no *subpoena* lieth.[12]

For instance, a writ of *subpoena* could not lie against a statute, nor against the maxims of common law.[13] One such maxim was that judgments given at common law could not be annulled except by writ of error, attaint or certification of *novel disseisin* – a maxim given statutory sanction in 1285 and 1402.[14] Chancery should thus avoid reviewing decisions at common law, even if proved erroneous or unjust. Such argument is the supreme expression of the proverb 'equity follows the law', although in St German's mouth it reflected equally that author's concepts of positive human law and national sovereignty, as unveiled during the jurisprudential battles of the Henrician Reformation.

To conclude, I wish to return to my remark that two-thirds of cases in the present Chancery proceedings offer no documentation other than the bill of complaint. The rate of survival actually varies from

[12] Quoted by D. E. C. Yale from St German's autograph in 'St German's *Little Treatise concerning writs of subpoena*', in *Irish Jurist* 10 (1975), 331 n.30.

[13] 'A Little Treatise concerning writs of *subpoena*', in *Doctor and Student*, ed. W. Muchall (1815), p. 30.

[14] *Ibid.*, p. 31.

category to category: for instance, as many as 91 per cent of town and borough suits for Wolsey's years have the bill alone. This insufficiency makes any valid generalisations about suits, particularly as to their equitable nature, virtually impossible at present. For the future, however, a substantial (and unlisted) class of Chancery miscellanea (C 4) has recently turned up at the Public Record Office, the first 23 bundles of which comprise several thousand assorted answers, replications and rejoinders, along with some surrejoinders, interrogatories, writs and certificates – the bulk covering the very period 1450-1550 here discussed. From these new-found bundles, complete pictures of many hundreds of individual Chancery suits can now be compiled for the first time, and, when interlocked with the relevant Chancery files (especially the *Corpus cum causa* series), a deeper understanding both of equitable principles and procedure can be constructed.

With the arrival into the equation of C 4, it is appropriate to offer a final *caveat* on the technique of case-counting. Statistics based on such counts tend to be of two kinds: (1) casual statistics designed to provide a quantitative foundation for the broadest generalisations; and (2) more systematic statistics from specific counties or bundles intended to prove a point by learned argument. But when two-thirds founded on bills of complaint alone, are such statistics of much value? First, the data gained are almost wholly *ex parte*. Secondly, it should be better realised that legal cases, like Jacobean manors, are not at any one time equivalent units like pounds, dollars or bags of cement. At any given historical moment, some suitors were pleading to long-established areas of jurisdiction in Chancery, others probing new areas with varying degrees of tentativeness; some cases were long and complex, others short and trivial; some suits were never intended (or allowed) to progress beyond bill of complaint, others were earnestly pursued to judgment over many years; some were genuine Chancery suits, others short-term or collateral actions for advantage with respect to suits pending elsewhere – and so on. The pitfalls are ubiquitous, and I close with a useful adaptation of the late J.P. Cooper's comment on the counting of manors: the counting of cases 'seems to have effects dangerously similar to the counting of sheep. It introduces us to a dream world in which, as in our own dreams, reality may not be entirely absent, but appearances are often deceptive'.[15]

[15] Quoted by J. H. Hexter, in *Reappraisals in History* (1961), p. 129.

CENTRAL COURT SUPERVISION OF THE ANCIENT DEMESNE MANOR COURT OF HAVERING, 1200-1625

M.K. McIntosh

One of the functions of the English central courts during the later medieval and Tudor periods was the supervision of justice as provided by lower courts.[1] The common law courts and the equity courts could issue writs to lower courts, calling up for review the record of a private suit about which one party had submitted a complaint. Various types of courts were subject to central court review: county courts, the courts of hundreds, boroughs, and liberties, and the courts of ancient demesne manors. I have encountered the question of central court supervision while studying an ancient demesne manor, and it is therefore upon the latter that this paper will focus.

Review jurisdiction has not yet been thoroughly explored by scholars, in part because the records are so widely scattered among the great mass of central court materials and are seldom detailed.[2] Any study of review will presumably need to include consideration of three related questions: to what extent did the king's central courts see themselves as responsible for the quality of justice offered by lower courts; what procedures were made available whereby a person who felt himself wronged in a lower court could complain to the central courts; and what circumstances would induce a party to go to the bother and expense of appealing to the central courts for review? It is hoped that the following discussion may stimulate interest in the subject of review on a broader level.

Tenants of the ancient demesne, those lands which had been in the crown's possession before the Norman Conquest, enjoyed certain legal privileges. One of these, established during the thirteenth century, was the right to a review by the central courts of the

[1] The research for this study was completed thanks to a Grant-in-Aid from the American Council of Learned Societies in the summer of 1979. I am grateful to S.F.C. Milsom and John Baker for discussing the subject of review with me and to Richard Helmholz and John Guy for their comments on a draft of this paper.

[2] Thus, although Margaret Hastings identifies one of the three classes of business of the Court of Common Pleas in the fifteenth century as its 'supervisory jurisdiction over the older local courts and the justices of assize', she says only that it 'has left few traces in the rolls', just an occasional memorandum of a writ or an entry re a land action: *(The Court of Common Pleas in Fifteenth Century England* (Ithaca, New York, 1947), p. 19). Supervision of thirteenth-century lower courts is discussed by Robert C. Palmer, 'The emergence of a national legal system in England', a paper read at the 1979 meeting of the American Society for Legal History.

procedures and judgments of ancient demesne manor courts. Writs were formalised to implement review of ancient demesne justice, directed either to the sheriff or to the suitors of the manor court.[3] An aggrieved party could complain to the central courts against the withholding of justice, against improper procedures, and against the non-execution of judgments. The central courts in the thirteenth century were thus prepared to exercise direct supervision over ancient demesne courts and to examine substantive local issues.

As time went on, however, the forms of review seem to have become far narrower in scope. The court of Common Pleas issued writs of *recordari facias* upon a complaint of false judgment, but apparently only for land actions, many of which were collusive.[4] Writs of *certiorari* from Chancery also initiated review, but most commonly on behalf of a successful plaintiff in a land action who had been unable to obtain execution of judgment. The court of King's Bench began to exercise supervision over ancient demesne manor courts only in the later fifteenth century, with the extension of writs of error.[5] There appears, therefore, to have been no mechanism during the later medieval years which enabled an unhappy party in an ancient demesne suit to complain to the central courts on grounds of defective justice. Review of substantive issues became possible again only with the expansion of the equity jurisdiction of Chancery and, to a lesser extent, of the King's Council in the later 1400s. By around 1500 petitions to the equity courts and writs of error from King's Bench must have been impinging upon local legal autonomy. Many lesser courts which previously had been functionally independent, in boroughs, liberties, and counties as well as in the ancient demesne, were now finding that their procedures and judgments were being carefully scrutinized by the central courts.

The operation of review jurisdiction in the medieval and Tudor eras may be illustrated by looking at the ancient demesne manor of Havering, lying 14 miles east of London in Essex. Havering was unusually large, with several thousand inhabitants occupying its 16,000 acres. The market town of Romford served as the focus of the

[3] *Early Registers of Writs,* ed. Elsa de Haas and G.D.G. Hall, SS 87 (1970), p. 115.

[4] An appeal concerning a collusive manorial land action must have been entered by agreement of the parties, presumably to achieve an enrolment of the land transfer on the central court rolls. See also M.K. McIntosh, 'The privileged villeins of the English ancient demesne', in *Viator* 7 (1976), 295-328, esp. p. 319.

[5] The application of writs of error to ancient demesne judgments may have resulted from a change in the King's Bench definition of what constituted a court of record. This subject was not discussed by Marjorie Blatcher in *The Court of King's Bench, 1450-1550* (1978) but is consistent with her general thesis.

community's thriving economic life. The Havering manor court was similarly active. It was empowered to hear all types and degrees of private suits, short of appeals of felony. All land held directly of the king was transferred or contested via little writ of right close in the court. During the fourteenth and early fifteenth centuries, the Havering court was hearing annually 100 to 150 personal suits and 10 to 15 land transactions.[6]

Havering tenants had an enterprising attitude towards the law. They were prepared to travel to Westminster to bring suit in one of the central courts, they made regular use of the Marshalsea court when it was nearby, and they seem to have been quick to take advantage of new procedures.[7] It is not surprising, therefore, that one finds an exceptional number of complaints to the central courts from Havering people, more than from other ancient demesne manors. Yet there was considerable variation in the number of Havering appeals from one period to another, depending both upon the methods of review open to the tenants and upon conditions within the manor itself. During periods of internal legal and political stability, Havering people made scant use of their right of appeal. When, however, new procedures were being introduced into the manor court or when the authority of the local oligarchy was being challenged, parties were more likely to obtain a writ of review.

I should make clear that the information which I have about Havering's relation with the central courts is not exhaustive. While working on a general study of Havering's economic, social, and legal history from 1200 to 1625, I have found references to about 80 Havering appeals. Some of the information comes from the manor court rolls, other cases were mentioned in the auxiliary records of the central courts, and the remaining instances were recorded on the plea rolls.[8] Certainly there must be additional cases which I have not encountered. Yet since there is no obvious, systematic distortion of the information which I have accumulated it seems reasonable to

[6]The Havering manor court rolls, extant in series only from the 1380s, are preserved at the PRO, SC2/172 and 173, and at the Essex Record Office (hereafter ERO), D/DU 102.

[7]E.g. CP 40/270/12, CP 40/1011/35, C1/12/186, C1/442/37, and C1/1157/52; M.K. McIntosh, 'Immediate royal justice: The Marshalsea court in Havering, 1358', in *Speculum* 54 (1979), pp. 727-733, and cf. below, Havering's adoption of the entry/recovery procedure.

[8]The clerk of the Havering court often noted on the roll when a 2 s. payment was made upon the delivery of a writ or when the record of a case was called into a central court for inspection. PRO classes KB 140/10-15 and KB 145 were made available to me through the kindness of David Crook. Several colleagues have generously told me of Havering references on the plea rolls, supplementing my own sampling of selected years.

assume that a major change in the level of activity among my references is indicative of some actual change in the volume of Havering appeals.

The beginning of review mechanisms for this manor lay in the 1230s, the same decade in which the Curia Regis authorised for use within Havering the characteristic ancient demesne land procedure by writ.[9] During this decade, one which saw considerable uncertainty within the Havering court, the king and his courts were prepared to receive complaints against the substance of law as administered locally. They pondered issues such as whether the Havering court had refused to proceed in a case because the defendant was a friend and relative of powerful suitors, and they questioned whether a complicated land inheritance case had in fact been decided in accordance with local custom, as the suitors claimed. Although writs of review had not yet been formalised, the orders from the king to the Havering court or to the sheriff are clearly near ancestors to the later writs. By the end of the 1230s the new manorial procedures had apparently become familiar and the more influential suitors of the court had acquired an accepted local position. Complaints to the king therefore subsided.

During the two and a half centuries which followed, the central courts seem to have been asked to review Havering decisions only rarely. Between 1237 and 1480 I have found just five instances of central court supervision: two writs of false judgement in land actions, and three writs of *certiorari* into Chancery, two of them involving land.[10] During the later medieval years the right to a review seems to have meant little to the tenants of this manor and to have provided minimal opportunity for central court supervision of local justice.

The level of central court involvement rose sharply around 1480. In part this was due to a pair of procedural changes. The first was the adoption within the Havering court of the newly-devised action of entry sur disseisin in the *post* leading to a recovery, used here as in the central courts to break an entail.[11] The first announcement in Havering that the ancient demesne land writ would be prosecuted as an action of entry came in 1491, followed by a flood of similar writs and announcements.[12] Almost at once, the defendants in such cases

[9]McIntosh, 'Privileged villeins' and references.

[10]CP 40/27, 2d; CP 40/851, 460; SC 2/172/26; C 260/144/9; and ERO D/DU 102/37, 4d.

[11]This form of the action of entry with a common vouchee came into regular use in the court of Common Pleas between 1472 and 1500; *Spelman's Reports*, ed. J.H. Baker, SS 93, 94 (1977, 1978), 2. 204-5.

[12]SC 2/172/36, 5d ff., *passim.*

began to obtain writs of false judgment against the decisions, with at least 13˙ such writs between 1498 and 1515.[13] Since the original judgments in these cases were affirmed by Common Pleas, the appeals were probably collusive, brought to test the validity of the new procedure and to obtain an enrolment on the central records.[14]

The second procedural change after 1480 was the appearance within Havering of the writ of error, issued by King's Bench. Prior to 1489, I have not found a single Havering instance of review by King's Bench. From 1489 to 1497, however, King's Bench issued at least 14 writs of error for Havering personal suits.[15] It is not clear why it seemed worthwhile for a party to obtain review in a minor debt or trespass suit, especially since the ostensible grounds alleged for reversal were limited to superficial errors in the wording of the record. Perhaps the threat of review was enough to induce the other party to agree out of court, or perhaps the justices were in fact prepared to go further beneath the surface of the cases.

To understand the changes of the later fifteenth century, one must also look at developments within Havering. In 1465 the manor obtained a royal charter which confirmed Havering's existing privileges, granted it liberty status, and authorised the election of a broad array of local officials, including justices of the peace.[16] The charter gave new life to the manor court, which had declined during the 1430s-50s. The number of suits heard annually leapt from 20 or 30 to over 100. The efficacy of the court also improved, fostered by the building of a gaol in Romford for the use of the Havering JPs but quickly appropriated by the manor court.

The resentment engendered among some local people by this increase in the authority and compulsion of the Havering court may have contributed to the popularity of the new writs of error. A more direct expression of antagonism to the court was made possible by the growth of Chancery's equity jurisdiction. Around 1480 Chancery moved into the position of supervising the content of Havering justice

[13] E.g., SC 2/172/38, 25d; SC 2/172/39, 5d, 10, 23d, and 24d; 961/456 and 507; CP 40/1011/541, 542, 572, and 576.

[14] Fitzherbert suggested that a collusive writ of error against a recovery in an action of entry might be prosecuted simply to preclude the possibility of an actual review which could lead to reversal: *Spelman's Reports,* 2 205. I am grateful to John Baker for this information and for several CP references cited above.

[15] E.g. SC 2/172/35, 11 (*bis*) and 13; SC 2/172/38, 4d (*tris*), 11 (*bis*), and 12; KB 27/940, 35 and 69. Very few of the writs of error entered into the manor court can be traced onto the KB plea rolls; the original judgments were affirmed in those appeals which were prosecuted.

[16] *Calendar of the Charter Rolls, 1427-1516,* pp. 204-206.

which had last been filled by the Curia Regis two and a half centuries before. Between 1480 and 1530 Chancery received at least 20 complaints against the Havering court and its officials, most of them lodged by little men or outsiders. They alleged false imprisonment, practices unfair to non-residents, improper bases for judgment, and undue influence and favouritism on the part of the local ruling families.[17] Chancery's decisions in these cases have not been recorded, but surely this kind of substantive complaint and a flexible review procedure constituted a far graver threat to the autonomy of the Havering court than had the more formalistic common law supervision.[18]

After the extraordinary burst of appeals between 1480 and 1530, Havering returned to a relatively tranquil state. Late in Elizabeth's reign, however, serious unrest again broke out, for the last time. Between 1580 and 1625 Havering underwent drastic change, with a cluster of economic, religious, and political cleavages which finally destroyed the authority of the traditional ruling families and of the manor court.[19] It is presumably no coincidence that at least nine more writs of error were issued during these years.[20] Central court review undoubtedly contributed to the loss of power and independence which the Havering court experienced over the course of the sixteenth and early seventeenth centuries.

The post-1580 writs of error raise an interesting and rather troubling closing point. The Havering manor court rolls record a decreasing number of personal suits as the sixteenth century progressed. By the early 1560s the clerk was entering only those suits which reached a jury; after 1589 no more suits were recorded at all.[21] I had therefore thought that in Havering, as in certain other local courts, the Elizabethan years saw the end of personal suits. Yet

---

[17]E.g. C 1/64/87 and C 1/543/3; C 1/109/45; C 1/369/94, C 1/440/19, and C 1/442/37; C 1/188/34, C 1/551/26, and C 1/600/21. Chancery had been receiving petitions concerning disputes over Havering land since the early 1400s, a use of the court which continued into the 1600s.

[18]The Chancery Decree Rolls, which begin only in the 1540s, indicate the use of direct personal interrogation and pressure by the court to compromise (e.g. C 78/2/17, C 78/6/66, and C 78/9/35). For the 'record' submitted by Havering officials in the 1520s in response to writs of *certiorari*, see C 244/166/35, C 244/171/14, 24, and 31, C 244/173/28 A, etc. I am grateful to John Guy and F.L. Boersma for their generous assistance in tracing and obtaining this material. A few more complaints against the Havering court were submitted to Chancery during the 1530s and 1540s but none thereafter.

[19]M.K. McIntosh, 'The Liberty of Havering-atte-Bower, 1465-1620' (forthcoming).

[20]E.g. KB 27/1285/139, KB 140/12, Pt. 2 (*bis*), and KB 140/13, Pt. 2 (*bis*).

[21]ERO D/DU 102/67 (1563-4) – 102/84 (1589-90).

among King's Bench materials there are writs of error with an attached record from Havering for cases of which there is no mention whatsoever on the Havering rolls.[22] The record submitted to King's Bench is detailed and describes exactly the characteristic Havering procedures. Since it is unlikely that the suits were fabricated, one must conclude that the cases were actually heard in the Havering court but not entered on the rolls. The Havering clerk would thus appear to have ceased enrolling a formal record of personal suits by 1590, while still keeping some kind of written notes so as to be able to prepare a record if required. Perhaps we ought to re-open the question of the decline of local courts during the sixteenth century, considering as well the possibility of a change in record-keeping practices among local clerks: examination of the writs of review and their records would be one means of approaching the question. It seems clear that a more general study of the supervisory role of the central courts would yield valuable material not only on the degree and type of control exerted from Westminster but also on the nature of justice as administered locally.

[22]KB 27/1255/237 and the references in n. 20 above. The Havering estreat rolls from the early 1600s note a few sums from defaulting defendants in personal suits not recorded on the court rolls (LR 11/58/847 I and LR 11/78/904).

THE KING'S BENCH IN SHROPSHIRE AND STAFFORDSHIRE IN 1414

E. Powell

This paper approaches the question of public order in England in the late Middle Ages by examining the use of the court of King's Bench as a 'superior eyre' – the term coined by Professor Putnam to describe the occasional perambulations of the court outside Westminster.[1] These eyres produced abundant records which survive among the archives of King's Bench in the Public Record Office. The present study is based on an analysis of the last major superior eyre, which took place in Shropshire and Staffordshire in 1414.[2]

The significance of these visitations was first revealed by Professor Putnam, who identified in the PRO many rolls of proceedings before the justices of the peace, and correlated them with the movements of King's Bench.[3] She argued indeed, that their survival was attributable to such movements, for when a superior eyre was held, King's Bench called in the rolls of the county JPs to review undetermined cases. She suggested that the superior eyre was devised by Sir William Shareshull, Chief Justice of King's Bench from 1350 to 1361.[4] In this new capacity, she commented, the court became 'an almost revolutionary instrument for law enforcement' and an important device for the review of the local judicial institutions of the crown.[5]

Later research has confirmed and also modified these views. R.F. Hunnisett has shown that the late medieval coroners' rolls likewise owe their survival to the perambulations of King's Bench, but he was sceptical as to the degree of influence the court could exert through its irregular bursts of mobility.[6] His doubts were shared by Professor

---

[1]B.H. Putnam, *The Place in Legal History of Sir William Shareshull* (1950), pp. 80,110.

[2]This paper is based on my Oxford D.Phil. thesis, 'Public Order and Law Enforcement in Shropshire and Staffordshire in the Early Fifteenth Century' (1979), where fuller documentation may be found for the conclusions laid out below.

[3]Her findings are summarised in *Proceedings before the Justices of the Peace in the Fourteenth and Fifteenth Centuries: Edward III to Richard III* (Ames Foundation, 1938), pp. 1vii-1xxii.

[4]Putnam, *Shareshull,* pp. 73, 109-10.

[5]*Ibid.,* p.134.

[6]R.F. Hunnisett, 'The medieval coroners' rolls', in *AmJLH* 3 (1959), 205-21; *idem, The Medieval Coroner* (Cambridge, 1961), p.114.

Sayles, and it is clear that Professor Putnam overstated her case.[7] The superior eyre was only one of several judicial expedients used by the Crown after the breakdown of the general eyre at the end of the thirteenth century.[8] Furthermore, Professor Sayles demonstrated that the use of King's Bench as a superior eyre originated well before Shareshull's time. As early as 1304-5 the court was associated with the trailbaston commissions in the Home Counties, and from the end of Edward II's reign it often exercised trailbaston jurisdiction on its own account.[9] Professor Putnam was nevertheless right to stress Shareshull's influence, for it was he who codified the jurisdiction of King's Bench as a superior eyre at Kingston-upon-Thames in 1353.[10] Between Shareshull's fall in 1361 and the death of Edward III, King's Bench rarely left Westminster, but it became more active under Richard II, when the superior eyre was most frequent.[11] Henry IV, perhaps fearing the opposition such visitations might provoke, never took his Bench into the country, and the superior eyre was not revived until 1414, when Henry V ordered King's Bench to accompany Parliament to Leicester to begin the sessions which are the subject of this paper.

The despatch of King's Bench to Leicester was part of a campaign to restore public order in response to petitions made in Henry V's first Parliament in May 1413.[12] To deplore the lamentable state of public order was a favourite pastime of medieval Parliaments, but in this case their complaints were heeded. Henry reacted with characteristic vigour, no doubt wishing to ensure peace at home before re-opening the war in France.[13] King's Bench played a central role in his strategy: it was in this court that the Lollard rebels were prosecuted after the

[7] *Select Cases in the Court of King's Bench,* ed. G.O. Sayles, SS 55, 57, 58, 74, 76, 82, 88 (1936-71), 6. ix-xii.

[8] For example trailbaston commissions, keepers of the peace and special oyer and terminer commissions: see 'Early trailbaston proceedings from the Lincoln roll of 1305', ed. A. Harding, in *Medieval Legal Records Edited in Memory of C.A.F. Meekings,* ed. R.F. Hunnisett and J.B. Post (1978), pp. 143-68; *Kent Keepers of the Peace, 1316-17,* ed. B.H. Putnam, Kent Records 13 (1933); R.W. Kaeuper, 'Law and order in fourteenth-century England: the evidence of special commissions of oyer and terminer', in *Speculum* 54 (1979), 734-84.

[9] *King's Bench,* ed. Sayles, 4.xxxviii-xlvi, 1 iv-1 xvi; *South Lancashire in the Reign of Edward II,* ed. G.H. Tupling, Chetham Soc., 3rd Series, 1 (1949) provides a calendar of trailbaston proceedings in King's Bench at Wigan in 1323.

[10] *Les Reports des Cases* (1678-80), part 5: *Liber Assisarum,* 27-28 Edward III; see Putnam, *Shareshull,* 109.

[11] *King's Bench,* ed. Sayles, 7, Appendices I-III; *Proceedings,* ed. Putnam,, pp.32-3.

[12] *Rot. Parl,* 4.4.

[13] See the review of Henry V's first five Parliaments in the Chancellor's speech of 1416: *Rot. Parl.,* 4. 94.

Oldcastle rising in January 1414, and that inquiries into disorders in Devon, Norwich, Yorkshire, Nottinghamshire and Derbyshire were returned for determination in the following months.[14] The revival of the superior eyre was the most striking feature of this strategy.

The superior eyre of 1414 lasted for three months, from April to July, spanning Easter and Trinity terms. At Leicester, where it sat first for nearly four weeks until mid-May, there was little criminal business, but at the sessions of Parliament held there at the same time petitions were presented which indicated serious disorder in nearby Staffordshire and Shropshire.[15] Probably as a result of these complaints, King's Bench was ordered into the two counties, spending three and a half weeks at Lichfield in Staffordshire from 18 May until 12 June (the sessions continuing throughout the Easter vacation); and a fortnight at Shrewsbury in Shropshire from 15 June. The court then turned for home, pausing only at Wolverhampton for the octave of St. John the Baptist (1 July) and arrived back in Westminster by the quindene of St. John (8 July), the final return day of Trinity terms.[16]

On arriving in each county the court called in for review all coroners' rolls and undetermined indictments from peace sessions. Presentments were also taken *coram rege* from a county grand jury and juries of each hundred, borough and liberty.[17] Apart from a few lost coroners' rolls, all the county records called in from Shropshire and Staffordshire in 1414 survive. There are thirty-three coroners' rolls for the two counties, many dating from Richard II's reign, some even from that of Edward III.[18] A peace roll survives for each county, and both have been printed.[19] Their spread is far narrower than that of the coroners' rolls; the Shropshire roll contains proceedings from 1400, the Staffordshire roll only from 1409. Each is written in a uniform hand throughout, and includes a copy of the latest peace commission.

---

[14] KB 27/611-26, Rex sections, *passim.* The returned commissions of inquiry are at KB 9/204/1 (Lollard commissions for several counties); KB 9/204/2 (Notts. and Derbs.); KB 9/205/1, ms. 1-14 (Yorks.); *ibid.*, ms. 37-8 (Norwich); KB 9/205/2-3 (Devon).

[15] *Rot. Parl.*, 4.30-3.

[16] KB 27/612-13, *passim.*

[17] *Liber Assisarum,* 27 Edward III, pl.2; *Registrum Omnium Brevium tam Originalium quam Judicialium* (1687), Jud. 77v.

[18] Hunnisett, 'Coroners' Rolls', 342-3.

[19] The Shropshire roll (JUST 1/752) is printed as *The Shropshire Peace Roll, 1400-1414,* ed. E.G.Kimball (Shrewsbury, 1959). The Staffordshire roll (JUST 1/815) is printed in *Proceedings,* ed. Putnam, pp. 295-333.

The juries of presentment *coram rege* made their returns to articles of enquiry which were probably similar to those drawn up by Shareshull in 1353.[20] These formed the largest and most comprehensive group of indictments, with charges ranging from treason and counterfeiting on the Welsh Marches to the construction of illicit fish-weirs on the River Severn.[21] The memory of the jurors was sometimes so long as to suggest access to written records: for example, of twenty-four offences recorded by the jury of Newcastle-under-Lyme in Staffordshire, ten were dated before 1399.[22]

The numbers of indictments contained in each record are about the same for both counties: some 300 homicides on the coroners' rolls, nearly 200 peace sessions' indictments and just under 400 *coram rege* presentments, so that the total for each county is between 850 and 900. The rate of duplication (i.e. of indictments for the same offence laid by different juries) is very high at 22 per cent or over one in five. This is most frequent in homicide cases: since coroners' inquests survive for most slayings, homicide indictments on the peace rolls or *coram rege* files are almost invariably duplicates. As a result, and because of the large number of coroners' rolls, there are more than 500 homicide indictments in each county – well over half the total of indictments for all offences.

A collation of the information given in the duplicate indictments confirms the need for caution in their use, as has been stressed in relation to similar records by J. S. Cockburn.[23] Nevertheless, many of their apparent inconsistencies disappear on closer examination: for although it is often necessary to root out the offender hiding under an alias, the jurors' local knowledge of his home and occupation can usually be trusted. Indictments rarely conflict in their location of offences, though they give little topographical detail. But in two important respects – the date and character of the offence – they should be treated with the greatest suspicion. There are usually as many different dates for an offence as there are indictments; while in cases of homicide, for example, it was not uncommon for one jury to view as justifiable killing what another set down as murder.[24]

---

[20] *Liber Assisarum,* 27 Edward III, pl.44. The presentment file for Shrops. is at JUST 1/753, for Staffs. at KB 9/113.

[21] Treason: JUST 1/753, m. 29(1) nos.1-6. Illicit fish-weirs: *ibid.,* m. 22 no.1.

[22] KB 9/113, ms. 37-8.

[23] J.S. Cockburn, 'Early-modern assize records as historical evidence', in *Journal of the Soc. of Archivists* 5 (1975), 215-31.

[24] For a detailed analysis of the indictment evidence, see Powell, 'Public Order', pp. 187-202.

98

On receiving the indictments, the officials of King's Bench sorted and classified them to prepare for writs of summons. Offences were divided into felony, trespass and accessory to felony, since the nature and timing of process differed in each case. Because many offences were several years old a rough form of limitation was imposed, and indictments dated before 1404 were usually omitted from process.[25] Treason, murder and rape were, however, an exception to this; process upon them issued irrespective of the age of the indictment. The reason for this lay in the statute of 1390, which excluded such crimes from the scope of general pardons.[26] J.M. Kaye and T.A. Green have viewed this statute as a landmark in the evolution of the law of murder and manslaughter, since it distinguished simple homicide, for which a general pardon was sufficient, from serious homicide or 'murder', which required a specific individual pardon.[27] There have been suggestions that the statute remained a dead letter, and its observance by King's Bench in 1414 is therefore of some significance.

Separate lists of summons, *venire facias* for trespasses and *capias* for felonies, were compiled for each set of indictments, sent to the sheriff for execution and entered on the controlment roll, the court's working copy of the plea roll.[28] It was on this copy that notes were made of the later progress of cases, through process to court appearance or outlawry.

Process of summons was issued with what can only be described, by medieval standards, as breakneck speed. Writs ordering exaction to outlawry were issued within days of the initial writ of summons, for trespass as well as felony.[29] The sheer volume of process, and its rapidity, demonstrate the vigour of Henry V's government. Over 1600 persons from Shropshire and Staffordshire were summoned before King's Bench.

[25] An indictment earlier than 1404 was marked 'antea perdonatus' by the King's Bench scribe, which indicated that the offence came within the scope of the general pardons of Richard II and Henry IV and should be omitted from process. Compare the *Shrops. Peace Roll*, ed. Kimball, pp.52-72, with the process lists on KB 27/613, Rex, ms. 13, 14.

[26] 13 Richard II, st.2, c.1.

[27] J.M. Kaye, 'The early history of murder and manslaughter', in *LQR* 83 (1967), 391-5; T.A. Green, 'The jury and the English law of homicide, 1200-1600, in *Michigan Law Review* 74 (1976), 457-68.

[28] KB 29/53, ms. 8-28.

[29] See, for example, the process issued on trespasses from the Staffs. peace roll: KB 29/53, m. 10d; KB 27/612, Rex, m. 26d.

Table 1 summarises the effectiveness of process arising from the superior eyre in the two counties. 43 per cent appeared on Staffordshire indictments, 29 per cent on those from Shropshire. In interpreting those statistics, allowance must be made for the number of 'cold' cases. 180 persons were summoned on indictments dated before 1404, of whom 160 were outlawed: many of these were probably dead.

Table 1: Total figures for appearance and non-appearance in court on process arising from all indictments submitted to King's Bench during the superior eyre.

	Staffordshire		Shropshire	
	Total	%	Total	%
Appearance	362	43	203	29
Non-Appearance	480	57	498	71
Total	842	100	701	100

Table 2: Appearance and non-appearance in court by percentage on indictments dated (i) before 1409, (ii) 1409 and after.

	Staffordshire		Shropshire	
	Before 1409	1409 & After	Before 1409	1409 & After
	%	%	%	%
Appearance	26	48.8	17.6	34.4
Non-Appearance	74	51.2	82.4	65.6
Total	100	100	100	100

Process on more recent indictments was, the evidence suggests, much more effective. Table 2 shows that the rate of appearance rose dramatically after 1409, in Staffordshire to almost 50 per cent, in Shropshire to 34 per cent. The difference between the two counties is attributable to the hundred or so Welshmen indicted in Shropshire, many in connection with border raids, only three of whom appeared in court. Some were resident in the county, but most lived in Wales or the Marches, and were thus beyond the sheriff's bailiwick. The appearance rate also varied greatly for different offences. Nearly 80 per cent (105) of the 133 persons indicted in Staffordshire for breaches of the statutes of livery appeared in court, and 70 per cent (57) of the 82 indicted in both counties for economic offences. For homicide, on the other hand, the rate was far lower: only 20 per cent (109) of the 536 indicted.

After the drama of the perambulation and the colour and variety of the indictments, the court proceedings themselves are an anticlimax. As Table 3 reveals, most of those who appeared in court proffered pardons or made fine, and the minority who stood trial were all, except one, acquitted. It seems that King's Bench was unable to cope with the flood of business that poured in as a result of the superior eyre. The problem was resolved in December 1414 by the proclamation of the second general pardon of Henry V's reign, which relaxed the conditions hitherto governing such pardons in two important respects. The clause excluding treason, murder and rape was dropped, and no time limit was set for the suing of pardons.[30] These changes may have been designed to help recruitment for the forthcoming French campaign. Certainly the pardon was at once in great demand, and nearly 5,000 were granted in the three years following,[31] 328 being obtained by persons indicted during the superior eyre in Shropshire and Staffordshire. Of these 328 only 208 presented them in King's Bench. The rest settled their cases by other means or were content to remain outlaws.

What then did the king achieve by the prodigious effect of sending his Bench to the provinces? Miss Kimball, noting the low appearance rate on indictments from the Shropshire peace roll, commented that 'the lack of law enforcement and general disregard for the law, generally associated with the middle of the fifteenth century, existed as early as the beginning of the century'.[32] This conclusion disregards the fact that the country did not suffer serious disorder during Henry V's absences in France after 1415. Both John Bellamy and the late K.B. McFarlane look to Henry's reign as a period of order and good governance contrasting with the middle years of the century.[33] The late E.F. Jacob described Henry's skilful blending of firmness and conciliation, qualities which are evident in the superior eyre of

[30]Contrast Edward III's jubilee pardon of 1376, where pardons had to be sought within six months of the proclamation: *Rot. Parl.*, 2. 364-5; 50 Edward III, c.3.

[31]C.67/37.

[32]*Shrops. Peace Roll*, ed. Kimball, p. 42.

[33]J.G. Bellamy, *Crime and Public Order in England in the Later Middle Ages* (1972), p.10; K.B. McFarlane, *The Nobility of Later Medieval England* (Oxford, 1973), pp. 118-9.

Table 3: Analysis of proceedings in King's Bench from the superior eyre in Shropshire and Staffordshire, 1414

	Appearance						Non-Appearance				
	Convicted	Acquitted	Pardoned	Pardoned & Acquitted	Fined	Indictment Insufficient	Outlawed	Dead	Indictment Insufficient	Untraced	No Process	Total
Staffs	0	76	150	3	132	1	472	22	0	8	262	1126
Shrops	1	24	110	3	62	3	484	44	5	14	415	1165

1414.[34] The tone of its proceedings is measured and authoritative, comparing favourably, for example, with the bewildered desperation of Edward I's trailbaston commissions.

Such a confident show of strength was no doubt a useful exercise in political management even if it did not produce many convictions. But it seems possible to define its purpose more precisely. The primary targets of the eyre in Shropshire and Staffordshire were not the lower classes, whose offences could be dealt with by the judicial machinery of the county. Although King's Bench cast its nets wide and caught a large number of small fry, its real catch was the big fish, the men who ran the counties and whose disputes had provoked the disorder to which the Leicester Parliament drew attention. Table 4 shows the rate of appearance in court of those styled knight, esquire or gentleman in the indictments, which averages over 80 per cent in

Table 4: Outcome of Process Issued during the superior eyre upon men styled knight, esquire or gentleman

	Appearance	Non-Appearance		Total
	Pardoned, Fined or Acquitted	*Outlawed*	*Dead*	
Staffs	47	4	4	55
Shrops	33	7	8	48

Shropshire and 90 per cent in Staffordshire.

Henry V's aim in the 1414 eyre was not so much to punish the warring factions as to resolve their disputes, or at least make peace between them. The local machinery of justice, based on peace commissions and assize circuits, as yet lacked the power to coerce the gentry. The maintenance of the king's peace therefore depended upon a fragile consensus in local society, promoted by arbitration and conciliation.[35] When such consensus broke down, as it did in Shropshire and Staffordshire before 1414, it was necessary for the crown to intervene to restore order. In Staffordshire the feud between

---

[34] E.F. Jacob, *The Fifteenth Century* (Oxford, 1961), pp.128-9.

[35] The importance of procedures for arbitration in the late middle ages was brought out by Dr. J.B. Post in a paper delivered to the Birmingham conference. See also Powell, 'Public Order', pp.318-32.

Hugh Erdswick and Edmund Ferrers of Chartley had wide ramifications but seems to have been a struggle for influence during the long minority of Humphrey, earl of Stafford.[36] These disputes figure prominently in the county indictments, and all the main protagonists appeared before King's Bench, usually to present a pardon.[37] In Shropshire the depredations of John Wele and Richard Laken, the lieutenants of the earl of Arundel in the marcher lordships of Oswestry and Clun, had created an opposition grouped round John Talbot, lord Furnival.[38] When members of these factions appeared on *coram rege* presentments, the county grand jury urged that they should be required to offer security for keeping the peace, and Arundel pledged £3,000 for the good behaviour of his seven chief adherents.[39] At the same time, of course, Henry V was recruiting troops, and some of those who had recently disturbed the peace in Shropshire and Staffordshire were diverted to service abroad. Edmund Ferrers served at Agincourt, Richard Laken and John Wele were employed in the subjugation of Normandy, while John Talbot, who had had the temerity to challenge the earl of Arundel in Shropshire, was punished by his appointment to the military command of Ireland.[40]

[36] For the petitions of Erdswick and Ferrers to the Leicester Parliament of 1414, see *Rot. Parl.*, 4.32-3.

[37] KB 27/613, Rex, ms. 15, 30d; 614, Rex, ms. 4d, 16; 617, Rex, m. 26.

[38] KB 27/613, Rex, m. 37 *et seq.*; JUST 1/753, m. 29(1) nos.8,9.

[39] KB 27/613, Rex, m. 36d.

[40] G.E. Cokayne, *The Complete Peerage of England* ... ed. V. Gibbs etc. (1910-59), 5. 305; E. 404/35/276, 288; *CPR, 1413-16,* p. 164.

THE DURATION OF CRIMINAL TRIALS IN MEDIEVAL ENGLAND

R.B. Pugh

To determine the average duration of a medieval suspect's trial for felony it might seem enough to sum the suspects subsumed under one date heading in a gaol delivery roll and divide that number by a predetermined number of hours of that day. That method, however, is unsound, since the headings may only show the day on which a commission was opened, trials proceeding thereafter day by day until at some unstated day the court adjourned.[1] The pitfalls of headings are mitigated where a roll covers the trials conducted on circuit place by place by a particular justice. If such a roll shows that A sat at x on Monday and at y on Tuesday and also shows the number of suspects tried at x, we are at least approaching a trial-duration figure. The present aim is to use the records of some particular trials in the hope of establishing some such figure. The conclusions, however, must not prejudice future investigations of the general issue, based as such investigations may be on a wider range of data.

The trials chosen for the immediate experiment number eleven and span the period 1292 to 1302. In each case two justices appear to have been appointed to deliver gaol y either on the same day as gaol x or on the next. On 4 September 1292 the justices sat at Bedford, tried twenty people in eleven groups, and adjudged nineteen.[2] Next day they were at Huntingdon.[3] On 31 January 1293 they sat at Wallingford and tried and adjudged twenty-two people in seventeen groups.[4] The same day they were at Windsor.[5] On 16 November then next sixty-three people in about twenty-two groups were tried and adjudged at Northampton county gaol.[6] Next day the town gaol was delivered of seven people in one group, and on the following the justices sat at Bedford.[7] On 22 March 1294 thirty-four people in ten groups were tried and adjudged in Worcester county gaol and on the same day thirteen in one group at the town gaol.[8] On 18 November 1294 twelve

[1] *Calendar of London Trailbaston Trials ... 1305 and 1306*, ed. R.B. Pugh (H.M.S.O, 1975 [*recte* 1976]) p. 8.

[2] Records of Justices Itinerant, etc., Gaol Delivery Rolls, JUST 3/89 rott. 11, 11d.

[3] *Ibid.*, rot. 15.

[4] JUST 3/91 rot. 1.

[5] *Ibid.*, rott. 14, 14d, 15.

[6] *Ibid.*, rot. 1d.

[7] *Ibid.*, rot. 15.

[8] JUST 3/92 rot. 3.

people in five groups were tried and adjudged at Windsor.[9] Next day the justices were at Reading.[10] On 4 August 1299 thirty-eight people in twenty groups were tried at Winchester county gaol and twenty-six of them adjudged.[11] Next day the justices cleared the city gaol. On 3 August 1302 fifty-two people in thirty-nine groups were tried at Old Salisbury and forty-six adjudged.[12] Next day the justices cleared New Salisbury gaol.[13] Finally on 16 September then next twenty-one people in fifteen groups were tried at Oxford county gaol and fourteen adjudged, and on the same day two people were separately tried in the city gaol and one of them adjudged.[14]

In making these and all comparable calculations there have been included as 'judgments' cases of men who turned approver but were none the less condemned and also *pro quali* trials in clergy pleas. Remands to later sessions, however, and mainprises to appear at such have been excluded, even though such proceedings must have occupied a little time, as must the opening of the commission if literally read. Appeals and indictments have not been distinguished although, if appellees could at this time still plead exceptions, appeals must have lasted longer. In fact at the chosen trials those prosecuted to judgment by innocent appellants were few indeed.[15] Although the number of groups in which the prisoners were tried has been expressed, its significance may be doubted. Sometimes it represents the delations of one approver about one incident, sometimes it seems no better than a jumble. Either way some suspects were acquitted and some not.

Cases where two gaols were delivered in one day provide the best data, because, where it is learnt that *x* was delivered on Monday and *y* on Tuesday, the delivery of *y* need not have begun until Tuesday evening and the trials at *x* may have extended into Tuesday; likewise trials at *y* might extend into Wednesday or beyond. It is best to limit investigation first to such trials, namely, those at Wallingford (1293), Worcester county (1294), and Oxford county (1302).

Before, however, judgments per hour can be established from the recited totals three questions must be pondered. First did the justices

[9]*Ibid.*, rot. 15.

[10]*Ibid.*, rot. 15*d*.

[11]JUST 3/98 rott. 4, 4*d*.

[12]*Wiltshire Gaol Delivery and Trailbaston Trials,* ed. R.B. Pugh (Wiltshire Record Soc. 33, Devizes, 1978), p. 82.

[13]*Ibid.*, p. 88.

[14]JUST 3/103 rot. 4; rot. 4*d*.

[15]Perhaps eleven among 1,735 judgments.

sit together or apart; secondly how many hours did they work daily; and thirdly in riding their circuits how fast did they ride? First it is reasonably deduceable from Smith's *De Republica Anglorum* that in the later sixteenth century the two assize judges sat together in both Crown and civil courts.[16] Not so later; each court then sat under a single justice.[17] What of earlier practice? Against single-justice sessions is the fact that, even where a special commission was issued to try a single prisoner, two justices were normally, if not invariably, appointed. Moreover it is doubtful whether many gaol halls had space enough for two concurrent sittings. Conversely the statistics, as will be shown, suggest that, if dual-justices courts must invariably be hypothecated, trial-times could often have been incredibly short. Could justices have sat sometimes together and sometimes apart? Now secondly. In the later seventeenth and earlier eighteenth centuries justices did not complete their work in daylight hours.[18] Might the same be presumed of medieval justices? Howbeit, daylight hours on the first test day were nine, on the second twelve and a quarter, and on the third thirteen. Justices, however, must eat and (that apart) their subordinates need time to produce documents and herd people into docks and pens. Consequently it is preferable to discard measured hours of daylight in favour of a normal span of seven hours a day.

Until the later seventeenth century not very much is known about travelling speeds. In the fourteenth century a writ-carrier from London to Newcastle upon Tyne could reach his destination after eight pernoctations, which implies a speed of just over thirty-four miles a day.[19] Such messengers, of course, travelled light; moreover their business was urgent and of national importance. Presumably they could commission horses and consequently stage.[20] At about the same time (*c.*1330) the Warden and Fellows of Merton College, Oxford, travelling on College business, might attain fifty-five miles a day (Nottingham to Doncaster); alternatively they might make no more than twenty-five (Oxford to High Wycombe). In 1356, at the summer solstice, the Warden, unaccompanied, did the whole journey from Oxford to London (60 miles, 28 June) in one day.[21] Such people

[16] Thomas Smith, *De Republica Anglorum*, ed. L. Alston (Cambridge, 1906), pp. 96, 101.

[17] J.S. Cockburn, *History of English Assizes* (Cambridge, 1972), p. 69.

[18] *Ibid.*, pp. 111, 300.

[19] *Red Book of the Exchequer* (Rolls Series 99), 3. 836.

[20] J.E. Crofts, *Packhorse, Waggon and Post* (1967), p. 58.

[21] G.H. Martin 'Road travel . . . 1315-1470', in *Jnl. of Transport History* 3 (1976), esp. 167, 170.

presumably could not stage. Could the justices requisition mounts? Probably at need they could.

The evidence, in fact, is very variable. Whatever its value, students must, in all the circumstances, remember that each day at least one meal break must be catered for, that hills have to be surmounted, and that judges and horses are not always in full vigour. In general, therefore, the safest conclusion seems to be that the pace could rarely have exceeded thirty miles a day, or ten to fifteen miles an hour, and that, as an average, fifteen miles is, if anything, too high.[22] Ten miles a day is a better working figure.

In calculating delivery-times the trials at Wallingford, the only ones at present to be affected by the third imponderable, come first. Windsor, twenty-seven miles away, was Wallingford's next staging-point. The intervening road is not exacting; nevertheless it climbs the Chiltern scarp. Out of the time allowed for Wallingford trials must be deducted about three travelling-hours and enough time to establish the Windsor court and try twelve prisoners. If Wallingford trials started at sunrise at 7.45 a.m. we reach about four hours in which to try twenty-two persons or about eight if the justices sat apart. The former assumption allows nearly eleven minutes a man, the latter nearly twenty-two. It might be, of course, that one justice rode ahead and at least opened the Windsor assizes. The record, however, does not hint at it.

Now to Worcester and Oxford. Perpetuating the assumption of a seven-hour day the results respectively are under thirteen or nearly twenty-five minutes, and thirty or sixty minutes. That these periods exceed Wallingford's can be attributed either to looser time-tables or to judicial distaste for the hypothecated day.

On to the remaining five cases, where x was delivered on the day immediately preceding y's delivery. Assuming again a seven hour day the results, reckoned in minutes, are given in the table overleaf. We ought to recall that at the stated season the justices visiting Northampton delivered the town gaol on the day following the delivery day for the county gaol. Since the trials at the first were few and those at the second many, it could have been that some county prisoners were tried on the second day even though the heading does not say so. If the delivery totals are aggregated and exactly divided into two, the rates-per-minute become twelve or twenty-four. Note also that Worcester city and Oxford town were at the same seasons

[22] Thanks are due to Miss Janet H. Stevenson for help at this point.

delivered on the same days as their county gaols. If the county and town deliveries are here also aggregated, though for other reasons, the rates-per-minute reach respectively nearly nine or nearly eighteen, and twenty-eight or fifty-six.

Table

	Justices sitting together	Justices sitting apart
Bedford	22.1	44.2
Northampton (county)	6.7	13.3
Windsor	35	70
Winchester	16.1	32.3
Old Salisbury	9.1	18.3

Let us now put all the eleven trials together and try to establish an over-all minutes-per-trial quotient. The foregoing supposition about Northampton will continue to be made so that the duration figures will be the higher ones. The quotient is 15.8 minutes per trial if the justices sat together or 31.6 if they sat apart. The range on the same assumption is 35 to 8.9 minutes or 70 to 18.9 minutes.

Crude mathematical averages obscure inherent difficulties between cases, the absolute length of calendars, and the lethargy of individual judges. The lists printed below, which extend much beyond the period covered by the trials examined above, show the justices sometimes hastening, even sitting on Sundays, but more often moving rather leisurely. In looking at the 1302 and 1303 lists, however, it must be remembered that after 1299 gaols were delivered by the same justices who had just taken the petty assizes. Tests suggest that those civil trials normally occupied the day before the gaol delivery session, though a case has been noticed where they were held on the same day.[23] The 1299 linkage does not seem to have lasted initially much beyond 1305 nor to have been permanently resumed until 1330.[24] Nevertheless, wherever it prevailed, it must affect trial-duration figures and circuit time-tables.

[23] On 1 Aug. 1299 twenty-six persons were adjudged at Old Salisbury gaol delivery and six civil pleas heard at New Salisbury; Pugh, *Wilts. Trials*, p. 80; Records of Justices Itinerant, etc., Eyre Rolls, etc. (JUST. 1), no. 1315 rot. 27A.

[24] R.B. Pugh, *Imprisonment in Medieval England* (Cambridge, 1970), p. 281.

Space is lacking in which to consider in detail anything beyond the above-defined deliveries of Edward I's reign. Figures, however, have been collected for the Old Salisbury gaol delivery of 6 September 1328 and for the Winchester county gaol delivery of 10 March 1329.[25] They show respectively eighteen and twenty-five judgments, representing forty-seven and thirty-four minutes a prisoner assuming single-justice sessions. Four one-day Cambridge county gaol deliveries between 1332 and 1334 show a total of nineteen judgments or, on the same assumption, a little over three hours for each prisoner.[26] The tardier pace, however, is probably not attributable to more meticulous standards observed by justices or jurors but to shorter calendars. In the case of Cambridge this was probably due in turn to a thinner population. Another student of such figures has examined six fourteenth-century deliveries of Norwich castle and has arrived at a daily average of forty-six with a peak of 142 over two days in March 1316.[27]

Perhaps after much labour very little has been said, no more, in fact, than that in Edward I's time trials could possibly average as little as nine minutes a man but that in his grandson's they averaged more because gaols were emptier. Taking, however, only the earlier period how do the figures match those of later times? In 1678 thirty-six persons were adjudged at the Old Bailey in two days.[28] Over eight test periods in 1738 daily judgments averaged twenty.[29] In 1750 between seventeen and eighteen suspects were adjudged daily at the Surrey assizes, and at the turn of the century the average length of Old Bailey trials was 'a few minutes'.[30] So, as Stephen said, criminal trials were 'short and sharp' until in 1836 counsel for the defence received ready access to the courts.[31] The present calculations suggest that in the Middle Ages trials were just as short and can have allowed jurors little time for debating issues. For, if judges really harangued prisoners, as the *Placita Corone* said they did, and if the harangues were delivered individually and each prisoner replied, four to six minutes must be

[25] JUST 3/121 rott. 2, 2*d*; rott. 10, 10*d*.

[26] *A Cambridgeshire Gaol Delivery Roll*, 1332-4, ed. Elizabeth G. Kimball (Cambridge Antiquarian Record Soc., Cambridge, 1978)

[27] Barbara A. Hanawalt, *Crime and Conflict in English Communities, 1300-48* (Cambridge, Ma., 1979), p. 41.

[28] J.H. Langbein, 'The criminal trial before the lawyers' in *University of Chicago Law Review* 45 (1978), 274.

[29] *Crime in England 1550-1800,* ed. J.S. Cockburn, p. 334 n.32.

[30] *Ibid.*, 165; J.H. Baker, *Introduction to English Legal History,* p. 417.

[31] By 6 & 7 Will IV c.114. For the Act's effect see Langbein, *Chicago Law Rev.* Stephen's remark is cited in Cockburn, *Assizes,* 122.

allowed for that process as part of each trial.[32] The highest average speed here advanced was nine minutes. Take six from nine!

How much debate, however, was needed anyway? Medieval juries were so unlike their successors. They were sworn to tell what is called 'the truth' and were supposed to know it before the trials began.[33] That is something that they can seldom have done. They must often have acquitted because they were convinced of their own ignorance rather than of a suspect's innocence. Often, too, they were impressed by notoriety, possibly conveyed by letters testimonial from a borough or manorial court.[34] They might acquit or convict simply on that ground.[35] To say 'I do not know' or 'He is a villain' does not take long. Other judgments might have been reached more slowly. Statistically, however, might not such laconisms have swamped them?

[32] Ed. J.M. Kaye, SS (1966), 16-18, 21-2.

[33] R.B. Pugh, 'Some reflections of a medieval criminologist' in *Procs. of the British Academy* 59, 97-8, 103.

[34] M.T. Clanchy, *From Memory to Written Record* (1979), pp. 32-33; *Court Rolls of the Manor of Wakefield* 1, ed. W.P. Baildon (Yorkshire Archaeological Soc., Record 29, [Leeds], 1901), 272.

[35] Pugh, 'Some reflections', p. 98.

DELIVERIES PRESIDED OVER BY JOHN DE LOVETOT
1276-8 [JUST 3/85]

Tues.	14 Apr. 1276	Norwich
Sun.	19 Apr. 1276	Colchester
Sun.	23 Aug. 1276	Colchester
Tues.	25 Aug. 1276	Bury St. Edmunds
Tues.	10 Nov. 1276	Tower of London
Tues.	10 Nov. 1276	Newgate
Thurs.	17 Dec. 1276	Guildford
Wed.	23 Dec. 1276	'Middlesex'
Sat.	2 Jan. 1277	Colchester
Sun.	10 Jan. 1277	Norwich
Wed.	13 Jan. 1277	Ipswich
Thurs.	14 Jan. 1277	'London'
Thurs.	21 Jan. 1277	'London'
Thurs.	28 Jan. 1277	Westminster
Sat.	13 Feb. 1277	Westminster
Fri.	26 Feb. 1277	Hertford
Wed.	10 Mar. 1277	Colchester
?Fri.	12 Mar. 1277	Rayleigh
Sat.	20 Mar. 1277	Westminster (Essex prisoners)
Fri.	2 Apr. 1277	Hertford
Sat.	3 Apr. 1277	St. Albans
Fri.	9 Apr. 1277	Westminster (Persons indicted at Wimbledon & Kingston)
Mon.	17 May 1277	
Sun.	23 May 1277	Newport
Sat.	29 May 1277	Royston
Fri.	18 June 1277	Colchester
Sat.	10 July 1277	Westminster
Thurs.	29 July 1277	Newgate
Tues.	17 Aug. 1277	Westminster
Thurs.	19 Aug. 1277	Newgate
Thurs.	7 Oct. 1277	Newgate
Fri.	14 Jan. 1278	Norwich
Sun.	16 Jan. 1278	Colchester
Tues.	8 Feb. 1278	Newgate
Fri.	18 Mar. 1278	Yarmouth
?Wed.	29 June 1278	Westminster
Wed.	20 July 1278	Westminster

DELIVERIES PRESIDED OVER BY ROBERT MALET
1291-4 [JUST 3/87-9. /91-2]

1291

Fri.	7 Sept.	Oxford county
Wed.	31 Oct.	Hereford
Mon.	5 Nov.	Leominster
Wed.	7 Nov.	Gloucester
Mon.	12 Nov.	Worcester

1292

Thurs.	10 Apr.	Warwick
Fri.	2 May	Reading
Mon.	5 May	Aylesbury
Mon.	19 May	Bedford
Sat.	2 Aug.	Reading
Thurs.	4 Sept.	Bedford
Fri.	5 Sept.	Huntingdon
Fri.	19 Sept.	Cambridge
Mon.	22 Sept.	Reading

1293

Sat.	31 Jan.	Wallingford
Sat.	31 Jan.	Windsor
Tues.	3 Feb.	Reading
Thurs.	12 Feb.	Tower of London
Fri.	13 Feb.	Guildford
Mon.	16 Feb.	Chichester
Wed.	18 Feb.	Southampton
Fri.	20 Feb.	Winchester
Mon.	23 Feb.	New Salisbury
Tues.	7 Apr.	Berkhamstead
Fri.	10 Apr.	Royston
Mon.	13 Apr.	St. Albans
Fri.	17 Apr.	Newgate
Wed.	13 May	Aylesbury
Fri.	22 May	Tower of London
Thurs.	28 May	Westminster
Thurs.	4 June	Newgate
Sat.	18 July	Reading
Mon.	20 July	Windsor
Thurs.	23 July	Newgate
Mon.	3 Aug.	Oxford county

1293 continued

Tues.	4 Aug.	Oxford town
Thurs.	6 Aug.	Worcester county
Fri.	11 Sept.	Aylesbury
Mon.	14 Sept.	Warwick
Wed.	16 Sept.	Northampton county
Thurs.	17 Sept.	Northampton town
Fri.	18 Sept.	Bedford county
Tues.	22 Sept.	Reading
Fri.	25 Sept.	Wallingford county
Fri.	25 Sept.	Wallingford town
Sat.	24 Oct.	Berkhamstead
Mon.	9 Nov.	Newgate
Mon.	28 Dec.	Tower of London

1294

Mon.	1 Mar.	Tower of London
Wed.	3 Mar.	Newgate
Thurs.	11 Mar.	Aylesbury
Mon.	15 Mar.	Windsor
Thurs.	18 Mar.	Oxford county
Thurs.	18 Mar.	Oxford town
Mon.	22 Mar.	Worcester county
Mon.	22 Mar.	Worcester city
Wed.	24 Mar.	Warwick
Fri.	26 Mar.	Northampton
Mon.	29 Mar.	Oakham
Wed.	31 Mar.	Peterborough
Mon.	5 Apr.	Wallingford
Fri.	14 May	Reading
Sat.	15 May	Windsor
Mon.	17 May	Newgate
Wed.	19 May	Tower of London
Mon.	21 June	Oxford county
Tues.	22 June	Newgate
? Fri.	25 June	Oxford county
Fri.	25 June	Oxford town
Sat.	26 June	Wallingford
Sat.	18 Sept.	New Salisbury
Sat.	25 Sept.	St. Albans
Mon.	27 Sept.	Newgate
Mon.	11 Oct.	Newgate
Tues.	12 Oct.	Tower of London

1294 continued

Tues.	19 Oct.	Oxford county
Tues.	2 Nov.	Aylesbury
Sat.	13 Nov.	Tower of London
Tues.	16 Nov.	Newgate
Thurs.	18 Nov.	Windsor
Fri.	19 Nov.	Reading

DELIVERIES PRESIDED OVER BY ROGER DE SUTHCOTE 1302-3 [JUST 3/103-4]

1302

Wed.	27 June	Windsor
Fri.	3 Aug.	Old Salisbury
Sat.	4 Aug.	New Salisbury
Sun.	16 Sept.	Oxford county
Sun.	16 Sept.	Oxford town
Mon.	17 Sept.	Wallingford
Tues.	18 Sept.	Windsor
Fri.	21 Sept.	Winchester county
Fri.	21 Sept.	Winchester city
Mon.	24 Sept.	Old Salisbury
Sat.	6 Oct.	Exeter county
Sun.	7 Oct.	Exeter city
Wed.	10 Oct.	Somerton
Sat.	20 Oct.	Guildford
Mon.	12 Nov.	Windsor
Wed.	14 Nov.	Wallingford
Thurs.	15 Nov.	Chertsey
Sat.	1 Dec..	Wallingford

1303

Tues.	15 Jan.	Battle
Mon.	25 Feb.	Chertsey
Thurs.	7 Mar.	Oxford county
Thurs.	7 Mar.	Oxford town
Thurs.	18 Apr.	Windsor
Sat.	20 Apr.	Wallingford
Tues.	23 Apr.	Oxford county
Sun.	28 Apr.	Guildford
Mon.	6 May	Winchester [county]
Wed.	8 May	Old Salisbury
Tues.	14 May	Somerton

1303 continued

Tues.	14 May	Exeter county
Sat.	1 June	Old Salisbury
Sat.	1 June	New Salisbury
Mon.	8 July	Windsor
Sat.	27 July	Reading
Mon.	29 July	Wallingford
Tues.	30 July	Oxford county
Mon.	16 Sept.	Old Salisbury
Fri.	27 Sept.	Exeter county
Fri.	27 Sept.	Exeter town
Mon.	30 Sept.	Somerton
Thurs.	10 Oct.	Guildford
Tues.	15 Oct.	Wallingford
Tues.	29 Oct.	Windsor

DELIVERIES PRESIDED OVER BY JOHN DE STONORE
1328-9 [JUST 3/121]

1328

Fri.	2 Sept.	Winchester county
Tues.	6 Sept.	New Salisbury
Tues.	6 Sept.	Old Salisbury
Sat.	10 Sept.	Somerton
Fri.	16 Sept.	Exeter county
Wed.	21 Sept.	Launceston
Tues.	27 Sept.	Dorchester
Thurs.	29 Sept.	Old Salisbury

1329

Thurs.	5 Jan.	Oxford town
Thurs.	5 Jan.	Oxford county
Fri.	10 Mar.	Winchester county
Fri.	10 Mar.	Winchester city
Tues.	21 Mar.	Old Salisbury
Fri.	24 Mar.	Dorchester
Sat.	1 Apr.	Exeter county
Sat.	8 Apr.	Launceston

THE EARLY DEVELOPMENT OF THE
PEINE FORTE ET DURE

H.R.T. Summerson

Late in 1322 Sir Robert Lewer, an active enemy of Edward II, was arrested in Southampton. Brought before royal justices, he refused to plead to any charge and was sent back to prison. 'The customary punishment, indeed', reported the *Vita Edwardi Secundi,* 'for those mute of malice is carried out thus throughout the realm. The prisoner shall sit on the cold bare floor, dressed only in the thinnest of shirts, and pressed with as great a weight of iron as his wretched body can bear. His food shall be a little rotten bread and his drink cloudy and stinking water. The day on which he eats he shall not drink, and the day on which he has drunk he shall not taste bread. Only superhuman strength survives this punishment beyond the fifth or sixth day.'[1] Such was the solution, known as *peine forte et dure,* eventually reached for the problem posed by suspected felons who would not accept jury trial when, after 1215, it had replaced the ordeal as the usual means of proof in criminal cases.[2] Initially such recalcitrance was dealt with in various ways. Sometimes a verdict was nonetheless taken, perhaps from an enlarged jury, sometimes the suspect was allowed to abjure the realm, often he was sent back to prison, where no doubt he remained either until suitable guarantors of his future good conduct presented themselves or until the problem of his disposal was solved by his demise.[3] This uncertainty continued for some years, but in the short term the first of these solutions prevailed.[4] Twice at the 1235 Essex eyre verdicts were given on prisoners who had refused to put themselves on a jury.[5] This practice was still the rule in 1251, when a verdict was given on a foreign merchant refusing to put himself on an inquest in Canterbury.[6]

---

[1]*Vita Edwardi Secundi,* ed. N. Denholm-Young (1957) p. 128. I am grateful for advice and assistance in the preparation of this paper from Professor R.B. Pugh, Mr. J.M. Kaye, Mr. A.D.E. Lewis and Dr. M.T. Clanchy.

[2]T.F.T. Plucknett, *A Concise History of the Common Law* (1956) pp. 118-21.

[3]E.g. *Pleas of the Crown for the County of Gloucester 1221,* ed. F.W. Maitland (1884) no. 316; *Rolls of the Justices in Eyre... for Lincolnshire 1218-19 and Worcestershire 1221,* ed. D.M. Stenton, SS 53 (1934) no. 1208; *Bracton's Note Book* ed. F.W. Maitland (1887) ii no. 136.

[4]*Curia Regis Rolls* XIII no. 2781.

[5]JUST/1/230 mm 2d, 10, C145/5 no. 25.

[6]C145/5 no. 25.

Soon after this, however, procedure changed. At the 1253 Northampton eyre Simon the shepherd of Thornhaugh, appealing Reginald son of Gilbert of wounding him, offered to proceed against him 'as a man maimed and lunatic'. Reginald's response was to offer to defend himself by his body, even though the appellor's self-confessed physical condition made a duel impossible, and he refused to accept any other form of proof. This time the justices did not feel able to impose a jury's verdict and adjourned the case to the following day, when the situation was saved by the appellor's withdrawal, after which a verdict was taken.[7] The change may simply have been prompted by dissatisfaction that suspects could forfeit lives, lands and chattels through verdicts they had not submitted to, but it may be significant that just as 1253 was the year when, according to Matthew Paris, Henry III was flirting with Savoyard practice in wanting to give victims of robbery the right to prosecute those whose duty it was to pursue the robbers – a proposal so closely paralleled by the sixth of the articles of the watch issued in the same year as to make it seem likely that the king was more successful in enacting his scheme than the chronicler was willing to allow[8] — so the requirement that no one should undergo jury trial without first consenting to it was in line with procedure in France, where, in the words of the *Livre de Jostice et de Plet,* 'no one is condemned by inquest unless he submits thereto'.[9] Perhaps the change resulted from one of the allegations of judicial high-handedness against Simon de Montfort with which the air had been thick the previous year.[10] The new procedure is soon apparent in the plea rolls, and at eyres in Shropshire in 1256, Berkshire in 1261, Northumberland in 1269, Kent in 1271, and Sussex in 1271/2 suspects refusing to plead were sent back to prison, to stay there until they changed their minds.[11]

These last three cases, however, reveal a less than satisfactory situation, since the Northumberland prisoner escaped and the Kent and Sussex prisoners were released by the officials to whose custody they had been committed, and so it is not surprising to find the first statute of Westminster of 1275 containing legislation on the subject.

[7] JUST/1/615 m 10d.

[8] F. Pollock and F.W. Maitland, *History of English Law* (Cambridge, 1952) i. 181; *CCR 1251-1253* p. 493.

[9] A. Esmein, *A History of Continental Criminal Procedure* (trans. J. Simpson, 1914) pp. 65-6.

[10] C. Bemont, *Simon de Montfort* (Paris, 1884) pp. 279-320.

[11] JUST/1/734 mm 23, 32d & 30; JUST/1/40 m 30; *Three Early Assize Rolls for the County of Northumberland,* ed. W. Page, SS 88 (1890) p. 359; JUST/1/371 m 22d; JUST/1/921 m 8d.

118

This provided 'that notorious felons, and which openly be of evil name, and will not put themselves in Enquests of Felonies', should have 'strong and hard Imprisonment – *prison forte et dure* – as they which refuse to stand to the Common Law of the Land: but this is not to be understood of such Prisoners as be taken of light suspicion'.[12] The earliest indication of what *prison forte et dure* may have meant in practice is provided by the tract *Placita Corone*, where a justice tells a gaoler how to deal with a suspect not to be persuaded into pleading by words alone – 'give him little to eat and less to drink; let him not drink on the day he eats nor eat on the day he drinks. In this way discharge your duty until our next session.'[13] Not only has this tract been dated by its editor to the years 1274/5, so that it may predate the statute, but the procedure it describes is in many respects like that of France in similar circumstances; in Normandy men refusing to put themselves on an inquest of the country were to be kept securely in prison for a year and a day with little to eat and drink, and Beaumanoir prescribes an almost identical treatment.[14] If the principle that suspects must plead before they could undergo jury trial had indeed originated in France, then it seems reasonable to assume that so too had the procedure used to enforce the principle, and that both were imported together. In all likelihood the statute did not innovate in its requirements for suspects who did not plead, rather it confirmed and underlined existing procedure in the hope of inducing officials to impose it, as they had not always done hitherto.

After *Placita Corone* there is no detailed description of the procedure that would become *peine forte et dure* for about fifteen years, and then, in the years around 1290, there are six, with one important exception identical in substance. *Fleta*, differing only in detail from *Placita Corone*, laid down that a prisoner refusing to plead 'shall be clad in a single garment and be unshod and, lying upon the bare earth, he shall have for food but a quatern loaf of barley bread every second day, nor shall he drink daily, but on the day when he does not eat, he shall drink only water'.[15] Britton's account is basically the same, but adds that the prisoner shall be in fetters, and a man refusing to plead to a homicide charge at Newgate in 1290 was condemned to have put on him 'a sufficiency of iron' as well as to live on the inadequate diet prescribed by *Fleta*.[16] To a man complaining in

[12]*SR* I p. 29

[13]*Placita Corone*, ed. J.M. Kaye, SS Supplementary Series 4 (1966) p. 18.

[14]Pollock and Maitland ii. 651 n. 4; Esmein pp. 65-6.

[15]*Fleta*, ed. H.G. Richardson and G.O. Sayles, SS 72 (1955) ii. 85.

[16]*Britton*, ed. F.M. Nichols (Oxford, 1865) i. 26-7; JUST/3/87 m 1d.

1292 of his ill-treatment in Dublin, and to a justice trying to induce a suspected rapist to plead at the 1293/4 Yorkshire eyre, the diet was the essence of the treatment, and there is no mention of irons, but in 1293, according to Bartholomew Cotton, when an inquest was held into the murder and robbery of Dutch sailors off the Norfolk coast and the hundred bailiff would not plead, he was sent to prison under the following conditions, 'that on the day when he ate he should not drink, and the bread should be the worst bread, and his drink should be stagnant water, and he should sit naked save for a linen garment, on the bare ground, and he should be loaded with irons from the hands to the elbows, and from the feet to the knees, until he should make his submission'.[17]

The obvious inconsistency among these accounts lies in the use of irons. If these were an essential part of the treatment, it would be strange if the justice at the Yorkshire eyre trying to intimidate a suspect into pleading had not threatened him with them. But the inconsistency may be more apparent than real. In all likelihood all such prisoners were in irons, and probably always had been, but not, at first, because they had refused to plead but because they were prisoners suspected of felony. Not only was it common – for Britton, prescribed – practice for suspected felons to be kept in irons while they were in gaol, but they had also to be kept in irons both while they were being brought from prison to the place of trial and while they were in court.[18] Twice at the 1272 Shropshire eyre prisoners paid to be allowed to come before the justices without fetters, and at a Warwick gaol delivery in 1300 the sheriff was put in mercy for bringing a suspected killer into court when he was not in irons.[19] Britton, in prescribing fetters for suspects refusing to plead, was surely doing no more than order the continuation of a condition they were already in, perhaps to ensure that they did not, as other prisoners were liable to do, pay fees to their gaolers for the removal of their irons.[20] A prisoner who 'comparuit in curia in ferro' at the 1293/4 Yorkshire eyre and on refusing to plead was remanded 'pene et penitentie', no doubt endured it still wearing the irons in which he had appeared in court.[21]

[17] Select Pleas in the Court of King's Bench under Edward I, ed. G.O. Sayles, SS 57 (1938) ii. 52; YB 30-31 Edward I ed. A.J. Horwood, Rolls Series (1863) p. 531; JUST/1/1098 m 76; Bartholomaei de Cotton . . Historia Anglicana, ed. H.R. Luard, Rolls Series (1859) pp. 227-8. Comparison with JUST/1/1286 mm 39, 40 reveals many discrepancies in the latter.

[18] Britton, ed. Nichols, i. 44; JUST/1/323 m 47; JUST/1/486 m 45; JUST/1/827 m 32d. (see also R.B. Pugh, Imprisonment in Medieval England [Cambridge, 1968] pp 178-80); JUST/1/934 m 21.

[19] JUST/1/736 mm 37d, 43; JUST/3/99 m 7.

[20] Pugh, pp. 178-80.

[21] BL Add. MS 31826 fols. 210v-211r.

Whether in chains or not, suspects standing mute were not always quickly persuaded into changing their minds about pleading. Two Newgate cases from the early 1290s show survivals of several months, while Richard of Harlow, a servant of the gaoler of Newgate, who refused to put himself on a jury when charged in July 1290 with killing a prisoner in his custody, did not finally plead until December 1291, when he was convicted and hanged.[22] A sojourn of this length, under the conditions described above, was exceptional, and probably indicates Richard's ability to profit from his inside knowledge of prison conditions.[23] Most of the suspects whose subsequent fates can be traced changed their minds and either turned approver or pleaded at the same eyre or gaol delivery at which they had originally stood silent. Even so, still greater harshness was to come to be inflicted on such prisoners. At the 1302 Cornwall eyre John de Dorley and Sir Ralph de Bloyou, both suspected felons, on refusing to plead were sent to prison under the same conditions – 'that he should be put in a house on the ground in his shirt, laden with as much iron as he could bear, and that he should have nothing to drink on the day when he had anything to eat, and that he should drink water which came neither from fountain nor river'.[24]

Clearly, 'as much iron as he could bear' represents a substantial increase in severity even over the treatment described by Cotton. Paradoxically, the cause seems to have lain largely in concern in the early 1290s about the ill-treatment of prisoners. *Fleta,* Britton, and the *Mirror of Justices* are all loud in their denunciations of gaolers who kill or torture prisoners, and occasional horror stories in the plea rolls show their concern to have been well grounded.[25] It would hardly be surprising, therefore, if such treatment of suspected felons who stood mute was not regarded in some quarters as excessively, even criminally, harsh, and in fact the *Mirror of Justices,* in declaring it an abuse 'that a prisoner should be loaded with iron or put in pain before he is attainted of felony', and denouncing as homicides 'those who kill a man by excessive pain', shows that there were those who did so regard it.[26] In such a climate of opinion, officials might reasonably have felt that, if they were going to avoid accusations of torture and

[22] JUST/3/36/1 m 3 & JUST/3/36/2 m 14 (Robert le Foulere); JUST/3/36/2 m 7; JUST/3/36/1 m 3; JUST/3/36/2 m 14; C144/30 no. 16; JUST/1/547A m 6d.

[23] I owe this suggestion to Professor R.B. Pugh.

[24] *YB 30-31 Edward I* p. 510.

[25] *Fleta,* ii. 68; *Britton,* i. 45; *Mirror of Justices,* ed. W.J. Whittaker, SS 7 (1895) pp. 23. 24, 52; JUST/1/877 m 64; JUST/1/1011 m 50d; JUST/1/1098 m 10 d. (see also Pugh, pp. 180-1).

[26] *Mirror of Justices,* pp. 160, 24.

homicide, then they must be able to find legal justification for their deliberately keeping prisoners, who had not been convicted of any felony, in sordid conditions and on an inadequate diet.

The plea rolls show that from 1292 onwards they found their answer to this problem in a restatement of the first statute of Westminster and in particular in an emphasis that, as the statute had said, those who declined to plead were refusing the common law. The phrase *tanquam refutans communem legem,* or variants, was first used of suspects standing mute on Hugh de Cressingham's circuit of northern eyres between 1292 and 1294, and *prison forte et dure* makes an occasional appearance in a plea roll at this time.[27] A case from the 1293/4 Yorkshire eyre not only gives the fullest example of this reapplication of the statute, but also gives an idea of where it might lead. Simon le Conestable, himself a former assize commissioner and gaol delivery justice, refused to plead to charges of robbery, abduction and killing his wife, 'so it is decided that Simon have hard and strong prison and the penance provided for such refusing the common law, and that his chattels remain forfeit to the king until Simon wants to stand to the common law etc'.[28]

The importance of this emphasis that a suspect standing mute was refusing the common law is indicated by its being recorded in the huge majority of such cases in the plea rolls after 1292, and it clearly signified a vital change in the status of the prisoner involved – by his action in declining to plead he was depriving himself of that protection against ill-treatment which the law afforded to ordinary prisoners and was thereby reduced to a condition not far removed from that of the outlaw. The one was outside the law, the other had refused it. Like the outlaw, the suspect refusing to put himself on a jury forfeited his chattels – which also meant that he lacked the wherewithal to pay for removal of irons or better food.[29] If he died it was nobody's fault but his own, so that a coroner's jury could say of a man dying of *peine forte et dure* in Northampton castle in 1323 that 'Michael died of lack of food and drink and of cold in that prison, and of no unreasonable pain inflicted on him'.[30] The parallel with outlawry is neatly brought out by a case from trailbaston proceedings in Sussex in 1306. One John Chaury, coming before the justices as an outlaw, successfully argued

---

[27] JUST/1/415 m 30; JUST/1/651 m 1; JUST/1/1098 mm 69d, 72d, 80d, 81d; JUST/1/1098 mm 80d, 87d; JUST/3/47/1 mm 1, 1d, 2, 2d, 3.

[28] JUST/1/1268 m 18d; JUST/1/1098 m 80d.

[29] In theory his chattels should have been returned to him if he changed his mind and pleaded, but no example has been noticed of this being done.

[30] JUST/2/110 m 3.

that as he had been in prison in Kent he could not have appeared in court in Sussex to defend himself. His outlawry was annulled and he was readmitted to the king's peace, but on being invited to acquit himself of the robberies for which he had originally been outlawed, he refused to plead and was sent back to prison as refusing the common law.[31]

The fact that the suspect who would not plead was regarded as having refused the common law not only cleared the officials charged with his custody of all responsibility in the event of his death, it also gave them an almost entirely free hand in any future treatment of him that they felt inclined to apply. In all probability he was already in chains, now they could heap more on him with no fear of the consequences. The extent to which they actually did so is brought out by another chronicler's account of the death of Sir Robert Lewer – in which nothing is said about his standing mute in court – 'tantoque ferri pondere compedum et catenarum oppressus. . . .miserabiliter infelicem vitam finivit'.[32] Medieval gaolers were frequently cruel men, quite capable of treating their charges with appalling savagery even without the excuse that their victims had chosen to deprive themselves of the protection of the common law, but they could plausibly have offered two reasons for making *peine forte et dure* harsher, besides the pleasure they found in indulging their lower natures.[33] The first was that suspected accessories could not be tried until any principals had been convicted; thus, when Matthew the carpenter, arrested for stealing horses, refused to plead at a Henhow gaol delivery in 1316, a woman suspected of harbouring him had to be sent back to prison, untried, to stay there until Matthew was convicted.[34] The second, closely related to the first, was simply the need to clear the gaols, to keep the processes of arrest, committal and gaol delivery ticking over. Gaols were not delivered only when they became full, but nevertheless they could become crowded to the point where hygiene and humanity required their clearance, as when in February 1306 a delivery of Warwick gaol was ordered 'because it is so full of prisoners that many of them have died and die from day to day'.[35] Suspects who stood mute were occupying prison space themselves and might be making it impossible for proceedings to begin against others, also

---

[31] JUST/1/934 m 21.

[32] *Flores Historiarum,* ed. H.R. Luard, Rolls Series (1890) iii. 211-12.

[33] See above n. 25.

[34] JUST/3/63/4 m 17d.

[35] C66/127 m 35A.

occupying prison space – two good reasons for making their lives as uncomfortable as possible.

How much more severe *peine forte et dure* actually became is shown by the case already cited from the 1302 Cornwall eyre. The development was not, however, a uniform one, and an exact standardisation of procedure took some years to emerge. When William of Podmore, remanded to *peine* at Stafford in December 1305, was found to be still alive the following July, his survival led to the sheriff's being suspected of having improperly supplied him with food and drink.[36] Yet William Parlebien, standing mute at Colchester, lasted from July 1301 to June 1302 without anybody expressing surprise.[37] Women may sometimes have been treated more leniently than men, or at any rate, to judge by variations in plea roll terminology, differently, while pregnant women appear to have been spared altogether.[38] But man or woman, *peine forte et dure* was an option open to every prisoner appearing in a royal court. Thus men appealed by approvers were not limited to choosing between battle and jury trial, they could opt for silence in preference to either.[39] As for the writ *de bono et malo*, if this was meant to ensure that suspected killers did not hold up proceedings by standing mute, it certainly did not always have that effect, a refusal to plead always taking precedence over the undertaking not to do so contained in the writ.[40]

Anybody could elect to endure *peine forte et dure,* but few did so. At twenty-four deliveries of Warwick gaol between April 1292 and July 1306, for instance, only nine out of the 1389 suspects attending would not plead.[41] At all the deliveries of Newgate gaol in the reign of Edward II from which records survive, only seventeen prisoners refused jury trial. The increasing severity with which premeditated silence in court was treated is probably sufficient to account for such reluctance to endure its consequences, but something may also have been due to the efforts made by justices to persuade suspects to plead, and to the steps they took to ensure that those who did not had acted

[36] *Select Cases in the Court of King's Bench* ii, p. clv; JUST/1/809 mm 9, 15.

[37] JUST/3/18/4 mm 4d, 5.

[38] JUST/3/1/3 m 5; *Crime in East Anglia in the Fourteenth Century,* ed. B. Hanawalt, Norfolk Record Society 44 (1976), p. 19; JUST/1/1001 m 3.

[39] JUST/3/109 m 5d.

[40] R.B. Pugh, 'The Writ De Bono et Malo', in *LQR* 92 (1976), 258-67; J.M. Kaye, 'Gaol Delivery Jurisdiction and the Writ De Bono et Malo', in *LQR* 93 (1977), 259-72; JUST/3/51/1 m 1; JUST/3/30/1 m 3.

[41] As far as possible these figures do not include suspects making more than one appearance.

deliberately, in full knowledge of the consequences. Hence, as early as 1293, the repeated questionings of prisoners, asked three or four times whether they would not put themselves on a jury, the opportunities given them of challenging jurors, eventually to the number of thirty six, after which number challenging jurors was deemed to have become refusing a jury, and the inquests – held perhaps as early as 1300, and certainly standard practice under Edward II – as to whether a prisoner was naturally dumb or was standing 'mute of malice'.[42] The Berkshire suspect found in 1302 to have been deaf and dumb from infancy was a rare exception to the rule that those who would not plead had deliberately chosen silence in preference to speech.[43]

Who, then did opt for *peine forte et dure*, and why? Those who stood mute were frequently people arrested in circumstances in which standing trial would have meant certain conviction, killers caught literally red handed, thieves arrested in possession of stolen goods. Some were clerics whose claims to benefit of clergy had been rejected.[44] Others, on the evidence of their names, were strangers to the neighbourhood of their arrest, understandably sceptical as to the impartiality of a jury chosen from the society of their captors. For such people, a refusal to plead must have been the product of desperation, a frantic attempt to defer execution, though with the faint chance of escape from prison or even of obtaining a pardon.[45] If they ever reappeared in court it was usually either to plead and be hanged or to follow the hazardous course of the approver. Wealthy men like Simon le Conestable in Yorkshire and Ralph le Bloyou in Cornwall had an obvious motive for dying unconvicted under the *peine*, since their doing so preserved their lands unforfeited for their heirs, but many suspects had no chattels, and of those who later changed their minds, pleaded and were convicted, very few had lands.[46] Some prisoners may have kept silent out of bravado, or because they were afraid of malice among jurors, or because they hoped to protect friends or accomplices.[47] Perhaps sheer panic sometimes kept a suspect tongue-tied – it is certainly hard to think of any other explanation of the conduct of the man who at the 1286 Cambridgeshire eyre endured *peine forte et dure* for a while rather than plead to a

---

[42] JUST/3/91 m 15d; JUST/3/118 m 4d; JUST/3/99 m 1.

[43] JUST/3/103 m 1.

[44] e.g. JUST/3/89 m 1d; JUST/3/41/1 m 28d.

[45] JUST/3/1/7 mm 1, 1d; JUST/3/39/1 m 22.

[46] *Calendar of Inquisitions Post Mortem, 1291-1300,* 193; *ibid., 1300-07,* 379.

[47] JUST/3/47/2 m 6d may be an example of this.

charge of homicide of which he had already been acquitted once.[48]

Later in the fourteenth century there were to be signs that the purpose of *peine forte et dure*, to induce suspects standing mute to plead, was in danger of being forgotten by some justices who saw it solely as a punishment for obstinate silence. At a delivery of Shrewsbury castle gaol in 1355, for instance, a suspected killer standing mute was 'sent to the king's prison, to his pain, to stay there for his whole life. . .'.[49] But if there were doubts by then as to purpose, procedure had apparently become standardised. The *Vita Edwardi Secundi* had described the treatment meted out to Sir Robert Lewer as 'carried out thus throughout the realm,' and with the appearance of the name (in circulation by 1312), the inquest as to 'mute of malice', the repeated questioning of suspects together with the opportunities given them of challenging jurors, the confiscation of chattels, the use of heavy weights and the starvation diet, all the essential features of *peine forte et dure,* which it was to retain until its abolition in 1772, were present by the death of Edward II.[50]

[48] JUST/1/92 m 12d.
[49] JUST/3/131 m 25d.
[50] JUST/3/112 m 7.

THE IMPORTANCE OF EIGHTEENTH-CENTURY CORONERS' BILLS

R.F. Hunnisett

It was not until 1752 that the majority of coroners became legally entitled to fees for holding inquests whatever the cause of death. Since 1487 they had been allowed 13s. 4d. for any inquest resulting from murder or manslaughter, from the goods and chattels of the homicide if he had any, otherwise from any amercements imposed on a township for his escape; but that remuneration had been introduced as part of a campaign against violent crime, not out of consideration for the coroners.[1] In contrast, the statute 25 George II cap. 29 expressly recognised that the limited fees authorised in 1487 were 'not an adequate reward for the general execution of the said office' and decreed that from 24 June 1752 coroners should be paid £1 for every inquest they held in any place in England which contributed to the county rates and 9d. a mile for their journeys from their usual dwelling-places, but that the total payment for an inquest on anyone dying in gaol was not to exceed £1. These new fees were to be paid out of the county rates by order of the justices of the peace at quarter sessions, and, additionally, the old fee of 13s. 4d. was still payable, in the manner laid down in 1487, in cases of murder and manslaughter. The coroners of the king's household, the admiralty, the county palatine of Durham, the city of London, the borough of Southwark, and of any city, borough, town, liberty or franchise not contributory to the county rates were excluded from the provisions of the act, although they might continue to receive any fees, salaries, wages and allowances to which they had previously been entitled. The payment of inquest- and travelling-fees, which was extended in a slightly modified form to all boroughs by the Municipal Corporations Act of 1835, continued until the end of 1860 when coroners became salaried officials.[2]

Whether or not the act of 1751 made coroners more conscientious in carrying out their duties, it certainly ensured that they made regular and complete returns to quarter sessions of a summary of all their inquests. These returns, or bills, were normally made yearly or half-

---

[1] 3 Hen. VII c.2. Cf. 1 Hen. VIII c.7, which provided financial penalties for coroners who took fees for holding inquests occasioned by misadventure. By the eighteenth century the practice was for the parish to pay the 13s. 4d. whenever a felon had fled leaving no goods, whether or not it had been negligent: E. Umfreville, *Lex Coronatoria* (1761), p.261.

[2] 5 & 6 Will. IV c.76 s.62; 23 & 24 Vict. c.116 s.4.

yearly, sometimes at other intervals. For many counties a high proportion of them survive, particularly from the eighteenth century.[3] This paper is based on the Wiltshire bills of the period 1752 to 1796. The county was divided into a northern and a southern district, each with its own coroner. Bills survive for all but 6 years 9 months for the northern district and 3 years 7 months for the south, out of just over 44 years. There are also some for the small borough of Wootton Bassett and the manor of Corsham, places which had their own coroners but which contributed to the county rates.[4] The surviving bills vary slightly from area to area and from year to year, but they all take the form of a list, in chronological order, of the inquests held by the returning coroner since the submission of his previous bill (or since his assumption of office) and they all provide certain basic facts about each inquest: its date; the place at which it was held; the nature of the death, omitted in only a few, very exceptional, instances; the distance from the coroner's home; and the fee claimed. Most coroners included brief additional details about many of the deaths, while some gave quite lengthy accounts of the more important or unusual ones.

The importance of coroners' bills for local historians, their archival history and their relationship to other local records are discussed elsewhere.[5] Here three other themes will be briefly illustrated: the wide range of historical interests which they can serve; the workload of the various coroners, about which they provide reliable evidence; and the light they throw on the way in which the coroners interpreted the 1751 statute or, rather, manipulated it to their personal advantage.

The Wiltshire bills of 1752-96 contain 2,779 inquests and 7 journeys to dead bodies which did not result in inquests.[6] It is impossible to categorise 22 of these 2,786 fatalities: because the

[3]Their existence is noticed in many of the published guides to county record offices.

[4]The surviving bills are Wiltshire County Record Office, A5/2/1/1-144 (nos 1-78 north Wiltshire; 79-122 south Wiltshire; 123-138 Corsham; 139-144 Wootton Bassett). They are published in *Wiltshire Coroners' Bills, 1752-1796*, ed. R.F. Hunnisett, Wilts. Rec. Soc., 36 (1981) (hereafter *Wilts. Bills*). Their contents are referred to hereafter by their entry numbers in that volume. The Salisbury and Marlborough coroners of the period have left no bills since those places did not contribute to the county rates. But original Marlborough inquests survive from the years 1773-1835: Wilts. Record Office, G22/1/204. A few are published in *Presentments of the Grand Jury of the Quarter Sessions, Leet and Law Days held at Marlborough 1706 to 1751, and Some 18th and Early 19th Century Inquests*, ed. B. H. Cunnington (Devizes, 1929), pp.46-54.

[5]*Wilts. Bills*, introduction.

[6]One further journey, which led to an inquest at Bath, in Somerset, is excluded from the following statistics: *ibid.*, no.1377; see below, p. 137.

record is incomplete or contradictory, no verdict could be returned or a special verdict defies classification. The rest comprise 1,442 deaths by misadventure, just over 50 per cent of the total; 706 natural deaths, excluding deaths in gaol, or just over 25 per cent; 309 suicides, including 3 in gaol, approximately 11 per cent; 139 deaths in gaol (136 natural deaths and the 3 suicides again), just under 5 per cent; 84 murders; 36 manslaughters; 31 accidental homicides; 11 stillbirths; 7 justifiable homicides and homicides committed in self defence; and 2 homicides committed by idiots. The figures for the two largest categories must be treated with caution since there is good reason to think that up to 70 of the verdicts of misadventure recorded in his earlier bills by one coroner were really natural deaths.[7] Moreover, deaths from inclement weather not associated with accidents, which total 124, and similar deaths from excessive drinking have been classified as natural deaths, not misadventures, since it is probable that in most cases the severe weather or alcohol – occasionally both – merely accelerated the death of someone already weak or ill. Indeed, the only coroner who regularly categorised either of them regarded deaths from inclement weather as natural deaths.[8] There were also, of course, a number of fatal acidents to which drink or the weather was a major contributory factor. With these minor reservations, the eighteenth-century coroners' bills obviously provide invaluable statistics for a period otherwise deficient, falling as it does between two centuries from which the majority of coroners' inquests survive and the era of regular statistical returns to the central government.[9]

As might be expected, males greatly outnumbered females as subjects of coroners' inquests, by between three and four to one (2,152 to 602, with 32 not known but probably nearly all men). Every category of inquest contained this imbalance to a greater or smaller extent, with one exception: of the 84 murder victims, 39 were male and 44 female, with one not known; but 44 of the murders were infanticides and 5 other victims were young children. As to the other categories, men were more likely to be involved in quarrels, to have

[7] They were mostly deaths which occurred out of doors, the bodies showing no signs of violence: e.g. *Wilts. Bills,* no.168.

[8] E.g. *ibid.,* no.2162. Twelve of the 124 deaths from the weather were of people specifically stated to have been ailing. One further death from the weather was categorised as a misadventure, probably because of other circumstances not mentioned: no.2374. The single death from lightning is in a completely different category and manifestly a misadventure: *ibid.,* no.1366.

[9] For the sixteenth and seventeenth centuries most coroners' inquests survive in the various classes of king's Bench Indictments, notably in Ancient Indictments (KB 9). When a death resulted in a trial for murder or manslaughter at assizes, the inquest, if it survives, should be among the Assize Indictments, where a few inquests arising from other deaths can sometimes be found.

occupations which carried the risk of accidents, and to die in prison or suddenly out of doors.

Twice as many men as women were found to have committed suicide (209 to 99, with one whose sex was not stated). Hanging, the method employed by just over half the total, was used by 120 men and only 39 women. Drowning, chosen by over a quarter, was the only method equally popular with both sexes (43 men, 41 women and the unknown). About 12 per cent (24 men and 14 women) cut their throats; 8 men and 4 women took poison; and 3 men and one woman threw themselves from windows. The remaining methods were used only by men: shooting accounted for 8 and stabbing for 3. The coroners' juries returned verdicts of felo de se in only 35 cases as against 274 findings of lunacy. A similar compassion doubtless transferred some suicides to the categories of misadventure and natural death. Nevertheless, a study of the undoubted suicides in the Wiltshire bills and those of a few other counties could indicate how the suicide rate varied from year to year and between town and country; whether or not one suicide led to others in the same neighbourhood, perhaps committed in the same way; and if certain seasons of the year were particularly conducive to suicide.[10] Despite the uneven survival of the Wiltshire bills, they firmly suggest that more suicides occurred between March and August than in the autumn and winter, with a peak in April and fewest in November and February. That would support the theory that good weather and the hope and happiness it inspires are more likely to induce suicide in the desperate, by emphasising their despair, than are fog, rain and cold.[11] An alternative or, since they are not exclusive, additional explanation of the April peak is that it reflects a sustenance trough, the time between the exhaustion of the winter food and the availability of new crops.[12] An investigation to discover whether the April suicide rate was normally higher in years of famine would be well worth making.

As already mentioned, severe weather led to 124 inquests and contributed to accidents which caused a number of others. The coroners' bills therefore provide useful supporting evidence for the history of weather in England, especially about micro-climatic conditions. One or two deaths from the cold in winter are of no significance, but when the north Wiltshire coroner held nine inquests

[10]Two men named Ferris hanged themselves at Rowde within ten days in 1775: *Wilts. Bills,* nos 964, 966.

[11]This theory is discussed in S.E. Sprott, *The English Debate on Suicide: From Donne to Hume* (La Salle, Ill., 1961).

[12]I am indebted to Professor J. S. Cockburn for this suggestion and for valued comments on other points in this paper.

in four days in February 1762 and eight of the deaths were attributed to the weather and the other occurred suddenly in a field, conditions must have been unusually severe.[13] Again, between 9 December 1767 and 26 January 1768 the same coroner held six inquests into deaths caused by the weather and two others resulting from sudden deaths in the open, while the severe weather led to another in the south.[14] The winter of 1783-4 must have been another bad one: in the county as a whole, between mid-December and mid-February five deaths were specifically attributed to the weather, seven other natural deaths occurred out of doors, and two accidental deaths were caused by a coach overturning in the snow and when a boy slipped on ice and fell into a well.[15]

All seven of the county coroners who held office in Wiltshire during our period were medical practitioners and one of them, Alexander Forsyth, was involved with smallpox inoculation in Salisbury.[16] It might therefore have been expected that the bills would be a valuable source for the medical historian, but their evidence is largely negative. They confirm the backwardness of forensic medicine in England and the lack of medical sophistication and even interest shown by coroners.[17] The 842 natural deaths tell us far more about social and economic conditions than about illness and disease.

The Wiltshire bills give precise causes of only a quarter of the natural deaths in gaol (34 out of 136), and the original inquests were probably no more informative if earlier centuries are any guide. Fever was said to have caused 23 of them (once combined with strangulated rupture and once with a sore throat), smallpox 7, and fits, consumption, dropsy and gangrene one each. Of greater interest is their chronological distribution, which shows when epidemics occurred, notably in 1785 when there were 17 inquests in the county gaol between 7 February and 2 September.[18] Specific medical conditions are mentioned as causing less than a fifth of the other natural deaths: fits 96, fever 12 (once with affection of the bowels and once with an overflowing gall bladder), dropsy 4, ruptured blood vessels 4, lung disease 3 (once with visceral disease), diarrhoea 2, and asthma, diabetes, the evil, gangrene, gathering in the throat, shock, smallpox, visceral disease and worms

[13] *Wilts. Bills,* nos 314-22.

[14] *Ibid.,* nos 557-9, 563, 565-8, 2302.

[15] *Ibid.,* nos 1382-7, 1391, 1395-6, 2560-4.

[16] Details about these coroners are given *ibid.,* introduction.

[17] J.D.J. Havard, *The Detection of Secret Homicide* (1960), pp. 1-10; T.R. Forbes, *Crowner's Quest,* Trans. American Philosophical Soc., 68 pt 1 (1978), 42-8.

[18] *Wilts. Bills,* nos 2587, 2589, 2591-3, 2595-6, 2598-9, 2601-3, 2606-9, 2612.

one each. This compares with 32 of the deaths attributed wholly or in part to drink. Likewise, fits are said to have contributed to 16 fatal accidents, fever to 2 and smallpox to one, but drink to 23.

Only when they had cleared someone of suspicion, and not always then, were medical findings set out in any detail. Only eight autopsies are recorded, and in every case there had been a strong possibility of murder or manslaughter: in three cases the deceased had made accusations and in two others there were named suspects.[19] In the event, the verdicts were four natural deaths, three misadventures and one special verdict. The autopsies found that three of the deaths were caused by lung disease (one accompanied by visceral disease), three by poison, one by bowel worms and one by injury to the abdomen. It is likely that for only two other inquests, resulting from the same accidental poisoning which caused one of the eight, were autopsies performed.[20] If so, only one of the coroners ever made use of them. Surprisingly it was William Clare and not Alexander Forsyth, a surgeon to whom the bodies of hanged felons were delivered for dissection by order of the assize judges.[21]

Some of the autopsies were performed upon children, but none on the bodies of newborn babies. The death of a newborn bastard was, however, always regarded with suspicion and invariably led to an inquest. The verdicts ranged from stillbirth, natural death and misadventure to murder. The large number of murder verdicts (44) proves that infanticide was not an offence that coroners' juries viewed with compassion, especially when committed by unmarried mothers. By law concealment of the death of a bastard child by the mother was murder, even if it had died naturally or been stillborn, but none of the Wiltshire cases seems to have been in this category.[22]

A detailed analysis of the deaths by misadventure, including the straightforward drownings and falls, would usefully supplement the work done for other areas by Professor Forbes and Professor Hair.[23] Here it must suffice to say that, taken together, they present a remarkably comprehensive picture of the life and conditions of the times. Road accidents were surprisingly numerous, while all work had

[19]*Ibid.*, nos 803, 836, 899, 950, 1077, 1081, 1281, 1583.

[20]*Ibid.*, nos 1078-9.

[21]E.g. *ibid.*, nos 1142, 1346.

[22]21 Jac. I c.27.

[23]Especially Forbes, *Crowner's Quest*; P. E. H. Hair, 'Accidental death and suicide in Shropshire, 1780-1809', in *Trans. Shropshire Arch. Soc.* 59 (1969-70), 63-75; 'Deaths from violence in Britain: a tentative secular survey', in *Population Studies* 25 (1971), 5-24.

132

its hazards, none more than quarrying which caused some 50 deaths, and the construction of the Kennet-Avon canal with 5 deaths in 13 months in 1795-6.[24] Unfortunately, the bills never named the deodand, even when one inquest was adjourned because the jurors could not agree on it.[25] Many, of course, are obvious, while others can perhaps be inferred from the wording of the verdicts: it is probably significant that one man is said to have been run over by one wheel of a waggon and another to have been killed by a waggon and horses, the waggon being loaded with flints.[26]

Two deaths by misadventure deserve particular mention for the reasons for which the coroner adjourned them. Altogether 34 of the inquests were adjourned to a later date, three of them twice and one three times. In at least 30 of the 34 cases there had been some degree of suspicion against particular individuals and 22 resulted in verdicts of homicide (14 murders, 7 manslaughters and one justifiable homicide). Most of the adjournments were for such time-hallowed reasons as to secure more evidence or because the jurors could not agree. In 1788, however, William Clare, county coroner in the north, held an inquest on a man drowned in the Avon at Chippenham. Because the footbridge from which he had fallen had been the cause of previous fatal accidents, Clare adjourned the inquest until after a vestry meeting, at which it was decided to widen and strengthen the footbridge as the resumed inquest was assured.[27] In 1793 the same coroner adjourned an inquest because the working methods used in a quarry in which a man had died seemed to be extremely dangerous. The master of the works and the proprietor of the land were summoned to the adjourned session and promised to make the necessary alterations which were then agreed.[28] These two cases have a very modern ring and William Clare obviously took his social responsibilities seriously and seems to have been in advance of his time in adjourning inquests solely in the interests of public safety. It is doubtful whether he had any legal right to do so. The only other case at all comparable was an inquest on a prisoner in Devizes Bridewell which the same coroner adjourned to the next day for further inquiry because the body was very wasted. The verdict exonerated the gaoler and his deputy, but attributed the death to the inclemency of the

[24] *Wilts. Bills,* nos 1981, 1990, 2002, 2042, 2061.

[25] *Ibid.*, no.783.

[26] *Ibid.*, nos 1050, 2105. For precedents for each of these awards see Umfreville, pp.453-8.

[27] *Wilts. Bills,* nos 1564, 1569.

[28] *Ibid.,* no.1881.

weather and lack of sustenance, the daily allowance of a twopenny loaf being 'a very short and scanty one, inadequate to and insufficient for the support and maintenance of the body of any man'.[29]

Because of the ways in which coroners' rolls were compiled in the middle ages and in which inquests have survived, however copiously, from the sixteenth and seventeenth centuries, it is impossible to assess exactly the workload of most coroners before 1752.[30] Thereafter the fact that coroners were not paid for inquests omitted from their bills and the survival of so many bills render reliable calculations possible for many. The following figures are based on the inquests proper held by the Wiltshire coroners between 1752 and 1796, to which have been added the 39 adjourned sittings and 8 journeys already mentioned: a total of 2,826 duties which will for convenience be referred to as inquests.

The workload of the two county coroners increased gradually, but irregularly, throughout the period. Between them they held some 73 inquests a year on average, ranging from a minimum of 42 in 1755 up to 98 in 1774, 99 in 1791 and 100 in 1794 among the 24 full years from which bills for both districts survive. However, the northern district, being the larger and more populous, consistently produced three times as many inquests as the south.[31] The northern coroners held an average of 57 a year, the fewest for a year from which all their bills survive being 28 in 1753 and the most 82 in 1794. The southern yearly average was only 17, with a minimum of 6 in 1755 and a maximum of 32 in 1786.

Not only did the northern coroners hold more inquests but they also had to make longer journeys – up to 38 miles for normal inquests as against a maximum of 26 miles in the south; and they much more frequently held two or more inquests on the same day, which could entail travelling as much as 50 miles when the venues were in different directions.[32] These distances represent the outward journeys only, as do all those recorded on the bills since the coroners were not paid for returning home. When they held inquests in that detached part of Wiltshire that lay in the east of Berkshire, as the northern coroners did twice and the southern ones 5 times, a single inquest

[29] *Ibid.*, no.1557. This verdict led to an increase in the prisoners' allowance: J. Waylen, *Chronicles of the Devizes. . .* (1839), p.318.

[30] R.F. Hunnisett, 'The medieval coroners' rolls', in *AmJLH* 3 (1959), 95-124, 205-21; above, p.128 n.9.

[31] For details about the districts see *Wilts. Bills,* introduction.

[32] E.g. *ibid.,* nos 1037-8 (Devizes to Ramsbury and Cricklade).

134

could result in a round trip of up to 118 miles.[33] Neither county coronership constituted a full-time job, but, when combined with another occupation, it must have contributed to a very busy life. Hence, possibly, the county coroners held as many inquests on Sunday as on any other day, despite the fact that Sunday was *dies non juridicus* and that any such inquests could have been adjudged void; and the two Clares 6 times held inquests on Christmas Day.[34]

In contrast, coroners of small boroughs and liberties had a very easy life. During the 44 years under review the Wootton Bassett coroners held only one inquest every four years on average and never more than two in one year, while their journeys were all of less than a mile. They would have been slightly busier had not the northern county coroners, for unexplained reasons, held at least eight inquests in the borough in the same period.[35] The county coroners never intervened in Corsham, but even so the coroners of the manor held inquests at average intervals of little under two years, with a maximum of four in a single year. They claimed travelling-expenses for less than a quarter of them, and then only for one mile.[36] Although without the pressures of their county colleagues, they also held inquests on Sundays.[37]

One Corsham coroner claimed 1s. for each of three journeys of a mile.[38] That was blatantly illegal, since the 1751 statute provided for only 9d. a mile. His bill was nevertheless approved by the JPs. Otherwise the Corsham and Wootton Bassett coroners had no opportunity to inflate their claims, unlike the county coroners whose increasingly successful peculation may well have been connived at by the JPs. At the very least the JPs were extraordinarily careless and uncritical, as is evidenced by their approving bills which contained errors of calculation, although the net results amounted only to the overpayment of one coroner by 3d. over his whole period of office and the underpayment of two others by 4d. and 1s. 3d.[39]

[33] *VCH Wilts.* 5 (1957), 1-2; *Wilts Bills,* nos 1014, 1735, 2189, 2242, 2325, 2504, 2645.

[34] Umfreville, pp.177-8; *Wilts Bills,* nos 185, 232, 681, 1023, 1168, 1467. They also held inquests on Good Friday: e.g. *ibid.,* nos 43, 369.

[35] *Ibid.,* nos 301, 564, 627, 633, 821, 881, 884, 1746.

[36] One missing Corsham bill presumably contained a claim for a two-mile journey, as the coroner was allowed £1 1s. 6d.: Wilts. Record Office, Treasurer's Accounts, 1758.

[37] *Wilts. Bills,* nos 2778, 2788, 2791, 2793-5.

[38] *Ibid.,* nos 2780-2.

[39] *Ibid.,* bills 4, 5, 15, 19, 22, 25, 27, 29, 30; 47, 64; 101, 109, 111-14, 116-17.

The county coroners inflated their claims in ways which ranged from the mildly unethical to the completely illegal. The 9 d. allowed by the 1751 statute was 'for every mile which [the coroner] shall be compelled to travel from the usual place of his. . . abode, to take' the inquest. In other words, the coroner was expected to travel by the most direct route. No doubt road conditions sometimes necessitated a more circuitous journey, but only one coroner, John Clare in the north, had any of his mileages amended and his claims correspondingly reduced at all regularly.[40] A few of the earlier bills of his son and successor William are similarly corrected, but he claimed and was allowed payment for a 40-mile journey from Devizes to Kingswood, normally 30 miles, because he went by way of Tetbury to get post-horses, as he stated in his bill.[41]

The statute had limited the coroner's fee for holding an inquest in a gaol to a maximum of £1. The south Wiltshire coroners never claimed more than £1 for any of the 76 inquests they held in the county gaol at Fisherton Anger, which was within their district, although they never claimed less. The restriction was no great hardship for them, since they all lived nearby: one at Salisbury, and he made no travelling-claims for other inquests held at Fisherton Anger; the others at Wilton, three miles away as one of them pointedly recorded in most cases.[42] The northern coroners all lived at Devizes and naturally claimed only £1 for each of the 45 inquests they held in Devizes Bridewell, as for most of their other Devizes inquests. But William Clare held 10 inquests in Marlborough Bridewell and always claimed travelling-expenses for 14 miles; and John Clare claimed for 23 miles for each of the 5 he held in the county gaol during vacancies in the southern office.[43] All these claims were allowed, seemingly without question.

The 1751 statute made no provision for payments for adjourned sittings. Only one inquest was adjourned by a southern coroner and it is impossible to interpret his consequent claim.[44] John Clare adjourned two inquests, in each case claiming only one inquest-fee but payment for two journeys.[45] That was a reasonable practice, well within the spirit, if outside the letter, of the statute, and William Clare made

[40] E.g. *ibid.*, bills 2, 4, 8, 13, 16.

[41] *Ibid.*, bills 35, 39; no.1430 (cf. no.10). Kingswood, geographically in Gloucestershire, was another outlying part of Wiltshire: *VCH Wilts.*, 5. 1-2.

[42] E.g. *Wilts Bills*, no.2311, nos 2297-8, 2300.

[43] E.g. *ibid.*, no.798; nos 539, 541, 552, 556, 561.

[44] *Ibid.*, no. 2461.

[45] *Ibid.*, nos 21, 488.

similar claims for his first five adjourned inquests.[46] His next adjournment was of three inquests, into three related deaths, from and to the same days. For these six sittings he claimed just one travelling-fee but six inquest-fees of £1.[47] Thereafter, except for the death in Devizes Bridewell mentioned earlier, for which he claimed two inquest-fees only, he invariably claimed two inquest-fees and two full travelling-fees when inquests had a single adjournment and three inquest-fees and three travelling-fees for those adjourned twice.[48] He thus became ever more demanding, but all his claims were allowed by the JPs, even those for two travelling-fees when inquests had gone on very late or for most of the night and were then merely adjourned to the next day.[49] If not positively in breach of the statute, these practices put an extremely generous interpretation upon it.

In 1756 John Clare for the first time held two inquests on the same day, the second at a place five miles beyond the first, and he claimed for journeys of 20 and 5 miles, not 20 and 25.[50] Thereafter he often held two inquests at different places on the same day, but only once again limited the second travelling-fee to the extra distance of the second place beyond the first.[51] Otherwise he did what William Clare and the southern coroners always did in similar circumstances: they claimed for the whole distance from their homes to each place, although on some days the venue of one inquest was on the direct route to the other and sometimes in an adjacent parish.[52] There may have been times when both journeys were genuine: when the coroner was not informed of the second death until after his return home from the first inquest. But that cannot always have been so.

It cannot have been true of most of those days when coroners held two or more inquests at the same place, and certainly not when the deaths were caused by the same event. The southern coroners were completely consistent and absolutely uncompromising, still taking full travelling-fees for every inquest. Thus when six people were burnt to death at Winterslow in 1791 and Alexander Forsyth held four inquests on one day and two more on the next, he claimed for six

[46] Ibid., nos 756, 783, 786, 848, 930.

[47] Ibid., nos 1077-9.

[48] Eg. ibid., no.1353.

[49] Ibid., nos 1619, 1702.

[50] Ibid., nos 127-8 (Devizes to Malmesbury and Crudwell).

[51] Ibid., nos 534-5 (Devizes to Alderbury and Landford).

[52] E.g. ibid., nos 703-4 (Devizes to Beechingstoke and Pewsey); 1849-50 (Highworth and Hannington).

complete journeys from Salisbury as well as six inquest-fees.[53] John Clare, in the north, was again more honest. His practice was to claim for full journeys for all unconnected inquests, but for only one when the deaths resulted from the same event.[54] Indeed, in 1755 he held inquests on a mother and her child at the same place on consecutive days and still, uniquely, claimed no travelling-fee for the second.[55] The inquests were held 20 miles from Devizes and he presumably stayed overnight, which would have involved him in some expense. William Clare was less consistent. On the first two occasions, in 1774, that he held two inquests at the same place on the same day he claimed for only one journey although the deaths were unrelated. Unlike his father, he specifically mentioned the fact in his bill.[56] Subsequently he claimed for separate journeys to all unrelated inquests and for most, but not all, of those caused by the same event.[57] Thus the southern coroners always and their northern colleagues usually extracted every possible penny from such situations. The claims were never disallowed.

The payments to coroners introduced by the 1751 statute were confined to occasions when they held inquests. William Clare, however, successfully claimed for the eight additional journeys already mentioned.[58] One was to Box where a newborn child, which had been secretly buried at night, had been exhumed. Clare found that it had been born at Bath, in Somerset, and brought from there dead. He therefore had it returned to Bath, informed the mayor who was also the city coroner, and himself attended the inquest there.[59] In six other cases he ultimately decided against holding inquests, for various reasons. He refused to exhume one body, which was putrified, because the deceased had been drowned accidentally; another, also putrid when buried, when his inquiry found that an accusation of poisoning was groundless; and a third, that of a child reported to have been overlain by its mother, because the mother was married and any overlying had been accidental.[60] In two other cases he decided that suspicions of violence were unfounded, one body of a newborn child proving on his inspection to be 'an imperfection of nature and . . . un-

[53] *Ibid.*, nos 2686-91.

[54] E.g. *ibid.*, nos 306-7, 545-6.

[55] *Ibid.*, nos 105-6.

[56] *Ibid.*, nos 887-8, 893-4.

[57] E.g. *ibid.*, nos 1082-3, 1760-1, 1767-8.

[58] Above, pp. 127, 133.

[59] *Wilts Bills,* no.1377.

[60] *Ibid.*, nos 871, 1615, 1759.

necessary and improper to be viewed by a jury'.[61] One journey he did not even complete: he was intercepted by a messenger with a report of a death in another part of the county and merely forwarded his warrant for the burial of the first body without a view because the deceased was an old man and there was no suspicion of unnatural death.[62] The eighth case was the most extraordinary. Clare was ill and sent his brother, a surgeon, to view a newborn child said to have been overlain by its mother. He found no marks or suspicion of violence and therefore left the coroner's certificate for burying the body.[63] It had always been illegal for anyone other than a coroner to hold an inquest;[64] dispensing with one after the coroner had been summoned should also have been his decision alone. Not only that, but Clare may have acted illegally in dispensing with inquests in some of the six other cases.[65] Indeed, except that some of the bodies had been buried before his arrival – itself an illegality[66] – the circumstances of all of them were identical to those of many deaths after which he and the other coroners normally held inquests.

That he also took fees for the journeys compounded the offences. For one journey of 26 miles he claimed £1 6s., or 1 s. a mile as against the normal 9d.[67] Another time, for a journey of 18 miles and expenses he claimed £1 11s. 6d.[68] Otherwise, with one uninformative exception, he claimed for the journey, without specifying the distance, and expenses. Once, when he was summoned from Salisbury assizes to Wroughton, the expenses were partly for being on the road for two nights; for the Bath case he claimed for the journey to Box and Bath and overnight expenses; and for his brother's journey he claimed £1 1s., which included the hiring of a horse.[69] Such payments were neither authorised by statute nor recognised in contemporary treatises.

The Wiltshire coroners' bills contain one further type of claim: for reimbursement of sums paid by three of the coroners to others in connection with inquests. Alexander Forsyth claimed £4 4s. for his

[61] Ibid., nos 724, 1704.

[62] Ibid., no.1053.

[63] Ibid., no.1482.

[64] R.F. Hunnisett, The Medieval Coroner (Cambridge, 1961), pp. 190-1; Umfreville, pp. 156-7.

[65] For specimen warrants allowing burial of bodies without a view see Umfreville, pp. 501-5.

[66] Hunnisett, Medieval Coroner, pp. 9, 11-13. Such a charge was brought against four men at Salisbury Lent assizes in 1787, but was not prosecuted: ASSI 23/8.

[67] Wilts. Bills, no.871.

[68] Ibid., no.1053.

[69] Ibid., nos.1615, 1377, 1482.

expenses resulting from an inquest three-times adjourned and for those of a constable and bailiff in bringing the murderers to justice; John Clare £1 1s. for a subpoena for a doctor and others to attend another murder inquest; and William Clare 13 separate sums which he had paid to constables and tithingmen for taking people charged at his inquests to one or other of the Wiltshire gaols, the sums being calculated on a rate of 1s. a mile, or 2s. when there were two suspects.[70] All these claims were allowed except for two made by William Clare in April 1792. They were deleted from his bill whose total was reduced accordingly, but Clare was ultimately allowed 6d. a mile for each.[71] Either because he had already paid the constables at the higher rate or because he was told that such claims were untenable, he made no similar claims for the rest of the period.

Some of the dubious practices of the late-eighteenth-century Wiltshire coroners were regularised during the next 50 years. In 1837 coroners were authorised to claim for reimbursement of the expenses they had necessarily incurred in holding inquests, and they were to receive an extra 6s. 8d. for each inquest if the JPs (or town council) were satisfied that the claim was correct. The coroners' expenses included the fees they were required to pay to medical witnesses for giving evidence or performing post-mortem examinations.[72] In 1844 coroners were finally allowed travelling-expenses for journeys made when they had been summoned to hold an inquest but decided on arrival that it was not necessary to do so.[73] In 1836 borough coroners were permitted to appoint a deputy when they were ill or unavoidably absent, and this provision was extended to county coroners in 1843.[74] The same period saw a marked decrease in the workload of the Wiltshire county coroners. In the 1830s Devizes regained its own coroner and Malmesbury began to exercise its long-standing right to have one[75] and in 1843 not only did Wiltshire gain a third county coroner[76] but inquests in the detached parts of the county became the responsibility of the Gloucestershire and Berkshire coroners.[77]

[70]*Ibid.,* nos.2461, 222, 775-6, 812, 847, 951-3, 1251, 1566, 1647-8, 1838-9.

[71]*Ibid.,* nos.1838-9; bill 70.

[72]1 Vict. c.68.

[73]7 & 8 Vict. c.92 s.21.

[74]6 & 7 Will. IV c.105 s.6; 6 & 7 Vict. c.83 s.1.

[75]J. Waylen, *Chronicles of the Devizes...* (1839), p.186; *List of Wiltshire Borough Records earlier in date than 1836,* ed. M.G. Rathbone, Wilts. Arch. & Nat. Hist. Soc. Rec. Branch, 5 (1951), 29, 33.

[76]C202/231/29. The third coroner is erroneously said to have been introduced in 1859 in *VCH Wilts.,* 5. 234.

[77]6 Vict. c.12 s.2. The detached areas were completely transferred to Gloucestershire and Berkshire in 1844: 7 & 8 Vict. c.61.

THE LATE VICTORIAN BAR: A PROSOPOGRAPHICAL SURVEY

D. Duman

In 1835 Alexis de Tocqueville wrote: 'Lawyers belong to the people by birth and to the aristocracy by habit and taste; they may be looked upon as the connecting link between the two great classes of society.'[1] This was neither the first, nor would it be the last attempt to describe the social composition and professional ethos of the English bar. Between the sixteenth and nineteenth centuries, scores of books, tracts and articles were written about the social structure of the bar. They ranged from social commentaries about one of England's premier professions, to the gossip of guide books and popular histories, to the polemics of authors who hoped to ameliorate what they perceived as the deteriorating state of the legal profession.[2] In every case their conclusions were based upon intuition and personal impressions, rather than upon any systematic analysis of the problem. By and large these descriptions can be grouped into four main categories. According to the first, the bar was being degraded by the infusion of non-gentlemanly elements, which would inevitably lead to its decline. The second presented the bar as the paradigm of professionalism based on merit: accordingly, intelligence and hard work, not birth and connection, were the ultimate determinants of success. The third contended that with few exceptions, the investment in time and money required by a prospective barrister prevented all but the wealthy from entering the profession. Finally, the fourth suggested that the members of the bar were primarily recruited from the sons of the middle classes – born neither to luxury nor to poverty.[3]

---

[1] Alexis de Tocqueville, *Democracy in America* (New York edn, 1961), p. 1 and p. 325.

[2] For the history of social critiques of the bar before the nineteenth century, see Paul Lucas, 'Blackstone and the Reform of the Legal Profession,' in *English Historical Review* 77 (1962), 456-89.

[3] Representative examples of these four categories are as follows:
1. John Ferne, *The Blazon of Gentry* (1586), as quoted in Lucas, 'Blackstone', 470; William Blackstone, *A Discourse on the Study of the Law* (Oxford, 1758).
2. Richard Edgeworth, *Essays on Professional Education* (1809); Thomas Ruggles, *The Barrister, or Strictures on the Proper Education for the Bar* (1792), 2 vols.; H. Byerley Thomson, *The Choice of a Profession* (1857); Samuel Warren, *Introduction to Law Studies* (1845), 2 vols. This view, that ability was the real determinant of success at the bar, was the prevailing one in the nineteenth century.
3. M. Cottu, *On the Administration of Criminal Justice in England and the Spirit of English Government* (1822); John G. Jeafferson, *A Book about Lawyers* (1867), 2 vols.
4. A. Polson, *Law and Lawyers: or Sketches and Illustrations of Legal History and Biography* (1840), 2 vols.

In the twentieth century, these same questions continue to interest sociologists and historians, who have begun to make use of quantitative methods in the search for answers.[4] While a quantitative analysis of the bar can yield more precise results than earlier impressionistic investigations, new problems have arisen, such as methods of classification and the inevitable missing data. These difficulties become more serious as we move down the professional hierarchy from the judges of the high court to the rank and file of the bar. During the past two decades, in particular, our knowledge of the social composition, education, career patterns and wealth of the members of the bar has been greatly enhanced, but much work remains to be done before any complete picture of the evolution of the profession can emerge.[5] My intention here is to add one piece to that picture by means of a prosopographical survey of the bar during the year 1885.

That year was chosen because of the availability of source material, in particular the biographical dictionary of the bar compiled by Joseph Foster, the nineteenth-century genealogist.[6] This provides a near-to-complete list of men who had been called to the bar at one of the four Inns of Court and were alive in 1885. The work includes 7,251 entries which contain basic biographical information. My survey is based on a 10 per cent random sample of those entries, that is a total of 725 barristers. The data provided by Foster has been cross checked and supplemented by information culled from a wide variety of professional, social and educational directories.[7]

[4] Some recent prosopographical studies of the High Court judiciary in nineteenth-century England are: Daniel Duman, *The Judicial Bench in England, 1727-1875: The Reshaping of a Professional Elite* (Royal Historical Society, 1982); Jennifer Morgan, 'The Judiciary of the Superior Courts 1820-1968: A Sociological Study' (Unpublished University of London M. Phil thesis, 1974); C. Neal Tate, 'Paths to the Bench in Britain: A Quasi-Experimental Study of the Recruitment of a Judicial Elite', in *Western Political Quarterly* 28 (1975), 101-29.

[5] Some studies of the English bar before the nineteenth century are: Wilfrid R. Prest, *The Inns of Court under Elizabeth I and the Early Stuarts 1590-1640* (1972); Thomas G. Barnes, 'Star Chamber Litigants and their Counsel 1596-1641' in J.H. Baker (ed.), *Legal Records and the Historian* (1978), pp. 7-28; E.W. Ives, 'Promotion in the Legal Profession of Yorkist and Early Tudor England', in *LQR* 75 (1959), 348-63; Louis Knafla, 'The Matriculation Revolution and Education at the Inns of Court in Renaissance England', in Arthur J. Slavin (ed.), *Tudor Men and Institutions* (Baton Rouge, 1972), pp. 232-64; Paul Lucas, 'A Collective Biography of Students and Barristers of Lincoln's Inn, 1680-1804: A Study in the "Aristocratic Resurgence" of the Eighteenth Century', in *Journal of Modern History* 46 (1974), 227-61.

[6] Joseph Foster, *Men at the Bar* (1885).

[7] For example, Frederick Boase, *Modern English Biography* (1965), 6 vols.; *Burke's Landed Gentry; Burke's Peerage and Baronetage;* Joseph Foster, *Alumni Oxonienses 1714-1886* (Oxford, 1887), 4 vols.; *Dictionary of National Biography;* J. and J.A. Venn, *Alumni Cantabrigenses 1752-1900* (Cambridge, 1940-54), 6 vols.; James Whishaw, *A Synopsis of the Members of the English Bar* (1835); *Who was Who.*

Before we can begin to discuss the composition of the English bar, one central question must be answered: How are we to define the profession? We may decide to count only those men who succeeded in establishing a practice from which they earned their livelihood; alternatively, we can widen our perspective to include all those men who at some time in their careers cherished the hope of gaining fame and fortune at the bar. The final possibility is to cast our net over anyone who was willing to eat his dinners and go through the formality of a call to the bar, regardless of any intention to pursue the career of an advocate. I propose to begin with the last definition in order to formulate as complete a picture of the profession as possible. Afterwards I will narrow the focus to permit a more detailed analysis of the structure of the practising bar.

Inns of Court men in 1885

Men who were called to the bar during the late Victorian era did not constitute an occupationally homogeneous profession. Table 1 indicates the variety of careers adopted by them: these include

Table 1: Occupations of Inns of Court men (1885)

	Practising Bar	Colonial Bar	Other Professions	Civil Service	Business	Land	Unknown	Total
No.	272	79	70	52	33	73	146	725
%	38	11	11	7	5	10	20	100

advocacy at home and abroad, membership of a host of major and minor professions, the home and colonial civil service, landowning, and almost every aspect of commerce and industry. However, it is not surprising to discover that within this diversity the legal occupations were by far the most popular choices. Thirty-eight per cent of the men in our sample practised as barristers in the courts of England and Wales, while another 11 per cent practised in Scotland, Ireland, and the colonies. Together these legal practitioners accounted for nearly half of the Inns of Court men. To their number can be added another group of men who did not practise law, but who did make professional use of their legal qualifications. This group, which is not categorised separately in Table 1, includes fifteen colonial civil servants who sat as local and high court judges, primarily in India, as well as four members of the home civil service and thirteen other professional men who filled offices in which a legal background was necessary. All in all, the call to the bar formed an essential step in the professional progress of 383 members of the sample, or 53 per cent.

In comparison to the legal contingent, the other occupational categories were small. Ninety men (12 per cent) were members of the professions in which their legal qualifications were not required, such as the armed services, the clergy, medicine, journalism, and the civil service. A further seventy-three men (10 per cent) derived their main income from landed estates. Of the sixty-eight for whom there are data 38 per cent belonged to the middle ranks of landed society, with estates worth between £1,000 and £3,000 per annum. In addition, 21 per cent had annual incomes of £3,000 to £10,000, 26 per cent were small landowners with rent rolls of between £300 and £1,000, 6 per cent possessed land worth less than £300 per annum, and finally 9 per cent were great landowners with annual incomes in excess of £10,000.[8]

The last major occupational category contains those Inns of Court men who made their careers in business. A total of sixty-four barristers, including men from almost every occupational category, were directors of public companies at some time during their careers; however, only thirty-three men (5 per cent) can be classified as full-time businessmen. Their principal interests were as follows: five were concerned with investment companies or stockbroking; four each in banking, brewing, insurance and manufacturing; three each were foreign merchants or in gas supply; two each in railway and land development; one was in mining; and in one instance the nature of the business was unknown. Furthermore, in one third of these cases, the man in question did not limit himself to a single business interest, but rather became involved in a number of ventures.

Having completed this brief occupational survey of the bar, we can now return to the question concerning the social origins of the members of the bar posed at the beginning of this paper. Barristers, like members of other occupations, were not drawn randomly from all social classes. Rather, the cost of education, the length of training required, the prospects for success, the availability of connections, and the eventual rewards help to determine the social composition of the profession by making it more or less attractive and accessible to the members of particular classes.

Even a cursory examination of the occupational origins of the members of the bar in 1885 indicates that they came from a very

---

[8] For an examination of the structure of nineteenth-century landowning, see F.M.L. Thompson, *English Landed Society in the Nineteenth Century* (1963), pp. 1-44. The landholdings have been traced in *Return of the Owners of Land 1872-73* (England and Wales), B.P.P. (1874), LXXII,(Scotland), B.P.P. (1874), LXXII,part III: *Return of the Owners of Land* (Ireland), B.P.P. (1876), LXXX.

Table 2: Origins of Inns of Court men
by fathers' occupations (1885)

	Bar	Solicitor	Clergy	Medicine	Other Professions	Civil Service	Business	Urban Gentry	Land	Rural Gentry	Other	Unknown	Total
No.	82	53	85	34	49	36	110	78	117	37	7	37	725
%	11	7	12	5	7	5	15	11	16	5	1	5	100

narrow stratum of English society. Almost 75 per cent were recruited from the urban middle and upper middle classes, including members of the professions, the civil service, businessmen, and the urban gentry.[9] The professions and the civil service alone accounted for almost 50 per cent of the bar, and within that category the lion's share belonged to the two branches of the legal profession. Together the barristers and solicitors represented 19 per cent of all occupations and 40 per cent of the professions. The prestige of the bar is emphasised by the structure of the professional component. Of the 339 barristers from professional origins, 189 or 56 per cent were the sons of members of the upper gentlemanly professions, including barristers, Church of England clergy and officers of the armed services. A further 135 men (40 per cent) were the sons of civil servants and members of the traditional non-gentlemanly professions including solicitors, court officials, medical practitioners, dissenting clergymen and teachers. Only fifteen barristers (4 per cent) were the sons of members of the new technical professions, including architects, accountants, surveyors, engineers and a dentist.

The predominance of the sons of professional men becomes even more striking when their numbers are compared to those of the next two largest occupational categories – the sons of landowners and of businessmen. The landed contingent in the 1885 bar amounted to 16 per cent of the total, and may have been as high as 21 per cent if the

[9]In addition to occupational categories, I have made use of two residual classifications for those fathers who are described in the directories as 'gentleman' or 'esquire', and for whom no other information has been found. Certainly by the nineteenth century, and perhaps as early as the seventeenth century, these titles were no longer associated exclusively with the landed gentry. In this study, therefore, I have divided the gentlemen and esquires according to their place of residence. Those who came from towns with 5,000 or more residents, according to the 1841 census, were classified as urban, while the remainder were considered rural. I have made the assumption that the urban gentry were professional and businessmen, while the rural gentry were landowners. In fact, this probably over-estimates the landed contribution to the bar, since even towns with less than 5,000 residents had professional and business communities. On this point, see Lawrence Stone, 'The Size and Composition of the Oxford Student Body 1580-1909', in Lawrence Stone (ed.), *The University in Society* (Princeton, 1974), p. 1, p. 48 and pp. 66-7.

thirty-seven rural gentlemen are included. However, nineteenth-century landed society was a rather heterogeneous social category, and it would be useful here if we could identify the socio-economic backgrounds of these men more precisely. With the help of the 'new domesday book' compiled in the 1870s, I have been able to discover the exact rentals of the paternal estates of 106 of these barristers. The results are displayed in Table 3 where they have been sub-divided into five income categories. In addition I have divided the barristers from landowning families according to whether they were first sons who would normally have inherited the estates, or younger sons who, in most cases, had to work for their livelihood.

Table 3: Inns of Court men from landowning families (1885)

Gross Annual Rental	Eldest Son		Younger Sons		Total	
	No.	%	No.	%	No.	%
£100 - £300	4	80	1	20	5	5
£300 - £1,000	18	62	11	38	29	27
£1,000 - £3,000	13	38	21	62	34	32
£3,000 - £10,000	10	36	18	64	28	26
£10,000 and over	4	40	6	60	10	9
Total	49	46	57	54	106	100

The picture that emerges from Table 3 confirms the description of the landholdings of barrister/landowners presented earlier. In both instances, most of the estates fall into the middle ranges, with the largest single category being those worth between £1,000 and £3,000 per annum. There is also a clear distribution of eldest and younger sons according to the size of the paternal estate. Almost two thirds of the sons of landowners with gross annual rentals of over £1,000 were younger sons, while for those with estates worth under £1,000 per annum, two thirds were first sons. The attractions of the bar were lowest for the groups located at the two extremes of landed society. The great landowners showed little inclination to send any of their sons to the Inns of Court in the second half of the nineteenth century, and this was probably true in earlier periods as well.[10] Their sons had no need to enter so competitive a profession as the bar, and the attractions of the Inns of Court could not compete with those of the grand tour. The lesser landowners also hesitated in sending their sons

[10] This was certainly the case among Lincoln's Inn barristers in the late seventeenth and eighteenth centuries. Lucas, 'Lincoln's Inn', 254.

to the bar, due to the costs of residence at the Inns, the uncertainty of success and the inability of fledgling barristers to earn enough during the early years to support themselves. To enter a son at the bar was to undertake a financial burden which was beyond the means of many smaller landowners, especially in regard to their younger sons.

The bar was most attractive to the middle ranges of the landed gentry. Residence at the Inns could serve to finish off the gentlemanly education of an eldest son, and perhaps provide the future JP with a useful grounding in the law. However, the bar was even more important for a younger son in search of a profession. Useful contacts could be made at the Inns, and if the young gentleman decided to pursue an active career at the bar, gentry connections were very useful in attracting a few early cases on the circuit or at the sessions.

The business contingent at the bar accounted for at least 15 per cent of the total, and would in all probability be higher if we knew more about the occupations of the urban gentry. The largest single group of businessmen is also the least specific – namely, the miscellaneous merchants. Included in this category are men variously described as 'merchants': wholesalers, domestic merchants of many varieties, and larger retail merchants. One third of the businessmen fathers belonged to this group. The remainder of the businessmen are divided into nine specializations, including banking and international trade – 10 per cent each, insurance – 8 per cent, utilities and railways – 7 per cent, publishing – 6 per cent, brewing and those serving as agents – 5 per cent each, and mining and miscellaneous – 2 per cent each. Some of these categories are rather vague, and one must be careful in ascribing socio-economic status on the basis of occupation alone. However, if we exclude the miscellaneous merchants, some of whom were probably closer to successful shopkeepers than to men of commerce, and the agents who could be practically anything, it would seem evident that by and large the businessmen fathers of the late Victorian barristers were from at least the middle ranges of industrial and commercial English society.

The last occupational category in Table 2 that requires separate notice has been labelled 'other' and contains a mere seven men or 1 per cent of the total. Included here are men who do not fit easily into the other categories: a colonial police colonel, a master sailor in the merchant service, a clerk, an organist, an auctioneer, a bookseller and a printer. With the possible exception of the police colonel, these are men who belonged to the lower middle or even to the artisan classes. Men born into these classes are notable chiefly as a result of their relative absence from the Inns of Court. Their scarcity helps to complete the picture of the social composition of the upper branch of the legal profession in the last quarter of the nineteenth century.

Barristers were recruited primarily from the upper and middle ranks of the urban professional and commercial classes, and secondarily from the middle ranges of landed society. They were men who had to seek a career, yet had the advantages of moderate wealth and in some cases connection to help speed them on their way. The really wealthy were apparently not interested in the bar as a profession or in the Inns of Court as social or educational institutions, while the cost, uncertain future, and perhaps social climate made them inhospitable to men from the lower echelons of the middle class and from the working classes.

The practising bar

In 1892, the *Law Journal* attempted to provide a working definition of the practising barrister:

> We incline to the position that any barrister who occupies business chambers anywhere, and no other barrister, is a 'practising barrister', but . . . there is some ground for saying that merely plying for hire, however long and continuously, will not turn a 'barrister' into a 'practising barrister', unless a moderate amount of professional success has been the result.[11]

I have tried to make use of both of these alternative definitions by dividing the practising bar into two groups. The first includes those men who achieved some success in the profession as measured by the receipt of offices and honours. The second is composed of all those men whose entries in the *Law List* give both a chambers address and a legal specialisation. In addition, the common law barristers have been cross checked in the separate circuit lists in order to eliminate those who had ceased to practise, but who had not bothered to revise the details given in the *Law List*.

Together these two groups comprise in theory the practising bar of England and Wales. However, in order to estimate the number of men who were actually practising in 1885, the data has been refined further. First of all, I have excluded all those barristers in the 10 per cent sample (Table 1) who are known to have retired from practice prior to 1885. Second, I have utilized the Chancery law reports for 1885 in order to separate those men who tried their luck at the bar for a few years before moving on to other careers, from men who made the

---

[11]*Law Journal* 28 (10 December 1892), 778.

bar their principal occupation.[12] Applying the resulting sample data to the entire bar (7,251 individuals) we find that in 1885 there were approximately 1,440 practising barristers who occupied business chambers in England and Wales of whom 660 received professional honours and offices during their careers. A comparison between the estimates of the maximum and minimum sizes of the late Victorian bar and the situation fifty years earlier, indicates a significant decline in the percentage of Inns of Court men who succeeded in establishing themselves in practice. In 1835, the ratio of practising barristers to qualified barristers under the age of sixty-five ranged from a maximum of 1:2.5 to a minimum of 1:5, while in 1885 the maximum was 1:4 and the minimum 1:9. From this evidence it would seem that the endemic problem of overcrowding at the bar became more serious between Queen Victoria's coronation and her Golden Jubilee.[13]

With the chances of success at the late Victorian bar limited to between 1:4 or 1:9, it seems essential to ask whether recruitment of practising barristers was random or whether men from specific social, educational or professional backgrounds were favoured in attaining a secure place at the bar. In order to help us answer this question, the social, educational and political histories of four groups of judges and practising barristers are compared in Table 4. The groups are as follows: (1) the judges of the Supreme Court appointed between 1875 and 1901;[14] (2) the elite of the bar in 1885 including QCs, Serjeants-at-law, and Supreme Court judges; (3) the definitely practising bar, those who achieved some degree of professional success or recognition; and (4) the entire practising bar.

[12] For equity practitioners, there is no way to cross check continued practice at the bar as there is for their common law colleagues. Therefore I have made use of the Law Reports of the Chancery Division of the High Court for 1885 in order to estimate the size of the equity bar.

[13] Of course it is possible that the decline in the proportion of practising barristers between 1835 and 1885 may reflect an expansion in alternate sources of employment, which drew Inns of Court men away from the bar, rather than an increase in overcrowding. In fact, overcrowding is a very difficult phenomenon to measure, due to problems of definition and data. However, nineteenth-century barristers were in no doubt that its existence could not be ignored.

[14] In this category are all judges appointed to the High Court between the inception of the Judiciary Acts in 1875, and the death of Queen Victoria in 1901. I have included all Lord Chancellors, Masters of the Rolls, Lords Justices of Appeal, Chief Justices and the puisne judges of both the Common Law and Chancery Courts. In addition, 6 Lords of Appeal who never sat on the High Court Bench were appointed to the House of Lords in this period, but only one of these men, Lord MacNaghten, has been added to the list of judges. I have excluded 5 Scottish and Irish judges who were not members of the English profession, as well as Arthur Lord Hobhouse, who gave up legal practice twenty years before his appointment to the bench. He took his seat in the Lords after a career in India, and as a member of the Judicial Committee of the Privy Council, and he only sat in India appeals cases.

Table 4: The Late Victorian practising Bar

	N=53 Judges 1875-1901		N=54 Elite of the Bar		N=97 Definitely Practising		N=272 Total Practising	
	No.	%	No.	%	No.	%	No.	%
Father's Occupation								
Bar	7	13	7	13	15	15	42	15
Solicitor	6	11	5	9	10	10	25	9
Clergy	12	23	7	13	12	12	34	13
Other Professions	4	8	10	19	12	12	29	11
Civil Service	0	0	3	6	6	6	16	6
Business	14	26	12	22	19	20	38	14
Urban Gentry	0	0	3	6	8	8	29	11
Land	8	15	4	7	11	11	27	10
Rural Gentry	0	0	1	2	2	2	15	6
Other	0	0	0	0	0	0	4	1
Unknown	2	4	2	4	2	2	13	5
Education								
Top 22 Public Schools	22	42	14	26	29	30	70	26
All Public Schools	28	53	24	44	43	44	104	38
Others & Unknown	25	47	30	55	54	56	168	62
Cambridge	15	28	20	37	37	38	85	31
Oxford	18	33	10	19	20	21	78	28
Other	13	28	13	24	18	19	44	16
Total University	46	87	43	80	75	77	207	76
Trinity, Cambridge	9	17	8	15	19	20	47	17
Balliol & Christ Church	10	19	1	2	5	5	16	6
Inner Temple	14	26	24	44	41	42	109	40
Middle Temple	7	13	11	20	24	25	67	24
Lincoln's Inn	30	57	14	26	27	28	88	32
Gray's Inn	2	4	5	9	5	5	8	3
Politics								
M.P.	22	42	19	35	23	24	24	9
Non-M.P.	31	58	35	65	74	76	248	91

Dynasticism played only a limited role in determining a man's chances for success at the late Victorian practising bar. For example there were almost twice as many clergymen's sons as there were barristers' sons represented on the judicial bench between 1875 and 1901. Although barristers' sons did form the largest single occupational category among the three other groups of practising barristers, men from clerical families were not far behind. Even if we widen our definition of dynasticism to include the sons of solicitors as well, then approximately one quarter of the barristers in each group were the sons of lawyers, as compared to 19 per cent in the entire 1885 sample, indicating that they had a slight advantage over most other members of the bar.

All Inns of Court men were not equal in the race for the few places at the practising bar, and while dynasticism as such was only of limited significance, social and educational background could have a marked influence on a barrister's chances of success, even in this comparatively open profession. The connection between social factors and professional success becomes clear when we compare the origins of the High Court judges with those of the members of the professional order from which they were largely recruited – the elite of the practising bar. The advantage of good birth in obtaining appointments to the judicial bench is undeniable. There were, for example, twice as many landowner's sons, and 80 per cent more clergymen's sons on the bench than there were in the elite. Gentlemen by birth, here the sons of barristers, Church of England clergymen, armed forces officers, and landed gentlemen accounted for 47 per cent of the judges, but only for 37 per cent of the elite of the bar. Interestingly enough, the elite and the judges represented the two social extremes of the bar, with the elite being the least exclusive of the four categories and the judges being the most.

Another occupational group whose sons were proportionately over-represented in the upper echelons of the legal profession were the businessmen, although in this case, there was only a slight difference between the judges and the elite.[15] Only 15 per cent of the total practising bar in 1885 were recruited from the business community, compared with 20 per cent of the definitely practising bar, 22 per cent of the elite and 26 per cent of the High Court judges. This rather unexpected connection between business origins and professional success may be explained in part by the ability of some businessmen fathers to provide their sons with a steady flow of business, directly or

[15] Barristers of business origins who eventually reached the bench were inordinately successful in being appointed to the Court of Appeal and the House of Lords. Tate, 'Paths to the Bench', pp. 118-22.

indirectly. However, this advantage alone was probably not sufficient to explain the marked success of this group of Inns of Court men.

A comparison of the educational careers of the judges and the elite suggests, as in the case of the gentlemen by birth, that a social gap separated them. Beginning with secondary education, we find that 40 per cent of the judges attended one of the twenty-two elite public schools, while a further 13 per cent had been educated at other public schools – thus a total of 53 per cent of the judges were public school old boys.[16] Among the elite of the bar, 26 per cent went to a leading public school, and 44 per cent to all public schools. At the university level, Oxbridge graduates were slightly more numerous on the bench (62 per cent) than they were in the elite (56 per cent). Although Oxford men predominate on the bench, while Cambridge men are most common within the other categories of practising barristers, it is, however, when we compare the attendance patterns of the judges with those of members of the elite at three leading colleges – Trinity College, Cambridge, Christ Church and Balliol – that the social gap again becomes striking . Thirty-six per cent of all the judges were students at one of these three colleges, representing 59 per cent of the Oxbridge men, while only 17 per cent of the elite were members of these colleges, or 30 per cent of the Oxbridge contingent. Additionally, 91 per cent of the judges were university men, compared to 80 per cent of the elite of the bar. The social superiority of the judges is even apparent in regard to the Inns of Court. The most popular choice among the judges (57 per cent), Lincoln's Inn, was also the most fashionable. However, only one quarter of the elite members of the bar were Lincoln's Inn men, while 44 per cent went to the Inner Temple.

It seems clear that while the professional elite was recruited from the practising bar more or less randomly, the gentlemen by birth and to a lesser extent businessmen's sons were more likely than other barristers to gain entrance to the judicial bench. This naturally raises the question: did social bias play a part in the appointment of High Court judges in nineteenth-century England? In order to answer this question, we must briefly examine the connection between politics and a career at the bar. As is clear from the last section of Table 4 and from Table 5, there was a direct correlation between professional eminence and membership of the House of Commons. Although only

---

[16] In a recent study of the public schools community, the traditional means of classifying these schools has been severely criticised. I have adopted an alternate scheme suggested in that work. The elite 22 schools are those that appear in Table 4, group 1, while the other public schools are those included in Table 4, group 2-4, and Table 5. J.R. de S. Honey, *Tom Brown's Universe, The Development of the Victorian Public School* (1977), pp. 264-8.

Table 5: Politics and professional advancement at the practising Bar (1885)

	Queen's Counsel		Local Judge		High Court Judge		Total
	No.	%	No.	%	No.	%	No.
M.P.	19	83	3	13	7	30	23
Non-M.P.	33	45	20	28	3	4	74
Definitely Practising	52	53	23	24	10	10	97

a quarter of the definitely practising barristers were MPs, over one third of the elite and nearly one half of the judges had sat in the Commons.[17] The relationship between political involvement and professional success, however, was not straightforward. First, only a minority of both the judges and the Queen's Counsel were House of Commons men. Second, most Queen's Counsel who sat in Parliament were first elected only several years after they took silk. Third, in only a small minority of cases did a man receive an appointment to the bench of the High Court without having established a reputation at the bar.[18] In fact the earlier a man took silk, the higher was the probability of his appointment to the bench of the High Court and especially to a senior judgeship. On the other hand, a Queen's Counsel who also sat in Parliament clearly had a better chance than his non-political counterparts of reaching the judiciary.[19] Political partisanship alone could not

[17]In addition to those men who sat as members of Parliament, 8 judges (15%), 5 members of the professional elite (9%), 10 definitely practising barristers (10%), and 11 members of the entire practising bar (4%) stood as parliamentary candidates, but were never elected. Combining this data with the last section of Table 4 gives the total percentage of politically active men as follows: Judges 57%, elite 44%, definitely practising bar 34%, and total practising bar 13%.

[18]There were several exceptions to this rule during the Chancellorship of Lord Halsbury. For example, the appointment of Edward Ridley to the High Court in 1897 was condemned as 'a political job' at the time. *Law Journal* 32 (17 April 1897), 215.

[19]The importance of the age at which a barrister took silk as an indication of his professional prospects is clearly indicated with regard to the bench of the High Court in Tate, 'Paths to the Bench', pp. 117-28. However, I believe that Professor Tate has underestimated the significance of political associations for a legal career. First, he has excluded the most political judgeships – the Chancellor, Chief Justice, and Master of the Rolls. Second, he has taken the entire period 1876-1973 as a single unit. This masks the fact that until the 1920s, a seat in Parliament was much more important in determining a barrister's chances for judicial appointment than it was after that time. However, by combining the relatively high percentage of judges who sat in Parliament in the earlier period with the low percentage of judicial MPs in the later one, Tate derives an average which misrepresents the importance of politics in a late nineteenth-century career at the bar.

make a judge, but a seat in Parliament was certainly advantageous if not absolutely essential for the most ambitious members of the bar.

Barrister/MPs stood apart from the rank and file of the bar, not only by virtue of their easier access to the highest professional offices, but also as a result of their distinctive social profile. On average, these men were more often gentlemen by birth or the sons of businessmen than were other members of the bar. As a result, membership in Parliament acted as a social and professional sieve, favouring barristers from the landed classes, from the high status professions, and from the wealthier segments of the commercial community. In addition, men from these classes were more likely to have the advantage of valuable social and professional connections which could be counted upon to bring an early and steady flow of clients to their chambers. The result was inequality of opportunity. However, it must be emphasized that this phenomenon was due not to overt social bias, but rather to advantages in the opening stages of a career, and to a judicial selection process, which indirectly and perhaps unconsciously benefited barristers who were gentlemen by birth.

Conclusion

In 1857, a commentator on the professions wrote:

> In the present day the bar has become more than ever a profession of the middle classes; not a very great number of the present race of barristers can boast of family. . . among the successful advocates [we have] several who have been small schoolmasters, wandering lectureres, newspaper-reporters, and others who have honourably raised themselves from occupations even less exalted.[20]

Ten years later, another author wrote as if to answer this view of the bar:

> These advocates who have raised themselves from plebeian rank are made to sustain a theory (fruitful of disappointment in the lower grades of the middle rank) which teaches ambitious boys to regard the bar as a profession in which men of ability and courage, unsupported by private means or connexion, have many chances of winning fame and power. A more fallacious or disastrous theory cannot be imagined.[21]

[20] Thomson, *The Choice of a Profession* (1857), p. 93.
[21] Jeafferson, *A Book About Lawyers* (1867), p. 2, p. 331.

For both men, the essential question was: Does the bar serve as a path of upward social mobility? Their answers, based as they were on a few outstanding examples, supplemented by general impressions concerning the state of the profession, were bound to be incomplete. In this respect we have an obvious advantage over them being able to base any conclusions on a firm, if not completely unimpeachable, quantitative foundation.

At the point of entry to the bar stood an almost impermeable social barrier. The sons of artisans and tradesmen who were able to pass through were no more than isolated exceptions. As Professor Harold Perkin has recently noted, social mobility did not usually occur in great leaps but in a slow movement over several generations.[22] The upwardly mobile members of the bar were the sons of solicitors, doctors, engineers, and middle and small scale businessmen. Their fathers had already some independence and perhaps even prosperity. In many cases, they were in a position to aid their sons in the early stages of a career at the bar with money, connections or both.

Once a man had passed through the portals of the profession, social origins receded as a determinant of success. Only a minority established themselves as advocates in England, but it would be ungenerous and incorrect to view the majority as failures. Some never intended to try their hand at the bar, preferring to retire to their family estates, or to pursue a career in business or in the professions at home or abroad. Others were attracted by more gratifying and less tedious vocations than that of a fledgling barrister, sitting in chambers hoping for a few paltry briefs. The relative unimportance of social origins for the career prospects of a barrister is indicated by the social profile of the tiny elite of counsel who achieved conspicuous success in the profession. These men were not noteworthy for their superior background, and were in fact descended from less exalted forebearers than were the rank and file of the Inns of Court men. Rather their success must be attributed to subjective and non-quantifiable factors – ambition, talent, temperament, and luck.

If one social barrier blocked open access to the Inns of Court, then another though less formidable one stood at the entrance to the judicial bench. The former excluded the vast majority of Englishmen from a career at the bar, while the latter favoured the sons of gentlemen and businessmen. The bar served as a path of upward social mobility for the professional, commercial, and industrial middle classes, but in the quest for its greatest prizes, the advantage belonged to the social and economic elite.

[22] Harold Perkin, 'The Recruitment of Elites in British Society Since 1800', in *Journal of Social History* 12 (1978), 232-3.

SCOTTISH LEGAL EDUCATION IN THE NINETEENTH CENTURY

P.S. Lachs

The new professionalism of the nineteenth century, often described as an evolution from 'status professionalism', based primarily on birth and social class, to 'occupational professionalism' based primarily on training and tested skills, affected the development of the modern legal profession in Scotland.[1] In this country, where law was valued for its universal qualities and as an expression of Scottish cultural nationalism, the growth of the modern profession reveals certain tensions in Scottish life.[2]

The first is one of open versus restricted opportunity. On the one hand the well-known Scottish tradition of democratic access to the universities, located in the principal cities, provided students with the opportunity to board cheaply in town while paying relatively inexpensive fees for instruction. Neither tuition nor university life-style were absolutely beyond the means of a boy of modest income who had talent, ambition, and industry. These conditions produced a university population in Scotland that was about the same size as the university population in England, which had a population five times greater. Figures for school population tell the same story. The Argyll Commission found in 1864-5 that one Scot in 250 had a secondary education; one Englishman in 1,300.[3] Against these general conditions of accessible education is juxtaposed the Scottish tradition of aristocratic membership in the legal profession. At the opening of the nineteenth century the Faculty of Advocates and the Society of Writers to the Signet were still largely associations of landed families or those with close landed connections, and they were linked to

[1] Philip Elliott, *The Sociology of the Professions* (1972), pp. 29-54; Brian Henney, *A Different Kind of Gentlemen: Parish Clergy as Professional Men in Early and Mid-Victorian England* (1976), p. 4.

[2] John Clive and Bernard Bailyn, 'England's Cultural Provinces: Scotland and America', in *William and Mary Quarterly*, 3rd series 10 (1954), 200-13; T.B. Smith, *Studies Critical and Comparative* (Edinburgh, 1962), pp. 46-71.

[3] R.G. Cant, 'The Scottish Universities and Scottish Society in the Eighteenth Century', in *Studies in Voltaire and the Eighteenth Century* 58 (1967), 1953-66; Christopher Harvie, *Scotland and Nationalism* (1977), p. 78; George S. Pryde, *A New History of Scotland*, (1965), pp. 166-7. Scottish emigration to study at English universities was partly offset by English dissenters choosing to study at Glasgow or Edinburgh before the removal of disabilities against dissent at Oxford and Cambridge in 1854. In general the higher figure for advanced education in Scotland continues well into the twentieth century (see Fritz K. Ringer, *Education and Society in Modern Europe*, [Bloomington and London, 1979], pp. 212, 229-30).

inherited tradition so strong and established that it has properly been called dynastic.[4] In the nineteenth century there were a number of families in both bodies whose association with the profession went back seven generations. The network of legal families was horizontal as well as vertical. Advocates and Writers with fathers and grandfathers in the profession usually had brothers in the other branch. These sons and brothers enjoyed opportunities of entering established practices against which the newcomer could barely compete.

The second set of circumstances derives from the distinctiveness of Scottish law, preserved intact after the Union of 1707 as a corpus separate from the common law. Before the Napoleonic Wars, young Scots intent on a legal career frequently studied for a year or two on the continent and then returned for practical training at home. Going to London to study law was not unknown in the eighteenth century, but it was relatively rare, and it virtually meant opting for a different system and thus deciding on a career based in England.[5] In the nineteenth century the southern route can no longer be considered rare or even unusual; for every three Scots who joined the Faculty of Advocates in the nineteenth century, two entered one of the Inns of Court.

The rate of emigration south to study law and other subjects worried those concerned about higher education in Scotland and was one of the principal reasons for the formation of the patriotic 'Association for the Extensions of Scottish Universities'. One of the aims of this group was the improvement of legal studies in Scotland by obtaining government grants for professorial chairs, with the hope of producing an expanded law school on the continental rather than the English model.[6]

A decision for England had to be made at a relatively tender age. (Nineteenth-century Edinburgh students entered the university in their early teens; twelve was not uncommon at Glasgow and Aberdeen). In making the choice, several factors were at work. Enrolment at Oxford or Cambridge would have been recognised as a

[4]G. Donaldson, 'The Legal Profession in Scottish Society in the Sixteenth and Seventeenth Centuries', *Juridical Review*, new series 21 (1976), 1-19; N.T. Phillipson, 'Lawyers, Landowners, and the Civic Leadership of Post-Union Scotland', in *Juridical Review*, new series 21 (1976), 97-120; Nan Wilson, 'The Scottish Bar: The Evolution of the Faculty of Advocates in its social Setting', in *Louisiana Law Review* 28:2 (Feb. 1968), 235-57.

[5]C.E.A. Bedwell, 'Scottish Middle Templars, 1604-1889', in *Scottish Historical Review* 17 (1920), 100-17, 251-2 is an incomplete list, even for the Middle Temple.

[6]George Davie, *The Democratic Intellect, Scotland and Her Universities in the Nineteenth Century* (Edinburgh, 1961), pp. 47-8; James Crabb Watt, *John Inglis* (Edinburgh, 1893), pp. 41-2, 187.

more advantageous beginning for a career as a barrister practising in London than study at Glasgow or Edinburgh. English university life, however, was more closely associated with the pocketbook and social connections of a gentleman.[7] Since the path to a legal career in London via one of the ancient English universities was the more expensive route, one might assume that it was be the option of the prosperous. But, since the law tended to be a family enterprise in Scotland, the prosperous were more likely to have opportunities available at home, and in a real practical sense the southern route had more to offer a young man whose fortune had yet to be made; one whose family had no career benefits to offer him at home.

This study examines primarily the two prestigious Edinburgh bodies, the Faculty of Advocates and the Society of Writers to the Signet, with some comparisons with those who took their training in London. The figures derive from an analysis of 930 biographies, just about one fourth of the total nineteenth-century membership of these professional associations. The data are obtained from the standard biographical dictionaries for England and Scotland, Edinburgh university calendars and the manuscript archives of the university (principally the matriculation rolls and class lists), the admissions registers of the Inns of Court, and the nineteenth-century apprentice petitions preserved in the library of the Writers to the Signet, all of which are rich in information on the educational and social profiles of the law students.

The Writers to the Signet were the largest and in many ways the most complex of the three groups under consideration. Of the entire nineteenth-century population of Advocates, Writers to the Signet, and Scots who entered one of the Inns of Court in London, forty-seven per cent were Writers, thirty-three per cent were advocates, twenty per cent entered the Inns.[8] Moreover, the Writers exhibit the extremes of social origin: they are at once the most dynastic and the most diverse in family background. Taking a view of the century as a whole, almost twice as many of the Writers followed the profession of their

[7]James Lorimer, 'Higher Instruction and its Representatives in Scotland', in *North British Review* 19 (May 1853), 219-42, contains observations on the relative costs and availability of fellowship at the Scottish and English universities and concludies that the position of the Scottish universities was being threatened by financial support availability of fellowship at the Scottish and English universities and concludes that although not necessary, for a career at the English bar, and lawyers in England were less well educated, in terms of university study, than lawyers in France and Germany in the nineteenth century (Fritz K. Ringer, 'The Education of Elites in Modern Europe', *History of Education Quarterly* 18:2 [Summer 1978], 159-72).

[8]Membership figures are obtained by tabulations from Sir Francis James Grant, ed., *The Faculty of Advocates in Scotland 1532-1943 with Genealogical Notes* (Edinburgh 1944); *The Society of Writers to His Majesty's Signet with a list of Members and*

fathers as the Advocates (22 per cent of the former – 12 per cent of the latter); 8 per cent of the Writers, 5 per cent of the Advocates were grandsons of the same profession. If one counts fathers in all branches of the legal profession, one includes 40 per cent of the Writers, 24 per cent of the Advocates. The mercantile interests are represented at about the same level in both groups (about 13-14 per cent), and local and national government as well as all branches of the civil service produce the same (4-5 per cent) of both. The other liberal professions account for almost 13 per cent of the Advocates' fathers; only 8 per cent of the Writers'. But among the Writers one finds sons of estate agents, tenant farmers, school-masters, insurance agents, artisans and even labourers (roughly 13 per cent) that constitute less than 4 per cent of the population of Advocates. Fathers who were landed gentlemen with no other occupational identity account for 36 per cent of the Advocates, 16 per cent of the Writers.

Figures for the century as a whole, of course, do not reveal the dynamics of changing social structures. As important as the presence of the sons of lower-middle and working-class families is the time that they appear in significant numbers. The picture is not of gradual and progressive democratisation of membership, but rather one of sharp fluctuation. For both Advocates and Writers, admissions rise to a peak in the decade of the 1820s and 1830s, fall in the hungry 40s; then rise slowly again until there is another fall off in the late 1870s followed by a period of stability and then another drop at the end of the century. In each case, the swing up and down is sharper for the Writers than for the Advocates. Severe economic depression can explain the declining admission of the 40s and 70s. The drop at the end of the century reflects severe overcrowding of the profession, which is well documented and which was popularly recognised as a serious problem.[9] New groups appear during the periods of prosperity and

Abstracts of the Minutes of the Society (Edinburgh, 1890; 1936); Joseph Foster, *Men at the Bar,* 2nd edn, (London, 1885); and from the following registers:
Gray's Inn: *The Register of Admissions to Gray's Inn 1521-1889,* ed Joseph Foster (privately printed, 1889). Gray's Inn Manuscripts, 1625-1900.
Inner Temple: Inner Temple Manuscripts. Admissions to the Inner Temple 1751-1850.
Lincoln's Inn: *The Records of the Honourable Society of Lincoln's Inn,* ed. W.P. Baildon (1896) II: Admissions 1800-1893.
Middle Temple: *Register of Admissions to the Honourable Society of the Middle Temple from the Fifteenth Century to the Year 1944,* ed Herbert Arthur Charlie Sturgess (1949), II.

[9] On surplus lawyers and briefless barristers, see Lenore O'Boyle, 'The Problem of an Excess of Educated Men in Western Europe, 1800-1850', in *Journal of Modern History* 42 (December 1970), 471-95 and Daniel Duman, 'A Sociological and Occupational analysis of the English Judiciary: 1770-1790 and 1855-1875', in *American Journal of Legal History* 17 (October 1973), 353-64.

high admissions (i.e., the 1820s and 1830s and the early 1880s); the professions are most 'closed' in the sense of having the highest proportion of legal fathers and grandfathers during the periods of restricted opportunity.

The rate of Scots who entered the Inns of Court, on the other hand, remained fairly steady throughout the century. Most of these men (53 per cent) were first sons; considerably higher than the Advocates (40 per cent) or Writers (20 per cent). Forty-eight per cent were the sons of landed families; another 39 per cent were of professional families (of whom just more than half had fathers who were Advocates or Writers). The remaining 13 per cent for the century as a whole (principally those of mercantile background) is the only sector of the Scots population at the Inns that shows a marked variation from decade to decade, rising in the very years during which the 'new' families decline among the two Edinburgh groups. Perhaps hard times dissuaded young men from entering the profession at home, but did not discourage them from trying to make their way southward.

The new professionalism rested on certain developments in the educational structure. The first was the strengthening and diversification of the university curriculum by means of additional courses, the elaboration of a variety of degree programmes, and the more marked professional qualifications of the law faculty. The thrust of the new education was to emphasise university instruction rather than apprenticeship. Time spent in articles was reduced from five to three years for those who obtained a university degree, or attended for three years. The second change was the adoption of one of the great nineteenth-century discoveries in social policy, the public examination, which implied a recognition of the principle of objective testing of acquired technical skills and academic knowledge.[10] The examination sought to impose a national minimum standard of competence, and at the same time to allow a greater latitude in the preparation to meet this standard. At least in theory, the profession became simultaneously stricter in its standards and more accessible to a broader social base.

A List of Clerks and Apprentices Entered at the Signet office (dated May 1798) indicates, indirectly, some aspects of the period of practical training.[11] The list contains two columns, one of the masters, and the second of the clerks and apprentices entered under their names. A few established writers had up to ten apprentices entered under their tutelage, but the most common pattern was a single

[10] John Roach, *Public Examinations in England, 1850-1900* (Cambridge, 1971).

[11] A List of Clerks and Apprentices Entered at the Signet Office in terms of the Regulations of the Writers to the Signet (May 1798).

apprentice, or a group of three or four. Checking each name on the list with professional directories shows that the attrition rate was heavy, and time in articles varied considerably. Of those who were admitted to the Society, all should have entered no later than 1803, since five years was the normal time in articles. Nevertheless, over a third served for six to ten years (a few even longer). The young men who were apprenticed for the longer periods were not in the service of members of their families, but with others.

By arranging all members of the Society admitted between 1800 and 1899 under the names of the masters who trained them (in effect creating a document for the nineteenth century to correspond to the 1798 list of the Signet Office) it becomes possible to compare changing patterns of apprenticeship. The longer period of nonfamily apprenticeship never entirely disappears. With rare exceptions, those who apprenticed to fathers or to other members of their family finished on time (three to five years, depending on prior educational level), while those who apprenticed to others account for five-sixths of the apprentices who had to go on for additional years before formal admission to the Society.

The masters themselves were of the same social and educational background as the Writers as a whole, with slightly more having fathers and brothers who were Advocates or who had some government connection. After 1870, those with university degrees and academic honours tend to turn up in the same firms. The more consistent correlation between masters and apprentices, however, is not educational background but family connection and county origin, showing that traditional social considerations outweighed other factors in determining which apprentice entered which chambers. The principal change which occurred during the century was a replacement of the characteristic single master training the single apprentice by partnerships (of two to four masters) training groups of three to twelve apprentices.

This rather conservative picture of the time spent in articles, compared to the innovations in university study, is offset by the adoption of the public examinations. The Writers' examination resulted from the Law Agents Act of 1873, which required uniform sets of examinations for all Scotland: a preliminary examination in basic knowledge, an intermediate examination of general educational achievement, and a final examination in professional competence. A graduate of a university, or one who had attended for three full years, was excused from the first two sets. Therefore, those who presented themselves for admission as apprentices on the basis of having passed the examinations were those who had not attended a university.

161

Although one of the arguments for the examination system was that it would open admission to apprenticeship to a more general population, it did not have this effect. Admission by examination was overwhelmingly the choice of the sons of legal families, the sons of clergy, and the sons of city merchants . . . the very young men who formed the traditional personnel of the profession.[12] The examinations, then, did not open the profession to working-class sons, nor to boys from the country. More than anyone else, these latter recognised their need for a few years at the university in order to bring themselves to the educational level that the profession demanded. The examination, evidently, provided a route of acceleration for those traditionally associated with the profession, who could dispense with the introductory two years at the university on the basis of a good school preparation such as Edinburgh Academy, and then combine the required law classes with the time in articles. The university matriculation rolls show that this is exactly what they did.[13] In so far as the examination option reduced university time spent in general Arts courses, its use reflects a trend away from generalism towards specialisation in legal education.

In conclusion, the new professionalism in legal education in the nineteenth century is certainly recognisable by the 1870s. It is more marked in academic training than apprenticeship, particularly by developments in the university curriculum, by a more academic faculty, and by a national standard of professional competence tested by examination. However, it is the forms and the programme that changed rather than the personnel. The young lawyers that emerged in the last quarter of the century were better trained than their predecessors, but to an overwhelming extent they were the descendants of their predecessors. What was new was the road they had travelled to get where they were.

[12] Society of Writers to the Signet, Apprentice Petitions, 1811-65; 1866-82; 1883-92; 1893-1905.

[13] Information drawn from Edinburgh University MSS.: Matriculation Roll of the University of Edinburgh, Arts, Law, Divinity, Vols. I-IV (1775-1858); 1858-69. First Matriculations 1869-77.

BRITISH JURISDICTION IN SOUTHERN GHANA, 1618-1901: ITS BASIS, DEVELOPMENT AND PROBLEMS

C.U. Ilegbune

Introduction

It is no doubt a startling result that persons who have been guilty of criminal homicide cannot be tried for their offence, but that is the effect of the very peculiar circumstances of this colony. We gradually glided into our jurisdiction.

These words of lamentation were spoken on 28 October 1908 by a British Chief Justice of the territory formerly known as the Gold Coast Colony in the southern part of present day Ghana.[1] They were spoken on a somewhat unhappy occasion in the administration of justice in the territory. A man, Kojo Ayensu, had wilfully killed a women, Ya Eja, at a place called Sefwi in the year 1892. In 1908, Ayensu was apprehended and brought to trial before the Supreme Court of the Gold Coast Colony sitting at Sekondi.[2] At the hearing, the defence counsel surprised the court with a most unexpected preliminary objection. He objected to the jurisdiction of the court to try the accused on the ground that at the time of the alleged offence, Sefwi was a foreign territory to which the King's Peace did not extend. Purcell, J., in a confessed show of surprise, refused even to call on counsel for the Crown to reply, and quickly over-ruled the objection, holding that he 'entertained no doubt whatever' that even well before 1892 the Supreme Court 'had always exercised jurisdiction' in Sefwi. He convicted Kojo Ayensu and sentenced him to death. His lordship, however, 'reluctantly consented' to the defence counsel's request to state a case on the issue of jurisdiction for the opinion of the Full Court. The question posed was whether in 1892 Sefwi was a part

[1] In this article, the expressions 'Gold Coast Colony' and 'Gold Coast' have been retained for the areas so called during the period under discussion. The expression 'Gold Coast Colony' originally referred only to the coastal Forts and Settlements and their immediate environs. Between these Forts and Settlements and the Ashanti territory to the north lay a vast expanse of territory which later became known as the 'Protected Territories'. The expression 'Gold Coast' was used as a generic name for these Protected Territories and the (coastal) Gold Coast Colony until 1901 when both territories were merged and reconstituted into the 'Gold Coast Colony' under an Imperial Order in Council of 26 September 1901. The expression 'Southern Ghana' as used in this paper, covers the territory of the 'Gold Coast Colony' as thus constituted in 1901. This use of the expression has been statutorily recognised in Ghana. See Ghana [Constitution] Order in Council 1957 art. 1(1).

[2] *Rex v Kojo Ayensu* (1909) Red 240.

of Her Majesty's Dominions and within the King's Peace or whether it was a foreign territory. In a well-considered opinion, Sir William Brandford Griffith, C.J. held that contrary to popular conception among judges of the Supreme Court, Sefwi was a foreign territory in 1892 and not within the King's Peace.[3] He quashed the conviction.

This case illustrates just one aspect of the many curious situations, uncertainties and problems which arose from the fact that the British Crown adopted a 'gliding process' in the acquisition and development of its jurisdiction in Southern Ghana. No British official from 1887 (when Kwamin Tandoh, the Chief of Sefwi, signed a very limited treaty of 'friendship and protection' with the British), would ordinarily have imagined that when Kojo Ayensu in 1892 wilfully killed Ya Eja, he was beyond the reach of British criminal justice. British jurisdiction was assumed as a matter of course. Yet no such jurisdiction in fact existed.

The principal objects of this paper are four. First, to discuss, in the light of British constitutional law and practice, the general nature and basis of British jurisdiction in overseas territories. Second, to describe in some detail the processes by which the British Crown developed its jurisdiction in Southern Ghana and the various legal and administrative problems which arose in the course of that development. Third, to discuss the extent to which, on general principles, the acquisition of sovereign powers by the British Crown over an overseas territory imports Crown rights in, or in relation to, the land of the territory. Fourth, to discuss the actual attitude which the Crown adopted or attempted to adopt towards land rights in Southern Ghana.

General nature and basis of British Jurisdiction Overseas

In British constitutional law, if a country is acquired by conquest or cession, the British Crown *ipso facto* displaces the local ruler completely and assumes the full sovereignty, both internal and external, over the territory, with unlimited powers of legislation and government.[4] Furthermore, the ownership of the territory itself (sometimes referred to as the *imperium*), the radical or ultimate title to all lands therein (sometimes referred to as the *dominium*), and the

---

[3] *Rex v Kojo Ayensu* (1909) Red 241. With him, Francis Smith, J., He conceded that from 1887 many cases were brought to British courts from Sefwi and heard without any objection being raised: (1909) Red. 241, at 243.

[4] The division of sovereignty into internal and external is a convenient form of expression, and seems well established in international law. See Sir Henry Jenkyns, *British Rule and Jurisdiction Beyond the Seas* (Oxford, 1902), p. 166n; W.E. Hall, *A Treatise on International Law* (Oxford, 1924), pp. 50-1.

immediate right of disposal over all unoccupied lands (unless otherwise abandoned), vest in the Crown.[5] The inhabitants of the territory become British citizens. The Crown's power to legislate for conquered or ceded colonies implies the right to establish any form of legislative, administrative and judicial machinery it chooses. The right of legislation may be exercised directly by Order in Council or Letters Patent, or it may be completely or partially surrendered to a local legislative assembly established by the Crown.[6]

A protectorate, on the other hand, signifies, in its strict sense, the assumption of external sovereignty only, that is to say, the control by the Crown of the external affairs of the protected territory. The nature of a British protectorate was thus stated by Sir Henry Jenkyns: 'A British protectorate is a country which is not within the British dominions, but as regards its foreign relations is under the exclusive control of the [Queen] so that its government cannot hold direct communication with any other foreign power, nor a foreign power with that government.'[7]

A protectorate therefore implies a jurisdictional limitation essentially different from a conquered or ceded colony. In the first place, the territory is not owned by the Crown. Secondly, the Crown's ruling powers are limited to the control of external affairs. Thirdly, the radical title to the land of the protectorate does not vest in the Crown. But these limitations exist more in theory than in practice. In practice only the first of them survived in English law as the only feature of *real* distinction between a protectorate and a conquered or ceded colony.[8] The other limitations lost all practical importance for two reasons. First, English law considers it always to have been competent for the Crown, if and when it chooses, to assume and exercise in a protectorate reins of internal jurisdiction as ample as those enjoyed by it in a conquered or ceded colony. In a 1956 case, *Nyali*

[5]*Amodu Tijani v Secretary, S. Nigeria* [1921] 2 AC 399; *Re Southern Rhodesia* [1919] AC 21; E.g. by adopting a policy of non-interference in land matters. The *Amodu Tijani cases* (above) would seem to support this qualification.

[6]Sir Kenneth Roberts-Wray, 'The Authority of the United Kingdom in Dependent Territories' in *Changing Law in Developing Countries*, ed. Anderson (1963), p. 25; E.W. Ridges, *Constitutional Law*, (1950), pp. 477 ff; O. Hood-Phillips, *Principles of English Law and the Constitution* (1939), pp. 491 ff.; Jenkyns, p. 6.

[7]*Ibid.,* p. 165.

[8]One consequence of this was that whereas the inhabitants of a conquered or ceded colony were regarded as British citizens by birth (see British Nationality Act 1948 s. 4), those of a protectorate were not (see Hood-Phillips, p. 496). But under the British Nationality Act 1948 s. 32, the inhabitants of a protectorate were accorded the status of 'British protected persons', which was said to carry some advantages; see Mervyn Jones, *British Nationality Law* (1956), pp. 185 ff.

Ltd. v Attorney-General,[9] Denning L.J. (as he then was) put this point beyond doubt. Second, although the Crown does not *per se* acquire title to any land in the protectorate, it is also recognised that it can in fact so use its sovereign legislative powers as to vest in itself title to all, or part of, the land in the protectorate.[10] Thus, the exact extent of internal jurisdiction exercised by the Crown in any given protectorate at any given time is accepted to be a question of fact to be ascertained by looking at the jurisdiction *in fact* exercised under the law in force.[11] The former Bechuanaland Protectorate was probably one of the best examples of a protectorate in which the Crown (from 1891) was held to have assumed full powers of internal government. The position of that protectorate is extensively discussed by the Court of Appeal in *R. v Crewe, ex parte Sekgome.*[12]

It may be asked: On what basis can this potentially unlimited jurisdiction of the Crown in the protectorate be explained? Viscount Haldane in *Sobhuza II v Miller* advanced two theories. According to him, it might be attributed to statutory powers given by the Foreign Jurisdiction Act 1890, or to an exercise of power by an act of State.[13] But the theory of the Foreign Jurisdiction Act as the basis of the Crown's power has been rejected by both judges and text-writers.[14]

What the Foreign Jurisdiction Act appears to have done was to make it clear statutorily that it was lawful for the Crown 'to hold, exercise and enjoy' any jurisdiction which it might have acquired in a protectorate 'in the same and as ample a manner' as if it had acquired that jurisdiction by conquest or cession.[15] This has been interpreted to mean first, that the Crown could exercise its jurisdiction in a protectorate with the same legislative *instruments* as in a conquered or ceded colony, namely Orders in Council and Letters Patent, and

[9] [1956] 1 QB 1. At p. 15. Also per Morris LJ at p. 22.

[10] See further pp. 184-6 below.

[11] Jenkyns, p. 196; *Tshekedi Khama v The High Commissioner* (1926-1953), HCTLR 9 at pp. 20 and 30; *Nyali Ltd v Attorney-General* [1956] 1 QB 1 at p. 15.

[12] [1910] 2 KB 576. See also *Tshekedi Khama v The High Commissioner,* n. 11 above, in which Watermeyer J at pp. 20-31 gave a detailed historical account of the development of British jurisdiction in Bechuanaland.

[13] [1926] A.C. 518, repealing and re-enacting with amendments, the earlier Foreign Jurisdiction Act of 1843 at pp. 523 and 528. For another reference to the Foreign Jurisdiction Act as the basis of the Crown's power see *R. v Crewe ex. p. Sekgome* [1901] 2KB 576, per Vaughan Williams LJ at p. 607.

[14] *Nyali Ltd. v Attorney-General* [1956] 1 QB 1 at p. 14, per Denning, LJ; *R. v Crewe,* per Kennedy, LJ, at p. 626; see Jenkyns, p. 154. See also Roberts-Wray, *Commonwealth and the Colonial Law* (1966), pp. 190-3.

[15] The Act itself recited that it was being passed to 'remove doubts'; see the Heading and Preamble to the Act of 1843; Foreign Jurisdiction Act 1890 s.1.

166

second, that where the Crown had *in fact* acquired unlimited jurisdiction in a protectorate, it might exercise it with the same degree of amplitude and irresponsibility as it could do in a conquered or ceded colony.[16] In that event, the Crown's powers in the protectorate and in the conquered or ceded colony became, for all practical purposes, conterminous and in legal effect indistinguishable.[17]

Viscount Haldane's second theory, the doctrine of an act of State, seems to have been preferred as a basis for the Crown's powers in a protectorate. The means whereby the Crown acquires jurisdiction in foreign lands are recited in the preamble to the Foreign Jurisdiction Act 1890 as 'treaty, capitulation, grant, usage, sufferance and other lawful means'. An act of State is one of these 'lawful means'. The true nature of this doctrine was stated by Fletcher-Moulton L.J. in *Salaman v Secretary of State for India* when he said: 'An act of State is essentially an exercise of sovereign power, and hence cannot be challenged, controlled or interfered with by municipal courts. Its sanction is not that of law, but that of sovereign power and, whatever it be, municipal courts must accept it as it is without question.'[18] The strength of an act of State as a means whereby the Crown acquires jurisdiction lies therefore in the fact that it is beyond judicial review. An act of State performed by the Crown may manifest itself in many forms.[19] Generally, however, it takes the form of a sovereign legislative act in the nature of an Order in Council or Letters Patent. Whatever powers and jurisdiction the Crown assumes in a protectorate through these means cannot be questioned in a court of law, and this is held to be so even if the power and jurisdiction so assumed are inconsistent with guarantees made by the Crown or its officials, or with previous jurisdictional limitations imposed by treaties with local rulers, or with earlier legislative acts of the Crown itself.[20] Sir Henry Jenkyns seemed therefore to have erred when he said that 'the validity of an Order in Council can be challenged on the ground that it is *ultra vires*'.[21] In British constitutional law, a sovereign

[16] W.E. Hall, *Treatise on the Foreign Powers and Jurisdiction of the British Crown* (1894), pp. 11 and 12; Roberts-Wray, pp. 189 and 194; *Nyali Ltd v Attorney-General* [1956] 1 QB 1 at p. 14.

[17] *Sobhuza II v Miller* [1926] AC 518 at p. 524.

[18] [1906] 1 KB 613 at p. 639.

[19] See Halsbury's *Laws of England*, (3rd edn) 7. 281 ff; *The English and Empire Digest*, 2, 613 ff.

[20] *Sobhuza II v Miller* [1926] AC 518. See also *Tshekedi Khama v The High Commissioner*, above, where the point fell squarely to be decided as one of the issues in the case, especially at p. 21.

[21] Jenkyns, p. 153.

legislative act of the Crown by which jurisdiction is acquired or exercised in a protectorate is proof against the doctrine of *ultra vires.*

But it must be noted that the legislative acts of subordinate legislatures established by the Crown, for instance, Proclamations or Ordinances passed by a colonial legislature, do not enjoy the status of acts of State. Consequently, their validity can be called to question and they may be declared *ultra vires* unless, as Lord Watson pointed out in *Sprigg v Sigcau,* it can otherwise be shown that on the true construction of the Order in Council or Letters Patent enabling such Proclamations or Ordinances to be made, the colonial legislature has the powers of 'an irresponsible sovereign or a supreme and unfettered legislature'.[22] This effect is not produced by the mere fact that in the enabling Order in Council or Letters Patent it is provided that the Proclamation or Ordinance when made, should take effect as if enacted in the Order in Council or Letters Patent.

In *Tshekedi Khama v The High Commissioner,* another Bechuanaland case, this point came up for decision.[23] The facts so far as here relevant, were as follows: The defendant in a preliminary objection, challenged the jurisdiction of the Court to enter into the question whether the High Commissioner had authority to promulgate the Proclamations there in suit.[24] These Proclamations were made in pursuance of an Order in Council of 9 May 1891 which contained the provisions, *inter alia,* that: 'Every Proclamation of the High Commissioner shall . . . have effect as if contained in this order.' The defendant contended that this provision meant that the Proclamations, since they had the validity of Orders in Council, were equivalent to acts of State.

Watermeyer J. rejected that contention. He distinguished the case from *Sobhuza II v Miller* (on which defendant's counsel had relied) on the ground that in *Sobhuza* what the plaintiff sought to be challenged were certain Orders in Council of the Crown, whereas in the present case what was being challenged was a Proclamation of the High Commissioner who was not vested with despotic or unlimited powers.[25] It is however a different and irrelevant question when once

---

[22] Cf. C.M. McDowell, 'Rights of the Crown in Northern Nigeria', read at an Advanced Seminar on Land Law at the Faculty of Law of the School of Oriental and African Studies, University of London, June 1971, pp. 43-4 (as numbered in the original, which starts with page 40); [1897] AC 238, at p. 246.

[23] (1926-1953), HCTLR 9.

[24] Native Administration Proclamation No. 74 of 1934, and Native Tribunals Proclamation No. 75 of 1934 (Bechuanaland).

[25] [1926] AC 518; (1926-1953), HCTLR 9 at pp. 11-12.

the power has been validly exercised by the subordinate legislature within the ambit of the enabling Order in Council or Letters Patent, that the effect of the Ordinance or Proclamation is revolutionary or unjust. These are not matters for the Court.

Two points in this section require special emphasis: First, the Crown's unlimited jurisdiction in a protectorate is only *potential*. It follows therefore that any jurisdiction in a protectorate beyond that strictly and ordinarily applicable in protectorates generally must first have been actually acquired and, either claimed by an Order in Council or Letters Patent, or else as Denning L.J. pointed out, made manifest in some 'other acts of the Crown'.[26] This means that a subordinate legislature established by the Crown would be acting *ultra vires* if it attempted by Ordinance or Proclamation to *exercise* jurisdiction not yet so acquired. Second, the power to acquire new jurisdiction inheres in the Crown alone. Again it follows that a subordinate legislature established by the Crown would be acting *ultra vires* if it purported directly or indirectly by Ordinance or Proclamation to *acquire* new jurisdiction itself. These two points have a special bearing on events in the Gold Coast, as we shall now see.

Development of British jurisdiction in Southern Ghana

The focal question explored in this section is, how in practice, and how far consistently with the general principles we have been discussing, did the Crown use its power in the acquisition and development of its jurisdiction in Southern Ghana?

The Gold Coast was one of the two earliest of the former dependencies of West Africa to be brought under British influence.[27] That influence at first was not exercised by the British Government, but grew out of the enterprise of individual traders and companies. Gold offered the earliest incentive to the earliest of the traders. The pioneers among these were Portuguese and before the British emerged on the scene, the Portuguese were said to have built forts and castles at the coastal towns of Elmina, Axim, Shama and Accra for the protection of their trade in gold.[28] Gradually, however, the slave trade which, for Britain, began with Sir John Hawkins's venture in 1562, replaced all legitimate trade in West Africa and got many European

[26] *Nvali Ltd. v Attorney-General* [1956] 1 QB 1 at p. 15.

[27] The other one was the Gambia. See C.P. Lucas, *A Historical Geography of the British Colonies* (Oxford, 1894), 3, 3.

[28] W.E.F. Ward, *A History of Ghana* (1967), pp. 66 and 70.

participants in it – the Portuguese, the English, the French, the Dutch, the Danes and the Swedes – involved for centuries in intrigues and competition, sometimes wars, for the control of that trade, not, as Sir Charles Lucas emphasised, for sovereignty.[29]

The castles and forts which the Portuguese had built originally for the protection of their legitimate trade became collecting centres for slaves, and new forts were soon built by nationals of other countries. The first British fort in the Gold Coast – the fort of Cormantin – was built in 1618, and this was the earliest British settlement in the country. In 1750, all British forts were placed in the hands of a body of merchants incorporated under an Act of Parliament and known as 'The Company of Merchants Trading to Africa', which began to receive a parliamentary grant of £10,000 to £15,000 a year for the upkeep of the forts.[30] By 1752, the number of British forts in the Gold Coast was eight, and interspersed among these were a number of forts belonging to the Danes and the Dutch. But the British forts lost their principal importance when, in 1808, the British slave trade was abolished.[31] A number of forts were abandoned, but four were retained at Dixcove, Cape Coast Castle, Anomabu and Accra.

Sir W.B. Griffith C.J. wrote that the traders who lived in these forts considered themselves, and were regarded by the local inhabitants 'as mere sojourners' and made no attempt to extend their influence beyond gunshot distance from the fort walls.[32] Also he and Crooks explained that the forts themselves were recognised as being on land belonging to the local inhabitants, and that before a fort could be built an annual ground rent was agreed on with the land owner.[33]

After the abolition of the slave trade, the forts continued to be run by the Company with increased parliamentary grant, until 1821 when, as a result of a quarrel between the Company and the British Government, the Company was dissolved, and 'all forts, castles,

[29]Ibid., p. 105.

[30]23 Geo. II, c. 31; By the same Act of Parliament an earlier company – the Royal African Company – which had been in charge of the British West African trade since 1662 was 'restrained' from further action. Two years later, in 1752, by another Act of Parliament (25 Geo. II. c. 40), it was completely dissolved with substantial compensation; see J.J. Crooks, *Records Relating to the Gold Coast Settlements from 1750 to 1874* (Dublin, 1923), pp. 10-20.

[31]See First Schedule to 25 Geo. II c. 40; The Slave Trade Abolition Act, 47 Geo. III, Seff. 1. c. 36 was enacted in 1807, but it came into force on 1 January 1808.

[32]*A Note on the History of British Courts on the Gold Coast, with a Brief Account of the Changes in the Constitution of the Colony* (Accra, 1936), p. 1.

[33]*Ibid;* Crooks, *Records,* p. 3. See also Casely Hayford, *Gold Coast Native Institutions* (London, 1903), pp. 136 and 138.

buildings, possessions, estates and rights' of the Company were 'vested' in the Crown by Statute 1 & 2 Geo. IV. c. 28. Accordingly, Letters Patent were issued by the Crown on 17 October 1821 annexing these forts and possessions to the leading British West African country of Sierra Leone, and on 29 March 1822, the Governor of Sierra Leone, Sir Charles McCarthy, issued a Proclamation announcing the new arrangement.[34]

For the purpose of administration within the forts and settlements, the Governor appointed justices of the peace with criminal jurisdiction from among the British local merchants and also petty debt courts, but in course of time these courts began to entertain cases from citizens in the neighbourhood of the forts. Governor McCarthy however was not destined to head the new administration for long. His main preoccupation seems to have been to prevent the incessant raids which the Ashantis to the north were making against the Fantis (occupying the land between Ashanti and the coast) whom the Ashanti King claimed to be under his dominion. For this purpose, the Governor pursued a policy of aggression towards the Ashantis, but in January 1824 during an invasion which he personally led against the Ashantis, he was slain. 'Such', wrote Sir W.B. Griffith, 'was the unpromising beginning of British interference in native affairs' in the Gold Coast.[35]

The failure of McCarthy's policy seemed to have discouraged the British Government, and for a time it was thought better to withdraw from the expensive and troublesome task of maintaining and protecting British settlements in West Africa. In 1828 an arrangement was made under which the government of the forts and settlements was transferred to a body known as the Committee of London Merchants, the members of which were chosen by the British Government. Under the terms of their mandate the Committee was to confine its administrative and judicial activities strictly to the forts, which were to continue to be treated as nominal 'dependencies' of Sierra Leone.[36] In 1830 Captain George Maclean was appointed President of the new régime. One of his first acts was to conclude a treaty with the Ashantis on 27 April 1831 under which the Ashanti King relinquished his claim to dominion over the Fantis, and recognised 'the English Governor as the future referee and arbitrator in the case of native quarrels'.[37] But by far the greatest work of Maclean lay in his system

[34] Crooks, *Records*, pp. 138-41.
[35] *A Note on the History of Courts*, p. 1.
[36] For the full text, see Crooks, *Records*, pp. 252-4.
[37] E. Hertslet, *Treaties*, 12, 13.

of judicial administration. Under him the justices of the peace at the forts increasingly heard cases brought by citizens from territories far beyond the fort, and their judgments in such cases were generally accepted. But it is clear from the terms of their mandate that the jurisdiction thus assumed was irregular.[38]

In February 1841 Dr. R.R. Madden was sent by the British Government to report on allegations, *inter alia,* that Maclean was unduly stretching his authority outside the limits of British territorial jurisdiction. His report, though strongly critical of Maclean's system, on the ground of its irregularity, acknowledged its beneficial working.[39] But he recommended the transfer of power and authority from the Committee of London Merchants to the Government, and the appointment of a Governor for the Gold Coast Settlements. A Select Committee of the House of Commons was next appointed in March 1842 to report on the West African Settlement as well as upon Dr. Madden's report. This Committee also concluded that Maclean's disregard of the terms of his mandate was done 'necessarily and usefully', and they endorsed Dr. Madden's recommendations, and further recommended that all jurisdiction outside the forts must be 'considered as optional and should be made the subject of distinct agreement . . . with the native Chiefs'.[40]

In consequence of these recommendations, the Crown in 1843 resumed the direct government of the Gold Coast Forts and Settlements, which continued to be administered by the Governor at Sierra Leone. Two Acts of Parliament passed in 1843 gave legal sanction to the new arrangement. The first, 6 and 7 Vict. c. 13, empowered Her Majesty to legislate by Order in Council for British Settlements in West Africa, and also to delegate Her authority by commission to resident officers. The second, the Foreign Jurisdiction Act 1843 was passed 'to remove doubts' as to Her Majesty's exercise of power and jurisdiction in foreign territories and 'to render the same more effectual'.[41] It rendered the exercise more effectual by providing that

[38] Colonel Ord described the jurisdiction as 'a species of irregular authority, partly tolerated from a conviction of its usefulness, and partly compulsory, from the nature of our position'. *Copy of the Report of Colonel Ord, the Commissioner appointed to Inquire into the Condition of the British Settlement on the West Coast of Africa* (1865), p. 20.

[39] See Crooks, *Records,* pp. 272-5.

[40] *Report from the Select Committee on the West Coast of Africa* (1842), part 1, p. vi. See also Crooks, *Records,* pp. 275-81.

[41] 6 & 7 Vict. c. 94. The circumstances of the passage of this Act did not particularly arise from events on the Gold Coast. For its background see, Hope Scott, Q.C., *Report on British Jurisdiction in Foreign States, dated 18 Jan, 1843,* reproduced in Jenkyns. App. VI, pp. 242 ff.

172

Her Majesty might exercise any power and jurisdiction which she might at any time have in such territories as if She had acquired such power and jurisdiction by cession or conquest of territory. Captain Maclean was then appointed to the post of Judicial Assessor to the Chiefs, and specific instruction was given to Commander H.W. Hill, who was also appointed Lieutenant-Governor for the Gold Coast Forts and Settlements that Maclean should maintain 'the exercise of that jurisdiction which had been established. . . in the case of crimes and misdemeanours committed among neighbouring tribes'.[42]

On 6 March 1844, in compliance with the recommendation of the Select Committee, a treaty, popularly known as the Bond of 1844, was signed between representatives of the Crown and some Fanti Chiefs whereby the Chiefs 'acknowledged . . . the power and jurisdiction' which had been exercised by the Crown 'within divers countries and places adjacent to . . . the forts and settlement'. The chiefs also gave formal consent to the trial of criminal cases 'before the Queen's judicial officers and the chiefs of the district, moulding the customs of the country to the general principles of British law'.[43]

It is perhaps important at this juncture to point out that up to this time, some of the means recited in the Foreign Jurisdiction Act, whereby the Crown acquires jurisdiction in foreign territories, had been at work in some areas of the Fanti county. The only element of *grant* so far, had been the Bond of 1844, but no new jurisdiction seemed to have been involved in the Bond. Sir W.B. Griffith's statement that the Bond was a 'document. . . of small intrinsic value. . made to satisfy the scruples of the Home Government', must be seen in this light.[44] Nevertheless, to the people of the Gold Coast, the Bond was a document of tremendous intrinsic value, not necessarily for what it granted, but for what it failed to grant. It did not, wrote Sarbah, grant exclusive judicial jurisdiction to the British.[45] Neither did it, argued the Chiefs and people of the Gold Coast in their

[42]Dispatch from Lord Stanley (Secretary of State) to Lieut.-Governor H.W. Hill 16 Dec., 1843 in Crooks, *Records,* pp. 285 ff. 'To take the opposite course,' explained the Dispatch, 'would. . . not only be most detrimental to the maintenance of order and civilisation at the moment, but render its restoration at a future period very difficult' (at p. 288). For an account of the development of British Gold Coast Jurisdiction under Maclean, see G.E. Metcalfe, *Maclean of the Gold Coast* (1962), especially Chapter 8.

[43]Crooks, *Records,* pp. 296-7.

[44]*A Note on the History of Courts,* p. 12.

[45]*Fanti National Constitution* (1906), p. 99.

numerous petitions against the Colonial Government's land measures of 1894 and 1897, grant any rights in the land.[46]

By 1847 it was estimated that the area over which British authority had extended in the Gold Coast was 6,000 square miles.[47] This was further extended when in August 1850 the King of Denmark 'ceded' to the Queen 'in full property and sovereignty' all forts and possessions still possessed by Denmark.[48] By Letters Patent dated 24 January 1850 the British Forts and Settlements on the Gold Coast were formally separated from the Settlements at Sierra Leone (as was recommended in 1841 and 1842), and a Legislative Council was constituted and empowered to legislate for the Forts and Settlements.[49] In 1853 the new Legislative Council passed the Supreme Court Ordinance No. 4 of 1853, whereby Fitzpatrick, the official at that time holding the office of Judicial Assessor was appointed Chief Justice.[50] 'From this date', explained Sir W.B. Griffith, C.J. 'there were two distinct jurisdictions.' As judicial assessor appointed by the Crown, Mr. Fitzpatrick dealt with cases *outside* the forts; as Chief Justice appointed under the Ordinance, he dealt with cases *within* the forts.[51]

But an interesting point about the Ordinance here seemed to have escaped Sir W.B. Griffith. Although, the Letters Patent of 24 January 1850 did not empower the Legislative Council to legislate for the territories *outside* the forts, the Ordinance, by s. 10, made a provision for appeals from decisions of the Judicial Assessor to the Governor in Council sitting, of course, within the forts. This provision would appear from the principles which we have seen, to be an *ultra vires* exercise of power. It has been suggested that the provision was properly made, in that it rested 'on the assumed fact that the condition of assent or sufferance required by the Foreign Jurisdiction Act 1843 had been satisfied'.[52] But this suggestion again ignores the point that if the condition of assent or sufferance was satisfied, the result was that

---

[46] For a detailed discussion of the nature, problems and local reactions to the Colonial Government's land policy in the Gold Coast up to 1915, see C.U. Ilegbune, 'British Concessions, Policy and Legislation in Southern Ghana, 1874-1915' (University of London Ph.D. thesis, 1974).

[47] West African Lands Committee (W.A.L.C.), *Draft Report*, para 35, African (West) No. 1046; CO/879/117.

[48] Crooks, *Records*, p. 322.

[49] *Ibid.*, pp. 320-21.

[50] Reproduced in Sarbah, *Fanti National Constitution* (1906), p. 160.

[51] *A Note on the History of Courts*, p. 15.

[52] *W.A.L.C. Draft Report*, para. 38.

174

power and jurisdiction accrued to Her Majesty. The Foreign Jurisdiction Act was not concerned with this accretion. It was concerned only with the *manner of exercise* 'by Her Majesty' of the power and jurisdiction so accruing and, like Maclean, the Legislative Council could not properly exercise Her Majesty's jurisdiction without being authorised to do so.

The first legislative manifestation of the extent of power and jurisdiction which the Crown was claiming to exercise outside the Forts and Settlements came in 1856. It came in an Order in Council of 4 April whereby 'the Governor' was empowered by Ordinance to legislate for the exercise by the Courts of powers and jurisdiction which Her Majesty had acquired or might exercise without the co-operation of any native chief or authority in the 'Protected Territories', subject to equitable regard being paid to native customs not repugnant to Christianity or to natural justice. The extent of jurisdiction thus conferred is difficult to assess. Apparently it comprehended such subjects as the hearing of cases voluntarily brought by citizens to the British courts, bankruptcy and the administration of the estates of foreigners living outside the Forts and Settlements. No general power of legislation or government was contemplated. Nevertheless, the Legislative Council, again without authority, proceeded to pass a number of Ordinances such as the District Assemblies Ordinance, No. 4 of 1858, the Municipalities Ordinance, No. 5 of 1858, and the Poll Tax Amendment Ordinance, No. 3 of 1858, all of which were intended to take effect outside the Forts and Settlements.

The next constitutional change took place in 1866 when, by a Royal Commission dated 19 February, issued as a result of the recommendation of a Select Committee of the House of Commons in 1865 for a policy of 'ultimate withdrawal of the Queen's Government', the Letters Patent of 24 January 1850 were revoked, and the Gold Coast Forts and Settlements were re-united to Sierra Leone, together with the Settlements in Gambia and Lagos, and known as the 'West African Settlements'.[53] But two events soon forced the British Government to abandon the policy recommended in 1865. First, in February 1871 the Government acquired the forts and settlements of the Dutch still in the Gold Coast, thereby removing all threats of

[53] Hertslet, *Treaties*, 13, 26; Crooks, *Records*, pp. 369-71. The Committee reported that 'all further extension of sovereignty or of protectorate was inexpedient' and hence made the above recommendation. The ports and island of Lagos were ceded to the Crown in 1861 by the then King of Lagos, Docemo; see Hertslet, *Treaties*, 2, 41-2.

external competition from other nations.[54] Second, in 1873-4 the British fought a war against the Ashantis and greatly reduced their military might, thereby silencing (for a time as events were to show) the most serious internal obstacle to territorial expansion inland.[55]

Accordingly, by a Royal Charter dated 24 July 1874 the Gold Coast Forts and Settlements (together with Lagos) were separated from Sierra Leone, and 'erected into' a colony, to be known as the 'Gold Coast Colony', with a separate Legislative Council.[56] On 6 August 1874 an Order in Council was issued empowering the Legislative Council (for the first time) to legislate 'by Ordinance' for the 'Protected Territories'. Such Ordinances were to be limited to 'such powers and jurisdiction as Her Majesty may, at any time before or after the passing of this Order in Council, have acquired' in such territories. Two questions arise from this Order in Council. First, what were the respective extents of the 'Gold Coast Colony' and the 'Protected Territories' under the new arrangement? Secondly, what now could be said to be the extent of 'power and jurisdiction' which Her Majesty had 'before' acquired in the Protected Territories?

Coming to the first question, the word 'Colony' so far as it related to the Gold Coast, was defined in the Charter of 1874 as 'all places, settlements, and territories belonging to US on the Gold Coast in Western Africa between the fifth degree of West longitude and the second degree of East longitude'. This definition was repeated in a subsequent Letters Patent of 13 January 1886 which 'erected' the Gold Coast alone into a separate Colony with a Legislative Council empowered to legislate for the Colony and (by an Order in Council of 29 December 1887), for the Protected Territories to the same extent as was stated in the Order in Council of 1874.[57] Sir W. B. Griffith, C.J. on three occasions, first, in two memoranda written in August 1899 and March 1900 and again in *Bainyi v Dantsi,* stated that this definition of 'Colony' comprehended 'the forts, . . the actual land which the Government had bought or otherwise acquired for public purposes under the Public Lands Ordinance 1876, the foreshore. . .

[54] See, the Convention of Transfer dated 25 Feburary 1871, and ratified at the Hague on 17 February 1872, printed as Appendix to *Correspondence Relative to the Cession by the Netherlands Government to the British Government of the Dutch Settlement on the West Coast of Africa* (London, 1872); C.670. See also Hertslet, *Treaties,* 13, 656.

[55] 'Kumasi was reached; but the war was not won.' Ward, p. 276.

[56] Reproduced in Sarbah, *Fanti Customary Laws* (1904), p. 295.

[57] *Government Gazette,* 29 February 1888, p. 31; Hertslet, *Treaties,* 17, 127.

and land within gunshot from the forts'.[58] To these may be added the few small territories 'ceded' to the Crown by treaty, for instance, the seaboard of Agbosome for two miles, and the seaboard of Afflao for one mile, from high-water mark inland.[59] Sir W.B. Griffith concluded however that in fact 'no one knew exactly how far the Colony extended', and thought that apart from the foreshore and what was got from the Dutch, the Gold Coast Colony in 1886 would be 'less than one square mile'.[60]

As for the 'Protected Territories', the Interpretation Ordinance 1876 provided that they should mean 'the territories near or adjacent to the settlement on the Gold Coast wherein Her Majesty may at any time before or after the commencement of this Ordinance have acquired powers and jurisdiction'.[61] 'This', said Sir W.B. Griffith C.J. in the memorandum of August 1899, 'was the beginning of the automatic action of the local law; as soon as Her Majesty acquired powers and jurisdiction over new territory it forthwith came under the definition of "Protected Territories", and the Ordinance applying to the Protected Territories thenceforth applied to such new territory'.[62]

---

[58] *Memorandum as to whether Ashanti should be regarded as a part of the Colony, 9 Aug., 1899.* Enclosure 5 in Confidential Dispatch from Hodgson to Chamberlain, 21 August 1899; CO/96/342; *Memorandum Advocating Proclamation of former Protected Territories on the Gold Coast to be part of the Gold Coast Colony, 22 March 1900.* Enclosure in No. 9 in *African (West) No. 649;* (1903), Ren. 287, at p. 291; This particular head is doubtful. It shows a confusion between *ownership* of (or title to) land and the constitutional *status* of a territory, a confusion not uncommon among officials during this time. See Ilegbune, ch. IV, pp. 147-58; See *Ancobra River Concessions Enquiries No. 638, 639, 641, 724, 725, 726, 731, 902 and 911 (Axim),* decided by Pennington, J. on 9 June 1906. The case is very inadequately reported in Ren. 247. The original record is much more useful. See SCT. 4/6/2 (Ghana National Archives); Sometimes referred to as 'artillery range'. There seems to be no conventional measure for this range. Some people put the distance at 3 miles, for example, *The African Times,* 1 March 1878, p. 31, while others put it at 5 miles, for example, F.A.R. Bennion, *The Constitutional Law of Ghana* (1962), p. 15. A judicial application of the principle was made by Earnshaw, J., in *Inkoom Company v. Attorney-General* (1910), Earn. 24, who used it in part tp support the ownership by the Crown of certain lands within 675 yards of the Cape Coast Castle.

[59] Both were ceded by treaties dated 2 and 6 December 1879 respectively. Hertslet, *Map of Africa by Treaty* (3rd edn 1967) 1, 68. There were a few other treaties in 1886 whereby the 'absolute domain and sovereignty' over certain lands, mainly in the Volta River Basin, were 'ceded' to Her Majesty 'freely, fully, entirely and absolutely'. *Ibid.,* p. 70. These words are reminiscent of the words used in the Treaty of Cession in Lagos in 1861; see Hertslet, *Treaties,* vol. 2, 41-2.

[60] Memorandum of 9 August 1899, above. Cf. *Rex v Kojo Thompson* (1944) 10 WACA 201 at pp. 210-211.

[61] This definition will be found in the 1887 edition of the *Gold Coast Ordinances,* p. 38.

[62] The distinction between 'colony' and 'Protected Territories', was recognised in Ordinances. Particular sections of Ordinances intended to apply to the Protected Territories declared that fact; see, for example, the Criminal Procedure Ordinances,

Presumably *any* power and jurisdiction acquired by Her Majesty in a new territory would bring this 'automatic application' principle into operation. For instance, if a chief in the hinterland signed a treaty giving Her Majesty jurisdiction in respect of slave-dealing within the chief's territory, Her Majesty would thereby acquire 'power and jurisdiction', and consequently the whole body of law applying in the Protected Territories would automatically come into force in that chief's territory. The 'automatic application' principle was no doubt a convenient and ingenious legislative device at a time when Her Majesty's jurisdiction was continually expanding. But its legal basis is suspect, as the Law Officers of the Crown were to show in October 1899.[63]

Coming now to our second question – the extent of the 'power and jurisdiction' which Her Majesty in 1874 already had in the Protected Territories – nobody seemed exactly to know, not even at the Colonial Office in London. Lord Derby, afterwards Secretary of State from 1882 to 1885, was quoted as saying in 1874 when he was Foreign Secretary in Benjamin Disraeli's Government: 'I greatly doubt whether any man in or out of the Colonial Office exactly knows or could define the limits of our authority . . . within the protected territories'.[64] In August 1874 Lord Carnarvon proposed to define 'the nature and extent' of Her Majesty's jurisdiction in the Protected Territories by Proclamation, and he forwarded a Draft Proclamation for that purpose to Governor C.C. Strahan.[65] The Draft Proclamation, dated 6 August 1874 'declared' that the power and jurisdiction which Her Majesty 'had acquired' extended 'among other things' to a very wide range of subjects there listed, including 'the protection of individuals and property', and the enactment of laws 'framed. . . with due regard to native law and custom where they are not repugnant to justice, equity and good conscience'. The Draft Proclamation was not adopted, but it was published for the British Parliament, together with Lord Carnarvon's Dispatch.[66]

1876, s. 1; Customs Ordinance 1876, s. 3. But in course of time legal draftsmen began to ignore (or to forget to make) such provision. Accordingly the Protected Territories Extension Ordinance 1888 was passed extending to the Protected Territories various Ordinances which had been meant to apply thereto: See *Bainyi v Dantai* (1903) Ren 287, per. W.B. Griffith CJ at p. 292.

[63] See below, p. 181.

[64] *Hansard,* Ser. 3, vol. ccxviii (1874), p. 1598 (per Sir S. Lawson).

[65] Carnarvon to Strahan, 20 August 1874, CO/96/113. This Dispatch is reproduced in Sarbah, *Fanti Customary Laws* (1904) pp. 288-92.

[66] One of the subjects listed in the Draft Proclamation was 'domestic slavery'. In December 1874, the Legislative Council (without the aid of the Proclamation) passed two measures on that subject, namely, the Slave Dealing Ordinance, 1874, and the

178

The Coussey Committee on Constitutional Reform in the Gold Coast pointed out that this publication of the Proclamation was done in an unusual way.[67] There is no doubt that it was. Nevertheless, it is arguable that despite the non-adoption of the Draft Proclamation, the fact that it was drafted and published at all would afford good evidence (as indeed it was intended to do) of the extent of power and jurisdiction which Her Majesty in 1874 had, or claimed to have, in those territories of the Gold Coast already under Her protection, which jurisdiction therefore the Legislative Council of the Gold Coast Colony could proceed to exercise in those territories by virtue of the powers conferred on it by the Orders in Council of August 1874 and December 1887. It does not seem to matter that the publication was made in London and not locally. In many of the cases raising questions as to the extent of Her Majesty's jurisdiction in foreign lands, the courts have accepted and relied on statements and affidavits of persons in authority made or sworn to in London as evidence of that jurisdiction.[68] Moreover, it is the view of English courts that any 'other acts of the Crown' apart from Orders in Council and Letters Patent, by which its intention as to jurisdiction is made manifest, are accepted as evidence of that jurisdiction.[69] In point of fact, the view at the Colonial Office was that the publication of the Draft Proclamation was 'sufficient notification of the claim to exercise the power and jurisdiction there claimed', and the Crown was thenceforth regarded as having acquired unlimited powers of legislation in the territories under its protection.[70] This also seems to have been the view of the local authorities, as their actions show. From 1874 onwards, 'the Legislative Council unhampered by any restriction, set

Slave Emancipation Ordinance, 1874, and the Government successfuly resisted the opposition of the native chiefs to the measures. The Colonial Office, gratified by the events, then felt that since the Legislative Council and the Government could force through such measures 'so vitally affecting the interests of the whole protectorate', there was no longer any need to proceed with the Draft Proclamation. Mainly for this reason, it was 'reserved'. See Minute of E. Fairfield, 9 May 1875, on Strahan to Carnarvon, 3 January 1875; CO/96/15, no. 2 C.1139. For the text, see Sarbah, *Fanti Customary Laws* (1904), pp. 293-5.

[67] *Report to H.E. the Governor by the Committee on Constitutional Reforms,* Colonial, No. 248, (HMSO, 1949), para. 14.

[68] 'The Courts rely on the representation of the Crown to know the limits of its jurisdiction and to keep within it'; per Denning, L J in *Nyali Ltd. v Attorney-General* [1956] 1 QB 1 at p. 15. In R. v Crewe [1910] 2 KB 567 the Court accepted Lord Crewe's affidavit. In *Tshekedi Khama v The High Commissioner* (1926-1953) H.C.T.L.R. 9, the Court accepted a written statement from the Secretary of State for the Dominions as 'conclusive'.

[69] See *Nyali Ltd. v Attorney-General* [1956] 1 QB 1 at p. 15.

[70] Minute of Sir A.W.L. Hemming, 10 June 1895 on Maxwell to Ripon, 9 May 1895; CO/96/257, no. 187.

about exercising its powers as freely as if Her Majesty's powers and jurisdiction in the Colony and the protected territories were co-extensive'.[71]

The position which we have described was how things stood up to 1894. Sir W.B. Griffith, C.J., in *Bainyi v Dantsi* described the problems which arose from the situation:

> Difficulties were constantly arising with respect to the difference between Colony and protected territories; draftsmen omitted to include the protected territories in Ordinances; questions arose as to whether the powers of the Executive in the Colony and protected territories were co-extensive or not; native Chiefs often found themselves in a false position, not understanding how far they were subject and how far they were independent; it was impossible to say how far the Colony extended and where the protected territories began; thousands of persons who claimed to be British subjects were only protected aliens; and altogether, the indefinite condition of things not only led to confusion and to the raising of many dificult legal problems, but it was also a real source of danger to the well-being of the Colony.[72]

In his memorandum of 9 August 1899 where he also referred briefly to similar problems, he explained that, 'the practice was not to settle them, and in that way to avoid hard and fast solutions'.[73]

In 1895 Sir Joseph Hutchinson, then Chief Justice, decided to cut the 'Gordian Knot' by using another and more dynamic automatic principle which the Law Officers of the Crown later aptly christened the 'automatic expansion' principle.[74] Sir W.B. Griffith C.J. in the *Bainyi* case described how Hutchinson C.J. did it.[75] According to him, Hutchinson, C.J. was then about to prepare an edition of the local Ordinances and, as a preliminary step, he drafted an omnibus revision Ordinance. Section 2 of this Ordinance – the Statute Law Revision Ordinance, No. 3 of 1895 – repeated the definition of 'Colony' and 'Protected Territories' in the Interpretation Ordinance 1876 and substituted therefor the following: ' "Colony" shall mean

[71] Sir W.B. Griffith, *A Note on the History of Courts*, p. 19.

[72] (1903) Ren 287 at 292.

[73] Enclosure 5 in CO/96/342.

[74] The 'automatic expansion' principle, as will appear presently in the text, differs from the 'automatic application' principle in that it involved two ideas: (a) the automatic expansion of Her Majesty's dominions and (b) the automatic application of *all* existing and future laws to territories affected by the expansion. The 'automatic application' principle, as we saw, involved only the second idea.

[75] (1903) Ren 287 at 292.

the Gold Coast Colony and shall include the settlement on the Gold Coast and the territories near or adjacent thereto wherein Her Majesty may at any time before or after the commencement of this Ordinance have acquired powers and jurisdiction.' Section 4 provided that every Ordinance then in force or thereafter coming into force was to apply to the Colony as thus defined. The Legislative Council, purporting to act under powers conferred by the Order in Council of 29 December 1887 passed Sir Joseph Hutchinson's Ordinance.

One thing which the Legislative Council intended Sections 2 and 4 of this Ordinance to do was to extend to the Protected Territories all Ordinances of the Gold Coast Colony, past and future, and thus expeditiously and amply to give effect to Her Majesty's jurisdiction in those territories. Another was to incorporate the Protected Territories within the Gold Coast Colony, that is, within Her Majesty's dominions, and thus do away with the troublesome distinction between Colony and Protected Territories. Under the provisions, every new territory over which Her Majesty acquired power and jurisdiction would *ipso facto* become part and parcel of the Gold Coast Colony and subject to all its laws. But there was one further interesting, though unintended, effect of the Statute Law Revision Ordinance 1895 which seemed not to have been realised. The Ordinance did not purport to repeal, and could not possibly have repealed, the definition of 'Gold Coast Colony' in Her Majesty's Letters Patent of 13 January 1886. Consequently, from 1895 the expression 'Gold Coast Colony' in fact came to have a double meaning.

From 1895 the Supreme Court, the Executive Council and the Legislative Council acted on the supposition that the intended aims of the Revision Ordinance had been perfectly accomplished. In 1898 the Legislative Council removed the last vestige of distinction between the Gold Coast Colony and the Protected Territories by the Statute Law Revision Ordinance No. 1 of that year. This latter Ordinance referred only to 'the Statute Law of the Colony' and in the revised edition of the 'Ordinances of the Gold Coast Colony' published in 1898 under this Ordinance, almost all reference to the Protected Territories were eliminated. All this time no one questioned the legality of the action of the Legislative Council. On the contrary the Chief Justice, Sir W.B. Griffith, relentlessly advocated the maintenance of the *status quo*.[76]

[76] His views are clearly represented in his judgement in *Bainyi v Dantsi* (1903) Ren 287 at 293; and in his two memoranda of 9 August 1899 and 22 March 1900, *op. cit.*

But the riot of jurisdiction resulting from the operation of the 'automatic expansion' principle soon became clear when British influence permeated into the hinterland of Ashanti as a result of British military occupation of Kumasi (the Ashanti capital) in January 1896 and the conclusion within the next few years, of treaties of 'friendship and protection' with various chiefs in other parts of Ashanti. Following these events, the Supreme Court, acting under the Revision Ordinance of 1895 held that since Her Majesty had acquired 'power and jurisdiction' in Ashanti, the whole of that territory had automatically become part and parcel of the 'Gold Coast Colony' within the meaning of Sections 2 and 4 of that Ordinance, and therefore within its jurisdiction.[77]

But the Secretary of State and his staff never ceased to be sceptical about the Revision Ordinance of 1895, although at the time it was passed, they did not advise Her Majesty to disallow it. The new Ashanti situation was to them too much to take without advice from legal experts. Accordingly, after receiving Sir W.B. Griffith's memorandum of 9 August 1899 defending the Revision Ordinance, Chamberlain referred the matter to the Law Officers of the Crown. He asked them specifically: (a) whether having regard to the terms of the Order in Council of 29 December 1887 it was *intra vires* the Legislative Council of the Gold Coast Colony to legislate in anticipation for future Protectorates; and (b) whether Sir W.B. Griffith's view that the effect of sections 2 and 4 of the Revision Ordinance 1895 was to effect an automatic annexation to the Colony of every new territory over which Her Majesty might acquire power and jurisdiction was correct.[78] The Law Officers returned a negative answer to the two questions. On the issue of automatic annexation they said:

> These sections [i.e. sections 2 and 4] do not and cannot convert into British Territory any region which Her Majesty had not acquired as British Territory. The only power conferred on the Colonial Legislature is, to provide for the exercise of the power and jurisdiction acquired by Her Majesty – there is no power to enlarge them, except in Her Majesty, and we are unable to see

[77]In 1899, for example, the Acting Resident of Kumasi sent the European manager and two native employees of the Ashanti Goldfields Corporation to Accra for trial on a charge of torturing persons in order to obtain evidence in connection with a robbery which had been committed at the Obuasi mine of the Corporation, and the Supreme Court held that it had jurisdiction to try the accused persons. See Confidential Dispatch from Hodgson to Chamberlain, 24 February 1900, CO/96/371; and Chamberlain to Major M. Nathan, 5 February 1901, CO/96/371.

[78]Chamberlain to the Law Officer of the Crown, printed in *Miscellaneous No. 86* (below, n. 79).

the ground for the theory of 'automatic expansion' of the limits of the Colony.[79]

Sir W.B. Griffith C.J. accepted the view, somewhat reluctantly.[80] The Government also did, and took immediate action to prevent further jurisdictional invasion of Ashanti by the Supreme Court.[81]

The climax in the gradual gliding process of the British to jurisdiction in Southern Ghana came in 1901. Following a fresh rising by some communities in Ashanti between April and June 1900, Secretary of State, Chamberlain, in February 1901 yielded to pressure already heavy on him for a complete annexation by the Crown of not only the Protected Territories of the Gold Coast, but also of the whole of Ashanti which he now, for the first time, claimed to have been 'conquered'.[82] Two Orders in Council effecting the annexations were issued on 26 September 1901, one annexing the Protected Territories and attaching them to the former Gold Coast Colony, under the same name, and the other annexing the whole of Ashanti, expressly declaring it to have been 'conquered by Her Majesty's forces'.[83] The two Orders in Council came into force on 1 January 1902, but Sir William Brandford Griffith C.J. has argued, as we shall presently see, that the Order in Council annexing the Protected Territories took effect much earlier.[84]

In order to cure the *ultra vires* exercise of powers by the Legislative Council in their Ordinances of the 'automatic expansion' period, the Revocation and Validation Order in Council of 23 October 1901 was issued also to come into force on 1 January 1902. By clause 1, the Order in Council of 29 December 1887 (the latest

[79]*Law Officers' Opinion on the Government of Adjacent Protectorates of the Gold Coast dated 21 October, 1899*, in *C.O. Miscellaneous No. 86* CO/885/14. In *Staples v The Queen* (P.C. 1899 unreported) Lord Halsbury, L C declared: 'I never heard that you can force a Sovereign to take a territory'. Cited by Kennedy, LJ, in *R. v Crewe* [1910] 2 KB 576 at 623.

[80]See *Bainyi v Dantsi* (1903), Ren 287 at 293.

[81]On 12 March 1900, the Governor, Sir F.M. Hodgson issued an Order of the Governor in Council, under s. 20(a) of the Supreme Court Ordinance, excluding Ashanti from the jurisdiction of the Court.

[82]Confidential Dispatch form Chamberlain to Nathan, 5 February 1901; CO/96/371.

[83]Gold Coast Order in Council, 26 September 1901. Reproduced in Sarbah, *Fanti National Constitution* (London, 1906), p.170; Ashanti Order in Council, 26 September 1901. Reproduced, *ibid.,* p. 173.

[84]See Proclamation in *Government Gazette,* 16 December 1901. To bring the development of its jurisdiction to completion, the Crown on the same date proclaimed a British Protectorate over the Northern Territories by the Northern Territories Order in Council, 1901, which likewise came into force on 1 January 1902. Reproduced, *ibid.,* p. 177.

Order empowering the Legislative Council to legislate for the Protected Territories) was revoked. By clause 2 it was provided that

> all Ordinances or reputed Ordinances enacted or purporting to have been enacted by the Legislative Council for the time being of the Gold Coast Colony, for the purpose of giving effect to any powers and jurisdiction as Her late Majesty may at any time before or after the respective dates of such Ordinances have acquired in the Protected Territories and which have received assent. . . shall be, and be deemed to have been, valid and effectual from the date of such assent for all purposes whatever.

Commenting on this provision in 1907 in *Mutchi v Annan*, Sir William Brandford Griffith C.J., in a determined and final attempt to circumvent the effect of the Law Officers' opinion on his automatic expansion device of 1895, stated that its effect was to validate what the local Legislature did or attempted to do in the Statute Law Revision Ordinances of 1895 and 1898 with respect to the Protected Territories.[85] The provision, according to him, validated the Legislature's attempt to extend to the Protected Territories all Ordinances of the Colony, past or future, and also their attempt to incorporate the Protected Territories within the Gold Coast Colony.[86] The Chief Justice went on to say that had His Majesty not made the Gold Coast Order in Council 1901 (i.e. the annexation Order), the Revocation and Validation Order in Council would, together with the enactments of the local Legislature it validated, have been held to have incorporated the Protected Territories within the Gold Coast Colony, because the validation was 'for all purposes whatsoever'.[87] Therefore, he concluded, 'the annexation of the greater portion of the Protected Territories dates back to 1895'.[88]

There is no doubt that this is a powerful argument. Nevertheless, his lordship seems to have given too much emphasis to the words 'for all purposes whatever' used in the Validation Order in Council, and no consideration at all to the fact that only such actions of the local Legislature as were taken *'for the purpose of giving effect to any powers and jurisdiction'* of Her late Majesty, were validated. As already explained, the Statute Law Revision Ordinance 1895 was enacted for two purposes, (a) to give effect to Her late Majesty's power and jurisdiction, and (b) to expand Her late Majesty's dominions. The Validation Order in Council affected, and was

[85](1907) Red 211.
[86]*Ibid.*, 225.
[87]*Ibid.*,
[88]*Ibid.*

intended to affect, only the first purpose. Hence His Majesty deemed it necessary also to make an annexation Order.

But what was the effect of this annexation Order on the Protected Territories of the Gold Coast? Before we attempt the answer, one preliminary observation may be made. This kind of 'peaceful annexation' by the Crown would seem to be constitutionally artificial and anomalous. It was artificial because 'annexation' as properly known in international and constitutional law is an incident of conquest or cession,[89] and neither of these two elements was present in the Gold Coast, either as a matter of fact or of claim. It was anomalous because British constitutional law traditionally knows only three kinds of Colonies, namely, settled, ceded and conquered colonies.[90] It is not surprising therefore that up to 1932 there were still voices which loudly insisted that 'countries like the Gold Coast are not colonies at all, but Protectorates'.[91] However, it seems to be accepted that a country so annexed assumes the same constitutional status as, and becomes subject to the same legal consequences as apply to, a country acquired by conquest or cession, with this qualification that 'special leniency' is in practice extended towards the *status quo ante.*[92]

Having now seen how the Crown used its powers in the development of its jurisdiction over the whole of Southern Ghana, we proceed to explore the third object of this paper, namely, the extent to which, on general principles, the acquisition of sovereign powers by the Crown over a territory imports Crown rights in, or in relation to, the land of the territory.

Sovereignty and Crown rights in, or in relation to, land

The first issue here is, what right in land does English law automatically accredit to the Crown by reason only of the fact that it has established itself as sovereign authority in a territory? Unfortunately, framed in this way the question may tend to involve wider issues of

[89] See Roberts-Wray, pp. 104-5; Oppenheim, *International Law,* vol. 1. para. 236ff.

[90] E.W. Ridge, *Constitutional Law* (1950), p. 477; E.C.S. Wide, *Constitutional Law* (1965), p. 418; Halsbury's *Laws of England* (3rd edn.) vol. 5, p. 544. Only Roberts-Wray, pp. 107-8, mentions annexation as an independent means of acquiring colonies.

[91] W.E.G. Sekyi in *West Africa,* 25 July 1932.

[92] *Mutchi v. Annan* (1907) Red 211 at 217. The difference between annexation after conquest and peaceful annexation was recognised by Alverstons, LCJ in *West Rand Mines v The King. The Times* 2 June 1905.

jurisdiction into which, happily, we have no need to wander.[93] The issue is really one to which reference has already been made when we distinguished Protectorate from conquered or ceded colonies. We saw that the acquisition by Britain of a territory by conquest or cession *ipso facto* constitutes the Crown the full internal and external sovereign, which carries with it the right to the radical title in the lands of the territory and of disposal of unoccupied or the so-called 'waste' land. We saw also that no such right, or indeed any right at all *in* land, is legally involved in Protectorate even if, contrary to claims sometimes made by colonial Government officials, the Crown has assumed sovereign (or paramount) powers of legislation and government.[94]

However, although the Crown's position as the sovereign ruling power in a protectorate carries no inherent rights in land, it puts it in a position legally to do anything it likes in relation to the land. The means whereby it arrived at that position of sovereignty is immaterial; it may have glided into it, usurped it, or assumed it as a matter of usage or sufferance. But once *de facto* in that position of sovereignty, it becomes its absolute discretion to choose what law to apply in the territory, and this involves a decision as to what rights to recognise or to abolish.[95]

The main factor in this connection is again the doctrine of an act of State which may manifest itself generally in the form of an Order in Council or Letters Patent. If the Crown or its subordinate legislature should through these means extinguish or modify the customary land rights of the people of the protectorate, English law recognises that no court of law can call the action to question, even if, as indicated earlier, it was done contrary to guarantees previously given. This was the substance of the Privy Council decision in *Sobhuza II v Miller* and the *North Charterland Exploration Co. v R.* in which it was held that a previous undertaking by the Crown not to interfere with native land rights, whether contained in a Convention or otherwise 'cannot

---

[93]For a discussion of such issues see Salmond, *Jurisprudence* (10th edn.) App. IV. pp. 520-1. (Omitted in subsequent editions).

[94]W. Buchanan Smith, Acting Commissioner of Lands in Southern Nigeria in 1912 expressed the view that title to all 'waste' and unoccupied lands as well as subsoil and mineral rights in the Protectorate of Southern Nigeria 'vested' in the Crown on the establishment of its sovereignty there: *Memorandum on the Existing Methods of Government Control of Crown and Other Lands in Southern Nigeria, dated 22 August 1912 in W.A.L.C. Correspondence and Papers,* p. 162, para 10. But C.W. Alexander, the Commissioner of Lands, rightly disagreed with him; *W.A.L.C. Minutes of Evidence,* para. 5301.

[95]This would seem to follow from the statement of Lord Dunedin in *Vajesingji Jeravarsingji v Secretary of State for India* (1924) LR 51 I A 357 at 360.

legally interfere with a subsequent exercise of the sovereign powers of the Crown, or invalidate subsequent Orders in Council'.[96]

The conclusion which must be drawn from the principles discussed seems to be that in English law, no legislative act of the Crown (or of its subordinate legislature, if *intra vires*) by which rights in, or in relation to, land in the protectorate are claimed, created, modified or extinguished, can be impugned on the *legal* basis that the Crown lacked the power. But how, one may ask, can this conclusion be reconciled with the established international law principles of respect for private property?[97]

The answer is that although this principle does in fact inhibit the action of the Crown, it does so on the same basis as do, for instance, moral, political and social considerations. This is because first, the Crown is not bound *always* to respect private rights of property, as the cases we have seen show; secondly, the principle itself does not create an obligation enforceable against the Crown in municipal courts since, if it repudiates it, no municipal court can review the action; and thirdly, the principle is subject to the important qualification that the supreme law maker in a State can always displace or alter existing rights and titles by altering the former law.[98]

Prince Brew of Dunquah, in the Gold Coast Protectorate, one of the staunch opponents of certain land measures proposed by the colonial Government in 1894 and 1897 did argue 'emphatically' in 1897 that the Crown possessed no right to deal with the lands of the protectorate 'because the country had not been acquired by conquest . . . or cession'.[99] It does not seem from what has been said above that this kind of legal argument could stand in British constitutional law. A more serious legal challenge to the land bills of 1894 and 1897, it is thought, should have been directed against the Gold Coast Legislative Council, on the basis of the extent of power which it was authorised to exercise at that time. This will be dealt with in the section that now follows.

---

[96][1926] AC 518; [1931] 1 Ch 169; [1926] AC 518 at p. 528.

[97]The principle is usually associated with territories acquired by conquest or cession. See G. Schwarzenberger, *International Law* (2nd edn). vol. 1, pp. 83 ff; J.G. Starke, *An Introduction to International Law* (6th edn.), p. 286. But there seems to be no reason in principle why, in view of the unlimited legal potentiality possessed by the Crown in a protectorate where it has assumed sovereign ruling powers, the principle should not apply to such a protectorate.

[98]Starke, p. 286.

[99]The Crown Lands Bill, 1894; The Lands Bill 1897; Dispatch from Brew to Chamberlain, 25 October 1897; CO/96/307.

The Crown's attitude to land rights in the Gold Coast

Although the assumption of sovereign ruling powers in a Protectorate theoretically puts the Crown in a position to introduce whatever land and other legislation it chooses, we have seen that in 1874 (the earliest date when such powers may be said to have been claimed over any part of the Protected Territories of the Gold Coast), the only type of power over land in those territories which the Crown intended or claimed to exercise, and which alone, therefore, the Legislative Council of the Gold Coast Colony could exercise, was the power to make laws 'for the protection of property'. It is well-known that up to this time (1874), the Crown never laid any claim to the ownership of any portion of land in the Gold Coast except the land in and around the sites of the Forts and Castles vested in it by Statute 1 & 2 Geo. IV. c.28. The land was recognised by Crown servants in London and in the Gold Coast as the property of the people.

After 1874, and up to 1894, the Legislative Council of the Colony faithfully respected this policy in its enactments. The Public Lands Ordinance No. 8 of 1876 recognised a citizen's right to receive compensation if his land was taken by the Government on behalf of the Crown for public purposes. It was claimed by Governor Maxwell in 1895 that section 7(6) of this Ordinance which precluded the right of compensation in respect of unoccupied land was intended as a statutory modification of the people's rights of absolute ownership of land.[100] But he seemed to be alone in this claim, at any rate among Government officials. H.C. Belfield in 1912 expressly rejected the idea, and noted that in any case, the provision was a dead letter.[101] Hayes Redwar in 1909 also treated the Ordinance as essentially a legislative recognition of the people's right of absolute ownership of the land.[102]

Another Ordinance passed after 1874 which contained a provision intended to recognise and preserve native land tenure was the Marriage Ordinance, No. 14 of 1884. Section 39 of it in effect excluded the operation of the doctrine of escheat in the Gold Coast in circumstances where it should have operated.[103] There was also the Native Jurisdiction Ordinance, No. 5 of 1883 which, by section 5 as extended by rule 1 of the Rules forming Schedule to the Ordinance, empowered the chiefs to make bye-laws for the regulation of mines and mining for gold and other minerals. The intention, no doubt, was to

[100]Maxwell to Ripon, 9 May 1895; CO/96/257, No. 187.

[101]*WALC Minutes of Evidence,* paras. 166-7.

[102]*Comments on Some Ordinances of the Gold Coast Colony* (1909) p. 68.

[103]See, *Laws of the Gold Coast* (1898 edn), vol. 1 p. 423.

recognise and protect the people's property in such mines and minerals. The Government itself did not exercise any such right of regulation.[104]

But in 1894 and 1897, following widespread and improvident dispositions of communal lands by Gold Coast chiefs and citizens in response to an unprecedented wave of concession scramble by foreign and local gold-mining concession hunters and speculators, the colonial Government introduced two revolutionary Bills to meet the emergency.[105] These Bills, the Crown Lands Bill 1894 and the Lands Bill 1897, represented the first and second attempts by the Colonial Government to pass pieces of legislation that raised questions as to their consistency with the people's right of property in land. The bills and the problems they raised are discussed in great detail elsewhere.[106] Here, the question to consider is whether, having regard to the terms of the Draft Proclamation of August 1874 (which evidenced the extent of power claimed by the Crown) the Ordinances proposed in the bills would have been *ultra vires* the Legislative Council. This is a question which, as we have shown, the Courts could entertain. The only relevant power claimed under the Draft Proclamation was power to enact laws which were for 'the protection of property' and were 'framed with due regard to native law and custom'. Accordingly, the proposed Ordinances would be *ultra vires* only if the Court could conclude (a) that they were not primarily or substantially intended for the protection of the people's land and minerals, and/or (b) that they were not framed with due regard to native law and custom.

On the first point – the issue of protection – this is largely a matter of individual judgment. The West African Lands Committee made a general reference to it, but declined to express an opinion.[107] The Crown Lands Bill was framed expressly to 'vest' all 'waste' land, all forest land and all minerals 'in the Queen for the use of the Government'. The Lands Bill was framed to place the administration of all 'public land' in the Government. Both Bills, however, contained provisions 'reserving' certain customary rights of user to the citizens. The Government contended that its primary purpose was to 'prevent improvident dealings' with lands and minerals, and supported its case by pointing to the unprecedented concessions scramble which was taking place in the Gold Coast at that time. The chiefs and their

[104] See, Redwar, p. 68.

[105] For a detailed account of the scramble, see Ilegbune, ch. I.

[106] *Ibid.*, chs. IV and V.

[107] *Draft Report,* paras. 45 and 46.

people replied by claiming that the Bills 'completely destroyed' their right of property in land and minerals, and supported their case by pointing to the express words of the Crown Lands Bill and to what they considered to be the 'practical effect' of the 'administration' proposed in the Lands Bill. The case might have been a difficult one no doubt, but, on the face of it, it seems clear that the Government would have had very great difficulty in satisfying the Court, at any rate as regards the Crown Lands Bill, that expropriation is consistent with the protection of property.

On the second point – the issue of 'due regard' to native law and custom – the views of the Government and the people differed. The principles which govern a decision on this kind of issue were discussed at length by Watermeyer J. in the *Tshekedi Khama case.* [108] They come to the following: (a) that such a requirement is not a mere discretionary direction, but imposes a condition which the Legislature concerned is bound to observe in its enactments; (b) that to require a Legislature to 'respect' (*a fortiori,* to give 'due regard to') native law and custom does not mean that the Legislature is prohibited entirely from altering or modifying such law and custom, but only that it is required to treat native law and custom with consideration, and not simply to ignore them; and (c) that once it is shown that as a matter of fact the Legislature has 'at all' considered native law and custom, the question then of how far the Legislature had done so, is a matter of discretion and cannot be inquired into in a court of law.[109]

The question therefore boils down to this: Did the Legislative Council of the Gold Coast give regard *at all* to native law and custom in the proposed Ordinances of 1894 and 1897? There seem to be two ways of looking at the matter. In the first place, in both proposed Ordinances, the intention, as expressly stated in the Lands Bills of 1897, was to introduce English land law and tenure 'to the exclusion of native law and custom' in respect of lands held from the Governor. Such land would have covered the bulk of the vast area of land within the ambit of each of the Bills. The scheme would seem clearly to involve a basic disregard of native law and custom. Secondly, in another sense, it could be argued that such a disregard was not really relevant to the question here at issue, in that native law and custom was left largely intact as between citizens *inter se* in regard to land not held from Governor. This latter point, however, seemed only fanciful

[108](1926-1953), HCTLR 9 at pp. 15-19.

[109]In that case, the requirement was that the High Commissioner in passing Proclamations should 'respect native law and custom'; See also *Minister of Health v R. ex. p. Yaffe* [1931] AC 494 at 533.

to the Gold Coast people, who raised a mountain of internal and external opposition against the Bills. And, fortunately for all concerned, the Bills were withdrawn and replaced in 1900 by a liberal Ordinance embodying only a mere supervisory control of land grants, administered through the Courts.[110]

It remains now to examine one issue of importance touching on the general question of the colonial Government's right of land control in British territories overseas. The question is, what normally is, or ought to be, the true nature of a Government's duty in relation to land within its area of authority, whether that area is Colony or Protectorate? This question assumes importance from the fact that during the hot controversy which followed the introduction of the Bills of 1894 and 1897 in the Gold Coast, some knowledgeable persons repeatedly proclaimed that the colonial Government possessed no right to deal with lands in the Gold Coast Protectorate.[111] The answer to the question, as it appears to the present writer, seems to be that there is, or ought always to be, implied in the power of government, an ultimate protective control over all matters within its territorial jurisdiction, including land. In the exercise of this control, the Government has, or ought to have, the right, and indeed the duty, to regulate *bono publico* the use to which an owner may put his land, or prevent him from using or disposing of those lands in a manner calculated to prejudice the social and economic welfare of the community as a whole. Where, however, in the exercise of its protective control over land, the Government arrogates to itself the right to say to the people, 'The Government will place your land under its ownership, or will administer your land for you, and alienate it to A, or alienate it to B, if they meet the Government's terms', this may provoke what Acting Governor H. Bryan in April 1906 referred to as a strong 'suspicion of ulterior motives'.[112] This, basically, was the trouble with the Colonial Government's attempt at land control in the Gold Coast between 1894 and 1898.

But the case will, perhaps, be different when it comes to minerals. Here, apart from the special circumstances of the Gold Coast which compelled the colonial Government throughout its existence to treat Southern Ghana as a special exception, there seem to be arguments, not easily controvertible on principle, which render minerals, because

[110]See Commissions Ordinance No. 14 of 1900. *Laws of the Gold Coast Colony* (1868-1906 edn).

[111]See e.g., the view of Prince Brew of Dunquah, a solicitor by training – cited at p. 186 above.

[112]*Colonial Reports – Annual, Ashanti,* 1905, p. 3.

of their location and mode of exploitation, specially adapted to State ownership and control.[113] These arguments were set out in an official document entitled, *Memorandum and Colonial Mining Policy,* which was circulated to Britain Colonial Governors by the Secretary of State in October 1946.[114] The document states:

> There are powerful arguments to be adduced for the vesting of all mineral rights in the Crown. In the first place, the development of minerals . . . frequently requires considerable Government expenditure, e.g. on survey, on transport or other facilities and it is undesirable that the results of such expenditure accrue to private mineral owners. Secondly, a multiplicity of owners is frequently an obstacle to the organisation of economic units of operation. Thirdly, the payments made under contracts between owners and mining companies do not necessarily accrue to the benefit of the members of the community which have the most substantial interest in the lands affected. Fourthly, minerals are important economic assets to a territory and being a gift of nature, their benefits should be shared by the community generally, to which they belong, and not to be enjoyed merely by limited groups of private individuals who are often not the members of the community concerned. Finally, Government by possession of the rights is in a position to control the size of concessions and the rate and terms of exploitation.[115]

In each of the countries of the former British West Africa, these reasons generally led to a policy of vesting all mineral rights in the Crown, but it was not until 1962 that the legislature of the Republic of Ghana, acting substantially on the same reasons, vested 'the entire property in, and control of, all minerals in, under, or upon, any lands in Ghana . . . in the President on behalf of the Republic of Ghana in trust for the people in Ghana'.[116]

---

[113] See, Dispatch from H.E. Sir Allan Burns to the Right Hon. The Secretary of State for the Colonies, 7 April 1947 (Gold Coast, No. 80), and the reply thereto, dated 26 August 1947 (Gold Coast, No. 193).

[114] Published as Colonial No. 206 (H.M. Stationery Office, 1946).

[115] *Ibid.,* para 5. For similar arguments see F.D. Lugard, *The Dual Mandate in British Tropical Africa* (1922), pp. 348-9.

[116] See, for example, Minerals Ordinance, 1916, cap. 93 in *Laws of Nigeria* (1923 edn); Minerals Ordinance, cap. 129 *Laws of the Gambia* (1955 edn); Minerals Ordinance, cap. 144 *Laws of Sierra Leone* (1946 edn); Except in the Northern Territories where minerals were vested in the Crown in 1936, by the Minerals Ordinance, 1936, cap. 155, *Laws of the Gold Coast* (1951); See (Ghana) *Parliamentary Debates* 1st Series, vol. 27, Session 1961-62, esp. pp. 352-68; Minerals Act 1962 (Act 126).

HISTORY OF THE COMMON LAW CONNECTION IN THE COMMONWEALTH CARIBBEAN

D. White

The peoples in the Commonwealth Caribbean are the inheritors of law and legal systems fashioned by Englishmen in the political and economic context of Empire.[1] This explains the unmistakeable identity existing between English law and the law in force in these territories and the frequent jibe that West Indian law is English law.[2] A glance at the West Indian law reports will reveal the closeness of this identity. West Indian judges more often than not apply rules of law which are identical with rules in the English legal system and rely on English decisions for guidance when applying these rules.[3] English legal history, therefore, defines significantly the legal history of most of these inheritor territories and sets the parameters in which these jurisdictions operate.

Although English legal history is definitive of the legal history of the common law Caribbean territories, there is a dimension to the legal history of these inheritor countries which at first glance can be said to have no exact parallel in English legal history unless it is accepted that the export of the common law is parcel of English legal history. It is submitted that the propagation of the common law in the Caribbean is an aspect of both English legal history and Caribbean legal history.

This conclusion finds support from the rule of colonial constitutional law that Englishmen in colonies founded in uninhabited territories brought such rules of English law as were applicable to their circumstances. This rule was a double-edged constitutional sword in the hands of the West Indian colonists. Firstly as a rule of reception it was constitutive of a number of colonial jurisdictions which were empowered to set up institutions analogous to English institutions and administer English law.

If contemporary appreciation ascribes to it a self-evident quality, history reveals that its effectiveness was largely the result of the limits

---

[1] Also referred to as West Indies, Common Law Caribbean.

[2] K.W. Patchett, 'English Law in the West Indies: A Conference Report', in *I. C. L. Q.* 12 (1963) 922.

[3] For example the *Rooks v Barnard* principles relating to punitive damages were applied in *Valentine v Rampersad* (1970) 17 WIR 12, *Marshall v Semper and Others* (1966) 10 WIR 129, *Douglas v Bowen* C.A.J.B. Vol. 11 p. 297, *Walker and Milligen v The A.G. and Burke* C.L. 1579/1972.

set to the royal prerogative, and that it is really telescoped with the greater rule of British constitutional law that it was the right of Englishmen in the colonies to be governed by English law.

The earliest form of West Indian government with the royal prerogative as its basis recognised no such right. Indeed the early colonists found themselves at the losing end of Charles I's prerogative claims as transmitted to the Earl of Carlisle. That was indeed barren soil for the propagation of rights of Englishmen generally, and in particular for those in the colonies.

The type of government first established in the Indies was proprietary in nature. Spurdle points out that originally 'proprietary and governmental rights in all these islands resided in the Earl of Carlisle. . . who in July 1627 was . . . granted letters patent over the whole of the Caribee Islands from 10° to 20° north latitude; a wide range which made express mention of Grenada, St. Vincent, St. Lucia, Barbados, Dominica, Guadeloupe, Montserrat, Antigua, Nevis, and St. Christopher. . .'.[4] The inclusion of Barbados was in defeasance of Sir William Courteen's rightful claim to that island and evidence of the superior political power of Carlisle.[5]

Spurdle argues that the terms of the constitution within the first Earl of Carlisle's patent were imprecise although 'for the better regulation of his people he was empowered to make laws which were to be issued only 'with the consent and approbation of the freeholders'. Spurdle claims that any safeguarding of popular liberty inherent in this particular provision 'was virtually nullified by the insertion of a further clause, empowering him upon emergencies to ordain laws without consent'. Since there was no definition of what constituted 'such emergencies, the provision in effect gave the Earl of Carlisle unlimited legislative authority'.[6]

Letters patent, in addition gave 'him unlimited power to tax and exact rents from his people'. Carlisle was empowered to govern either personally or by deputies and also to 'execute justice in all causes whatsoever'. Spurdle concludes that the terms of the letters patent can be 'reduced to one comprehensive statement that all legislative, executive, taxative, judicial and military authority centred in the Proprietor who was permitted to exercise it through deputies'.[7] Carlisle was an absentee properietor and governed through Governors

[4]F.G. Spurdle, *Early West Indian Government* (The Author, Palmerston North 1962) pp. 7-11.
[5]*Ibid.,* p. 8.
[6]*Ibid.,* pp. 8-11.
[7]*Ibid.,* p. 9.

194

whose commissions were said to be 'as devoid of institutional definition as was [Carlisle's] own patent'.[8]

This arrangement laid the foundation for harsh and arbitrary government. With respect to the governors and their subservient Councils Spurdle writes: 'a spirit of arbitrariness pervaded all their doings. A summary harshness marked the trials which were heard before them, the punishment extending even to whipping, branding and death. Popular liberties were practically non-existent, and life itself was cheap to those who dared protest'.[9] For example Sir Thomas Warner, Carlisle's Governor of St. Christopher executed an unknown man 'for defaming Colonel Jefferson'.[10] Spurdle's description of the exercise of the proprietors' taxative powers further emphasises the arbitrariness under which the early colonists laboured.

'In Barbados for example, Henry Hawley in 1634 demanded a poll tax of 40lbs of cotton or tobacco per head – 20 for the use of the proprietor and 20 for his own purse'. The pretext for its exaction was 'that it was to be used in the making of fortifications within the island, but it was never so used though it was continued annually down to the year 1641, when it was exacted by Governor Huncks for the last time'. In St. Christopher Sir Thomas Warner exacted a similar tax to be shared equally with Carlisle in addition to a further tax 'for the maintenance of a minister and a small party of guards'. This tax was exigible down to the year 1646, although it is believed to have been collected 'up to 1649 the year of Warner's death'.[11]

The taxes were collected in defiance of the colonists' liberty of property. 'As soon as the time arrived for the crops to be gathered in, the Provost Marshal in each island demanded the amount of duty and in default of payment had power to distrain upon the goods of defaulters for its satisfaction. Until the taxes were paid no person was allowed to dispose of his crops'.[12]

Not until 1641 when Governor Bell replaced Hawley was the Assembly, established in 1639 as a mere advisory body, given the right to initiate legislation. An Assembly was established in Antigua in 1644 and one in St. Christopher in 1647. Even up to 1654 there was no popular assembly in Montserrat where 'one Samuel Waad a brother-in-law to Governor Roger Osborne was by the latter ordered

[8]*loc. cit.*
[9]*Ibid.,* p. 10.
[10]*Ibid.,* p. 9.
[11]*Ibid.,* p. 10.
[12]*Ibid.,* p. 11.

to be shot, because he in a public gathering did solicit the governor. . . that they might be regulated by due course of law as other of the islands were, which was to be by common Council and Assembly'.[13]

In Barbados no interest was shown in the Civil War and 'Proprietor, Crown, and Parliament alike had their authority disregarded, [as] the island. . . pursued a course of virtual independence'.[14] Indeed Francis Willoughby commented in a letter to Charles II upon the Barbadians' disposition to believe 'that they were not to be governed by your Majesty's Commission, nor anything but their own laws'.[15] In fact the colonists had declared their independence of Britain.[16]

This was a reaction to the excesses of the royal prerogative as transmitted to the proprietor and his governors. By 1667 the Barbados Assembly was able to strike a bargain with the triumvirate of governors Henry Willoughby, Hawley and Barwick – who were only able to secure supplies 'at the price of a definite promise that the inhabitants should be governed according to the laws of England and the constitutions and laws of this place, and not otherways'.[17]

Jamaica, captured by the English in 1655 pursuant to Cromwell's Western Design was subjected to military government under Edward Doyley – an officer of the 1655 expedition. Civilian government was established in 1663 on the arrival of Lord Windsor who was appointed governor by Charles II and empowered to set up an Assembly. This Assembly was elected in October 1663 and inaugurated on 20 January 1664. The Assembly, fearful that the King might impose arbitrary taxation on the colonists because Jamaica was acquired by conquest, passed a number of laws granting revenue 'for the public use of this island' and then 'hastened to declare the illegality of any further or other tax or levy or assessment. . . imposed or levied upon the island or inhabitants thereof, without the assent of the Governor, Council and Assembly'.[18] This attempt was revolutionary because 'in framing these Acts of January, 1664, the Jamaican Assembly was not following English usage, for the House of Commons had not yet begun the practice of appropriating supplies. . . '[19]

[13] loc. cit.

[14] Ibid., p. 12.

[15] Ibid., p. 17.

[16] Williams, Documents of West Indian History 1492-1655, pp. 301-2

[17] Spurdle, p. 17.

[18] Ibid., p. 26.

[19] loc. cit. But it anticipated the decision in Campbell v Hall (1774) 1 Cowp 204.

When Sir Thomas Modyford arrived in June 1664 he summoned a new Assembly which at his instance nullified all the Acts passed by its predecessor. However, the revenue acts were re-enacted, with alterations which effectively restored the administration of the revenue to the Governor and Council.[20]

In addition an act was passed 'declaring the laws of England in force in' Jamaica. The aim of this measure was 'to stave off arbitrary interference from England and ensure that the constitutional liberties possessed by the older West Indian colonies would be enjoyed by' the Jamaicans. But Jamaica was not to be granted the laws of England by such an easy route because as a conquered colony the Crown which had unlimited power over it, was not minded to lose its right to raise revenue in such an easy manner.[21]

After much agitation and bargaining a compromise was eventually struck and the Assembly in 1728 approved 1 Geo. 11 Cap. 1 which granted the King a permanent revenue of £8000 per year in exchange for the recognition of the colonists' right to be governed by English law. Section 22 of 1 Geo. II Cap. 1 validated the colonists' prior unauthorised use of the laws of England and conferred on them the right to use such English statutes as were in force in England at the date 1 Geo. II Cap. 1 was passed.[22]

The Restoration brought the recognition of the 'serious problem of providing a suitable constitutional frame for every one of the royal provinces'. [23] Action by England in this regard was obviated because representative Assemblies had already emerged and were asserting the right to control the issuing of supplies to protect the liberties of the colonists from the arbitrariness of the exercise of the royal prerogative and to general legislative competence. The problem therefore was how to contain these legislatures and deal with colonial affairs. The *Acts of the Privy Council* records that 'the regular mode of dealing with colonial business from 1675-1696 was to refer it for consideration to the Committee for Trade and Plantations and to give an order in accordance with their report'.[24]

[20] Spurdle, p. 27.

[21] *Ibid.,* p. 31, *and see Journal of the Commissioners for Trade and Plantations, passim.*

[22] Spurdle pp. 31-2, *Cephas v Commissioner of Police and the Attorney General* (unrep.) S. 22 of 1 Geo. II Cap. 1 has been re-enacted as s. 41 of the Interpretation Act.

[23] Spurdle, p. 28.

[24] *Acts of the Privy Council (C.S.) 1680-1720.* This Committee was appointed in 1688. It was re-constituted in 1689 and dissolved in 1696 when its powers were transferred to a body known later as Board of Trade (Council of Trade) Lord Commissioners of Trade and Plantations which was dissolved in 1782.

During this period it was to this committee that all laws passed by the colonial legislatures were sent for scrutiny to ascertain whether they reflected 'powers undue and exhorbitant in the [Colonial] Assembly, and thereupon unfit to be confirmed by Her Majesty'.[25]

The committee took advice from the Law Officers of the Crown with respect to the legality or propriety of confirming them.[26] It also considered any *caveat* lodged by some interested person opposed to confirmation.[27] Ultimately the committee, according to the advice received from the Law Officers, prepared a representation for laying the act for royal confirmation or disallowance.[28]

Specifically, the Board of Trade was the instrument through which the Crown's long struggle with the Jamaican Assembly was waged and 'the confirmation of laws was used as a bargaining card' to pressure the Assembly into granting supplies.[29]

The circumstances existing in the colonies during the seventeenth century certainly did not augur well for the reception of the law of England into Carlisle's Caribee Islands. Although Carlisle's commission to his governors made vague references to the law of England the colonies were governed as if (and indeed they were), the personal estates of the first Earl of Carlisle.[30] Thus under the proprietary governments of the seventeenth century the right of the colonists to English law existed largely in the realm of constitutional theory. The right was not effectively recognised until the royal prerogative was bridled in the motherland and representative government emerged in the colonies.[31]

This right which was denied in practice to colonists in settled territories was a matter of law denied to those colonists who inhabited conquered or ceded territories. Furthermore, the laws of England were not bestowed as free goods. Revenue considerations were central to the enjoyment of that original grant which is said to have been received by force of 'silent principles of constitutional law'. The

[25] For example a Jamaican Act of May, 1739 to dissolve the marriage of Edward Manning with Elizabeth Moore and to enable him to marry again was disallowed.

[26] See CO 137/23 W13 for H.M. Law Officers detailed report on the Manning Divorce Act.

[27] The hearing on the Manning Divorce Act was a grand forensic display. *Journal of the Commissioners for Trade and Plantations* entry for 31 July 1740 the day appointed for the hearing.

[28] *Ibid.*, entry for 16 July 1741.

[29] See n. 23.

[30] Spurdle, p. 9.

[31] *Ibid.*, pp. 12-32.

198

silence here may have resulted from the effective lubrication which revenue imparted!

Doubtless, the Glorious Revolution served the cause of the colonists in their fight for the recognition of their right to be governed by the laws of England.[32] But in view of the original opposition it was thought necessary to put the matter beyond argument. For example, the Leeward Islands' Assembly on 20 June 1705 'declared that the common law of . . . England . . . is in force . . . and is the certain Rule whereby the Rights and properties of Your Majesty's good subjects inhabiting these Islands are and ought to be determined, and that all Customs or pretended Customs, or Usages, contradictory thereunto are illegal null and void'.

Since the constitutional right by force of which the original intake of English law was made possible did not ensure the reception of English law in a steady unimpeded stream beyond the date of settlement, and since this right was not enjoyed by English colonists in conquered or ceded territories, subsequent reception of English law in settled colonies, and its reception in conquered or ceded territories was by force of the enactment of the colonial legislature or by the extension of the Imperial Parliament.[33]

The need to extend the *corpus* of law in each colony was met by enacting from time to time statutes which brought in English law or by re-enactment *mutatis mutandis* of English acts.[34]

A variety of factors must have influenced this type of law-making. Firstly, it was an assertion of the Englishman's continuing right to be governed by English law. The function of the Board of Trade as scrutineer *par excellence* of laws passed by colonial legislatures, the absence from the colonies of expert draftsmen, are factors which can account for this approach to legislation. In the case of conquered or ceded territories where a selection had to be made between two competing traditions, Englishmen naturally selected the one which was familiar, theirs by right of nationality, and more facilitative of their interest.[35]

[32] See Spurdle, pp. 28-9.

[33] Eg. Supreme Court Ordinance (Antigua) S. 25 provided that 'All the enactments (omitting recital) contained in Section 25 of the 'Supreme Court of Judicature Act 1873' as amended S.10 of the Supreme Court of Judicature Act 1875 shall extend to, and be in force in, the Colony.'

[34] Eg. The Wills Act 1837, Sale of Goods 1893, Bills of Exchange Act 1882, Bills of Sale Acts 1878 & 1882 are only a few of the English Acts in force in the territories. See Patchett, 'Reception of Law in the West Indies', JLJ 17 (1973) for a catalogue of English statutes in force in the West Indies.

[35] E.g. Guyana, Trinidad; see Campbell, 'The Transition from Spanish Law to English Law in Trinidad Before and After Emancipation', paper presented at the 7th Annual Conference of Caribbean Historians 2-8 April 1975.

THE LEGAL CONTROVERSY SURROUNDING THE IRISH STATE PRISONERS 1848-1856

B. Touhill

William Smith O'Brien was the leader of the Irish Revolution of 1848. He was not an ordinary revolutionist. He was an Irish aristocrat, a wealthy landowner, an Anglican, a lawyer, and a member of the British Parliament for seventeen years.

The Irish Revolution of 1848 was short-lived. The Irish people did not support the revolution and after a brief skirmish at Ballingarry, the revolution ended. Four of the principal leaders, Smith O'Brien, Thomas F. Meagher, Patrick O'Donoghue, and Terence B. McManus were arrested. Within a year the four revolutionaries were tried and convicted of committing High Treason. The sentence was death.

No one really thought the death sentence would be carried out. British public opinion opposed capital punishment for political crimes and the officials of the British government opposed the creation of four Irish martyrs. The British officials decided to extend the mercy of the Crown to the prisoners by transporting them for life to a penal colony.[1]

O'Brien opposed the transportation order. He knew that so long as he was in jail in Ireland, his friends could effectively work on public sentiment and, in time, obtain pardons for him and his associates. He also knew that transportation to a penal colony thousands of miles from the British Isles could easily lead to oblivion for both himself and his cause, repeal of the Act of Union. At that point, O'Brien began to use his knowledge of English and Irish law to protect himself and his cause.

O'Brien doubted whether transportation was legally available to the authorities in connection with a conviction for high treason. He wrote to the Sheriff of Dublin calling on him not to allow any official to remove him from Richmond Prison except on legal authority.[2] He then wrote to his attorney, Sir Colman O'Laughlin, and directed him to obtain a writ of habeas corpus if any attempts were made to transport him.[3]

[1] *The Times* 10 August 1848, p. 6; Kevin B. Nowland, *The Politics of Repeal* (1965), p. 216; Earl Grey to Sir William Denison, 5 June 1849, CO 408/32.

[2] O'Brien to the Sheriff of Dublin, 5 June 1849, MS 443/2548, O'Brien Papers, National Library of Ireland.

[3] O'Brien to Sir Colman O'Laughlin, 5 June 1849, MS 443/2550, O'Brien Papers, NLI.

On 6 and 7 June 1849, O'Brien and his fellow prisoners formally protested against the transportation order by petition to the House of Commons.[4] They maintained that the statutes regarding transportation, and commutation to transportation, were different in England and Ireland, that the Irish statutes allowed transportation only in felony conviction, and that in Ireland treason was separate and apart from felony. In England treason was felony and, therefore, a transportation order could not be questioned there when an individual had been tried and convicted of treason in an English court. While the House of Commons refused to hear the petition of the State prisoners, the Whig government decided that it was 'better to remove all shadow of doubt' regarding the transportation of the Irish leaders. Accordingly Westminster passed an act which allowed persons convicted of committing high treason in Ireland to be transported for life.[5]

On the morning of 9 July 1849 the four revolutionaries started the 16,000 mile journey to Van Diemen's Land, (now Tasmania).[6] During the voyage, O'Brien decided to fight against oblivion and recognised that it would probably be necessary to suffer some form of martyrdom in order to keep his name before the public.[7] Earl Grey, the Secretary of State for the Colonies, had issued orders to the governor of the penal colony, Sir William Denison, which he hoped would place the State prisoners in 'gentlemanly oblivion'. They were to be treated as gentlemen and not forced to associate with the felons; unless, of course they became difficult to handle. In keeping with Earl Grey's directive the Irish State prisoners were all offered tickets-of-leave on their arrival in Van Diemen's Land, in return for a promise not to escape. This meant that they would be relatively free in directing their personal lives, although there were some minor restrictions. All the State prisoners accepted the offer of the ticket-of-leave except O'Brien, who maintained that he was not prepared to promise not to escape. Governor Denison therefore sent O'Brien to the Darlington Probation Station on Maria Island.[8]

Denison decided that the only way to get O'Brien to accept a ticket-of-leave would be to put pressure on him to ask for one.

[4] O'Brien to Speaker of the House of Commons, 6 June 1849, MS 443/2551; O'Brien to Mr. Redington, 7 June 1849, MS 443/2553, O'Brien Papers, NLI.

[5] *Hansard,* CV I, p. 160, p. 161, p. 437, p. 826.

[6] *Journal of William Smith O'Brien,* 6 parts, 9 July 1849, part 1, p. 1, MS 3923, O'Brien Papers, NLI.

[7] Sir William Denison, *Varieties of Vice-Regal Life,* (2 vols., London: Longman, Green, and Co., 1870), p. 134.

[8] *Journal,* I, 29 October 1849, p. 79; W. Nairn to O'Brien, 29 October 1849, MS 443/2570, O'Brien Papers, NLI.

Denison realised that if O'Brien were confined to a small house, if his exercise area were narrowly defined, if all his mail were inspected and censored, and if the officers and members of their families were forbidden to speak with him, Grey's directive ordering the State prisoners to be treated as gentlemen and kept apart from the felons would be carried out, yet O'Brien would effectively be placed in solitary confinement. In time, O'Brien would have to ask for a ticket-of-leave.[9]

When the new directive was put into effect on 8 November 1849 O'Brien realised the seriousness of the situation.[10] It was not until early January 1850, however, that he noticed that his health was deteriorating and he had found the martyrdom he was looking for. His legal background gave him a base from which to publicise his situation. On 7 January 1850 he sought legal assistance by hiring an attorney. He questioned whether the colonial laws authorised the government to consign him to solitary confinement for an indefinite period and whether he could obtain a writ of habeas corpus which would force Governor Denison to show under what authority he was kept in solitary confinement.[11]

By the end of February, O'Brien received the legal opinion of his attorney, Mr. Knight. Knight was an outspoken opponent of transportation and as such had made a particularly detailed study of the statutes governing transportation. Knight considered O'Brien's solitary confinement to be illegal. He knew of 'no British statute, nor any law of this Island that authorises an offender convicted in Ireland . . . to be kept in solitary confinement'. It followed, he thought, that no Secretary of State would issue such instructions to the Governor of Van Diemen's Land. Knight recommended that O'Brien should sue for a writ of habeas corpus in Van Diemen's Land and thereby force Governor Denison to disclose the instructions from the Secretary of State to the court. Knight told O'Brien, 'I cannot for a moment presume that any such order exists'. He thought that the courts would issue an order immediately releasing O'Brien from solitary confinement. Knight had some other opinions on the transportation law: he told O'Brien that the current law contained several obscure passages, which he believed required the Secretary of State to designate the specific place of confinement for the transported felon and from which the felon could not be released until the expiration of his term. Knight,

[9]Nairn to Superintendent Lapham, 6 November 1849, C O 280/249.

[10]*Journal*, II, 8 November 1849, p. 7.

[11]O'Brien to Pitcairn, 7 January 1850, MS 443/2610, 11 January 1850, MS 443/2613, O'Brien Papers, NLI.

was, by this interpretation, questioning the release of the felons by means of a pass and a ticket-of-leave.[12]

O'Brien decided not to sue for a writ of habeas corpus. After the local physician noted that his health was deteriorating, O'Brien had been released from solitary confinement. He knew that his current situation was sufficient to maintain his physical and mental health and planned to send Mr. Knight's opinion along with some other letters of complaint to his friends in the British Isles, hoping they would result in Grey issuing orders to Denison to refrain from placing him back in solitary confinement once his health was restored. O'Brien was willing to give the British officials time to issue such orders.

Denison was well aware of O'Brien's struggle to make his martyrdom known in England and Ireland and to rest his case on legal grounds. Denison carefully wrote to Earl Grey outlining what he had done and why. Denison thought very little of Knight's opinion: he believed that Knight had confounded the case of a prisoner who was sentenced to hard labour in the colonies with that of a prisoner sentenced to ordinary transportation.

Grey completely supported Denison's actions, but realising that O'Brien's friends in Westminster would raise questions he sought advice from his colleague, Mr. Hawes, and forwarded the appropriate correspondence to the officials at the Home Office for their perusal.

After reading the contents of Denison's dispatch, Mr. Hawes agreed with the Governor that Knight had quoted the wrong statute. But in his report to Earl Grey, Hawes acknowledged there was a vagueness in the current law governing transportation. Hawes was well aware of the rising public discontent in Van Diemen's Land over the continuance of transportation, and was worried.[13] It was not unthinkable that one of the State prisoners might use the courts as a way of protesting against his treatment as a transported offender and that the force of public opinion could intimidate the judge to rule in favour of the State prisoner and thus against transportation.

Meanwhile O'Brien's letters describing his treatment arrived in the British Isles. In general O'Brien's complaints received little sympathy in England but re-awakened support in Ireland. O'Brien also became a subject of debate in Westminster. His friends raised the question of a

[12]Knight Opinion, MS 443/2647, O'Brien Papers, NLI.

[13]Denison to Earl Grey, 17 April 1850, CO 280/258-7883; Note by Hawes, 24 September 1850, CO 280/258-7883; Note to Sir George Grey, 14 October 1850, C O 280/258-7883.

pardon, justified not for O'Brien's sake, but for the sake of the Irish people.[14]

By the end of the summer of 1850, O'Brien was aware that Grey had endorsed Denison's methods. The immediate question for O'Brien was whether his health could withstand continued martyrdom long enough to swing public opinion behind him and thus force the government to grant him a pardon. The answer was, no. No one knew that better than O'Brien. By September he was back in solitary. By November he was forced to admit that continued solitary confinement would leave him mad, an invalid, or dead. O'Brien accepted a ticket-of-leave.[15] Between his arrival in October 1849 and his acceptance of a ticket-of-leave in November 1850, O'Brien had mustered sizeable support from the free citizens of the penal colony. Part of that support was from the Irish immigrants in residence there and part of it was from the anti-transportation forces who disliked Governor Denison intensely for his continued stand in favour of transportation. O'Brien appeared to be Denison's victim and the anti-transportationists therefore considered him worthy of protection.

If martyrdom and legal controversy were to be continued as a way for the Irish State prisoners to struggle against oblivion, and thus obtain pardons, one of the other State prisoners would have to carry on the fight. O'Brien was exhausted.

Terence McManus accidentally assumed the mantle of martyrdom and the role of legal contestant. When O'Brien accepted the ticket-of-leave he took up residence in New Norfolk where McManus paid him a visit. Such a visit, however, was against the rules of the special ticket-of-leave which McManus held. When Denison learned what had happened he withdrew McManus's ticket-of-leave and ordered him to a probation station to serve three months at hard labour.[16] McManus reacted by employing Mr. Knight to obtain his release by means of a writ of habeas corpus. The anti-transportation leaders had found another martyr. They referred to Denison's actions as arbitrary and created an even larger public opinion which was anti-Denison and pro the Irish State prisoners not only in Van Diemen's Land but on the

[14]Duffy to Meagher, 13 September 1850, John Kiernan, *The Irish Exiles in Australia* (Dublin: Clonmore and Reynolds, 1954), pp. 93-4; *The Times* 8 October 1850, p. 8; Hansard, CXI, 786-795.

[15]Journal, III, 24 August 1850, P. 23; O'Brien to Reeves, Port Arthur, 9 November 1850, MS 444/2770, O'Brien Papers, NLI.

[16]Denison to Earl Grey, 28 February 1852, enclosing letter of Nairn to McManus, 24 December 1850, CO 280/289-6356.

mainland of Australia. Those citizens began to petition the Queen to pardon the State prisoners.[17]

Meanwhile Mr. Knight presented his case on behalf of McManus before the Supreme Court of Van Diemen's Land. Knight questioned whether there were any Irish statutes permitting the services of a transported felon to be assigned to the Governor of a penal colony, whether there were any statutes designating Van Diemen's Land as a penal colony, and whether Governor Denison had the power to revoke a ticket-of-leave at his own discretion.

As the government attorneys set to work to make the return they discovered that they did not have complete copies of the laws governing the transportation of convicts sentenced in Irish courts. Nor did they have copies of the legal proof of conviction; namely, the Certificate of Conviction, for most of the convicts, including McManus. Nevertheless, the Solicitor-General prepared the return as best he could. He was able to state that he had found two Irish Parliamentary Acts, one in 1773 and one in 1798, assigning the services of a transported felon from the Lord Lieutenant of Ireland to the Governor of a penal colony. Next he informed the Court that Van Diemen's Land had been designated as a penal colony by an Order in Council of Queen Victoria on 4 September 1849. And finally he maintained that to challenge the ability of Governor Denison to withdraw a ticket-of-leave on his own authority was untenable.[18]

On 21 February the Court announced its decision. The justices concluded there was an absence of important facts in the government's return relating to McManus's conviction for high treason, and subsequent transportation, and because of those defects, 'he is now free to go out of these Courts'.[19]

Denison reacted by immediately writing to Grey informing him that while the court had freed McManus the government attorneys were amending the return and he had just ordered McManus's arrest. Denison then spoke of the larger issues. He asked Grey to forward to him the complete versions of the Irish Acts governing transportation, as well as the proper certificates of conviction for all convicts being

[17]*Argus* (Melbourne), 14 February 1851, 26 February 1851; *Launceston Examiner* (Launceston), 15 March 1851, 19 March 1851.

[18]Denison to Earl Grey, 8 February 1851, CO 280/274-4286; 22 March 1851, enclosing letter of Attorney General's Office to Denison, 25 February 1851, enclosing Copy Return to Writ of Habeas Corpus, 14 February 1851, R. Ballantine, CO 280/275-7124.

[19]Denison to Earl Grey, 22 March 1851, Substance of the Judgement of the Supreme Court . . . McManus, CO 280/275-7124.

sent to Van Diemen's Land. Denison recognised that providing individual certificates of conviction for every convict who was transported was difficult and suggested a solution to the problem. Denison suggested that the Imperial Parliament pass a law whereby the proof of conviction would be the 'Assignment List'; namely, a list which named everyone on board the convict ships and their term of transportation.[20]

It was not until May 1851 that Grey first learned of the legal battle going on in Van Diemen's Land. About the same time as the officials in Earl Grey's office were turning their attention to McManus's legal battle, the officials in the Home Office under Sir George Grey were beginning to worry about Knight's previous legal opinion which challenged the power of Governor Denison to put Smith O'Brien in solitary confinement. As a result of those concerns the law officers of the Crown were alerted to the questions being raised by Mr. Knight in both O'Brien's case and in McManus's. The crucial question raised by Knight was not so easy to answer: namely, was the power of the Governor over transported felons without restriction? Could Denison place O'Brien in solitary confinement and revoke McManus's ticket-of-leave on his own authority?[21]

On 11 June the opinion was given. There were no clear legal guidelines respecting the extent of the power which the Governor had to enforce the government's right to the services of the convict. If a convict appealed to the courts of Van Diemen's Land alleging that he was being restrained and coerced in an illegal manner, it was up to the discretion of the judge as to whether the official means being employed were legal. It was indeed possible that both Smith O'Brien's solitary confinement and McManus's confinement at a probation station could be declared 'coercive' and that the court could rule that they should be freed from such restraints.[22] After reading the opinion, both ministers urged the legal councillors to begin work on legislation which would clearly define the power of the Governor and thus do away with the vagueness of the law which could result in the limitation of the Governor's power. The legislation would also solve the Certificate of Conviction problem by making the Assignment List legal proof of conviction. The new legislation was to be presented by

[20] Denison to Earl Grey, 28 February 1851, CO 280/274-5299; 18 April 1851, CO 280/276-8638.

[21] Waddington to Merivale, 27 May 1851. Note to Elliot, 29 May 1851, Note from Earl Grey to Merivale, 31 May 1851, Merivale to Grey, June 1851, Note from Earl Grey to Merivale, June 1851, CO 280/284-4668.

[22] A.E. Cockburn and W.P. Wood to Waddington, 11 June 1851, Merivale to Grey, 18 June 1851, CO 280/284-4668.

206

the Home Office to the Imperial Parliament at the ensuing session. It was also decided to forward to Governor Denison complete copies of all Irish statutes relating to transportation.[23]

The Ministers had been able to deal with the legal question raised by Knight regarding the vagueness of the law. But Knight's legal contest had uncovered another problem for the ministers. The general consensus in Van Diemen's Land was that the Supreme Court had announced its independence from the executive leadership of Governor Denison by releasing McManus from confinement. If the newly elected Legislative Council followed the lead of the Court, Denison and the British policy of continuing transportation to Van Diemen's Land would be in serious jeopardy. By the fall of 1852, the Legislative Council passed a resolution against transportation.[24]

Meanwhile McManus had escaped. When he learned that the Solicitor-General had amended the return and that Denison had ordered his arrest he decided that the time had come to leave Van Diemen's Land and fled to America where he was greeted warmly. His arrival set in motion a wave of public sympathy for the Irish State prisoners throughout the United States. The Americans petitioned both their Congress and their President to ask the British to pardon the State prisoners. The petition movement spread to Canada and Ireland. Once again the treatment which the State prisoners were receiving was debated in Parliament. Actually both the State prisoners and the anti-transportationists of Van Diemen's Land were the recipients of words of sympathy from the members of the opposition party. How long Russell's Whig ministry would last was unknown but there was a general feeling that new ministers would end transportation to Van Diemen's Land and pardon the Irish State prisoners.[25]

In February 1852 Russell's Whig ministry fell. The new Tory ministry formed under Lord Derby gave hope to both groups but no policy change was put into effect. It remained for Aberdeen and his coalition government to end transportation to Van Diemen's Land

[23] Waddington to Merivale, 4 December 1851, Earl Grey to Merivale, 9 December 1851, Merivale to Waddington, 22 December 1851, Merivale to Grey, CO 280/284-10152; Earl Grey to Denison, 28 November 1851, CO 280/275-9260 LPRO.

[24] *The South Australian Register* (Adelaide), 19 March 1851; *Launceston Examiner* (Launceston) 26 February 1851, p. 135, Sir William Denison to Mrs. Denison (mother), 13 October 1852; *Varieties of Vice-Regal Life,* pp. 195-197.

[25] *Launceston Examiner* (Launceston) 26 March 1851, p. 200; *Morning Herald* (Sydney), 21 August 1851, p. 4451; Daniel Webster to Abbott Lawrence, 26 December 1851, Harvard University, Houghton Library, Webster Papers, 035582-035583, Manuscript Division, Library of Congress; *Nation* (Dublin), 22 May 1852, p. 597; *Journal,* VI, 28 June 1852, pp. 50-55; *Hansard,* CXVI, pp. 588-590, CXVII, pp. 634-41, p. 1067.

and grant conditional pardons to the Irish State prisoners. Aberdeen was anxious to solidify both the Empire and the British Isles as the Crimean War approached. At the end of the Crimean War the British ministers granted full pardons to the Irish State prisoners. O'Brien returned to Ireland where he continued to advocate repeal.

The chances are that the Irish State prisoners would probably have been pardoned eventually. But there is little doubt that O'Brien's interest in law and his use of it had beneficial results. The fact that Westminster passed a law before sending him into exile probably did appear to some individuals as ex post facto legislation. Challenging his solitary confinement did reawaken support for him in Ireland and did allow his friends in Westminster formally to raise the question of pardon. In Van Diemen's Land his actions connected him to the leading advocates of the anti-transportation movement and they as well as O'Brien knew the importance of a martyr in stirring up public opinion. McManus's legal struggle tied the knot. The Irish State prisoners as a group won the support of the free citizens on mainland Australia. McManus's escape brought the sympathy of America and Canada.

The legal struggle also clearly displayed to the British ministry that the public in Van Diemen's Land no longer supported transportation. If the Courts and the Legislative Council were no longer acting in unison with the executive, a change in policy had to come. Transportation was doomed.

Smith O'Brien has been accused of being vain. He was. It was his vanity which took him to the barricades at Ballingarry. It was his vanity which set him on his course of action making him a martyr. It was his vanity which led him to claim the protection of the law. Ultimately it was the protection of the law which kept him safe, as well as his cause, repeal.

DESERTION AND DIVORCE: THE COLONY OF VICTORIA, AUSTRALIA, 1860

R. Campbell

Why did the Victorian Parliament in 1860 pass a Divorce Bill which provided, inter alia, in Clause 13, for dissolution of marriage on the grounds of four years' desertion by either party, without reasonable cause? Certainly desertion was rife – indeed *The Argus* newspaper in mid-1860 did not quibble at asserting bolding that 'in no country is the crime of wife desertion so common a crime as this. . . let the ministers of the gospel spare time from the stage and lecture-room. . . and chopping of texts – to look at this, one of the most frightful sores in our social condition'.[1] To make matters worse, went on *The Argus,* 'in no country is it harder for the poor woman to live and maintain herself and children in an honest way'.[2] Times were tough in the later 1850s and early '60s for both sexes. Men, despite their enfranchisement, had not succeeded in having the land unlocked from the grip of the squatters, and scratched for work, some still prospecting, others roaming the countryside in their quest. In Victoria, summed up *The Argus* in July 1859, 'half troglodyte, half nomad, their homes alternating between a tent and a right of way, and their occupations between the lottery of gold-digging and the competition for public works, men have neither homes nor occupation to spare. Meanwhile, the women, married and deserted, or tossed from Dan to Beersheba, fill up the ranks of prostitution.'[3]

The plight of women unable to find work – and employment opportunities for them were very limited – was often aggravated by isolation 'from the counsel and assistance of friends',[4] especially in the case of recent migrants. 'There is but one resource', *The Argus* again, 'and that, black as it is, is shut to all but the young and the well-favoured'.[5] In a letter to *The Argus,* a writer whose passionate pseudonym was 'One who Writes Feelingly on the Subject', estimated that there were thousands of deserted husbands and wives in Victoria –

[1] *The Argus,* 20-6-1860.

[2] *Ibid.*

[3] In 1860 nearly two-fifths of Victoria's population of over half a million were still to be found on the gold-fields; *Statistical Register,* 1860. By then of course many worked for mining companies, as surface gold could no longer be easily found; *The Argus,* 4-7-1859.

[4] *The Argus,* 28-6-1859 and 20-6-1860.

[5] For an example of such a woman in dreadful straits and quite friendless, see *The Age,* 10-9-1858.

though male desertees received scant attention in newspaper discussion.[6] We can only guess how many Victorians were deserted, but there seems no doubt that the number, especially of women, was 'alarmingly great' and not only among 'what may be termed the lower class', but 'also among those who [had] been reared with some pretensions to gentility'. So wrote one who signed herself 'A Sufferer'.[7]

Although evidence is lacking, I feel that it was the magnitude of the wife-desertion, along with its moral consequences that, more than anything else, probably secured the inclusion of the desertion provision in Clause 13 of Victoria's Divorce Bill of 1860. Somehow the problems had to be resolved. Central Government provided no means of subsistence for the wives and children of married men who left the Colony for distant gold fields, or other places, leaving their families unprovided for. Nor was poor relief available, for the traditional system had never been brought to Australia. As for charitable bodies, they could not adequately cushion the effects of such widespread desertion, as well as those of poverty in general. Although *The Argus* and newspaper correspondents called for the expansion of the area of female employment, it still remained narrow, and no one could forge supportive families or helpful ready-made friends for newcomers.[8]

Victoria was a dreadful place in which to be deserted. 'The greater cost of mere animal existence' than in England exacerbated the stresses of those left without funds, and so did 'the tyranny of distance'.[9] A husband seeking work or his freedom from family responsibilities could soon be hundreds of miles away, his 'destination out of [his wife's] power to follow'.[10] She would usually find it impossible to ascertain whether he were alive or dead. And many did die: 'the human remains of persons unknown are being. . . constantly discovered', wrote a correspondent, Agnes Mason, in 1861.[11] A locality often had its 'Dead Man's Gully'.[12] *The Argus* told of the lot

[6]*The Argus,* 15-6-1859. Mr. Horne, MLA, agreed, though Mr. Woolley, MLA, did not. Vic. *Hansard,* 6. 1358 and 1359; see though, the letter to the editor, by E.F.B., a deserted husband, in *The Argus,* 24-3-1860.

[7]*The Argus,* 1-6-1860.

[8]*The Argus* call, 9-9-1859; letter from 'A Sufferer', *The Argus,* 1-6-1860; letter from M.A., *The Argus,* 6-8-1860.

[9]*The Argus* 20-7-1860; The title of a work by Professor Geoffrey Blainey, University of Melbourne, 1966.

[10]Letter to *The Argus* 1-6-1860, by 'A Sufferer'.

[11]Letter to *The Argus,* 14-5-1861.

[12]A point made by a speaker for the Australian Broadcasting Commission, early 1978, discussing mid-nineteenth century life in the gold-mining area of Creswick, Victoria.

of the poor and the deserted, in 1860.[13] 'Among the instances which have come to our knowledge . . . are some which put to shame the imagination of domestic novelists and are too dreadful for a full recital – instances of well-born ladies driven to madness, or worse, out of sheer despair – of their children dying of hunger, or saved only by a resource too piteous and horrible to be told of a Christian people in a Christian land'. 'To the desolate mother of children, what does this fair and rich young colony offer?' asked the same paper.[14] Prostitution was one offering: 'marry, stitch, die or do worse', was a quotable quote from a *Times* leader, and it was predictable that 'doing worse' should flourish in Victoria, given the incidence of desertion, the dearth of jobs for women, and the disproportion between the sexes: less in 1860 than 1857, owing to female immigration and male emigration to New Zealand and elsewhere, but 'still considerable and still productive of serious evils'.[15] Much was written about the sin of great cities. 'Expectant', urging liberal divorce legislation as a curb, stressed that Victoria had 'the unenviable repute of being very lax in its morals'.[16] 'Cleopatra', another letter-writer, presented a Melbourne teeming with prostitutes, occupying 'the main thoroughfares of the City, obstructing the passage of respectable travellers: driving mothers and sisters out of the streets and compelling them to seek other and more quiet paths'.[17] Less socially aware than 'Expectant', Cleopatra demanded firm action by the Melbourne City Council, like strict orders 'forbidding bare heads and indecent dress'.

The Argus was more understanding. 'It is notorious', it claimed, 'that the most prolific source of misery and vice in Melbourne is the desertion of wives by husbands', a statement which might have prompted, a week later, 'A Deserted Wife' to lay bare her despairing tale – and to plead for four years' desertion as a ground for divorce.[18] 'Married as I was about eighteen years of age, with the consent of my mother and approval of friends, to an apparently most eligible husband, fair business and everything outwardly prosperous, in a few months difficulties intervened and swept all away. My husband leaves, disappointed, for the diggings, writes to me at first, then at long intervals, and for the last four years never deigns to write a word.

[13] *The Argus,* 20-7-1860.

[14] *The Argus,* 20-6-1860.

[15] *The Argus,* 28-6-1859; Balls-Headley. Dr. W., 'Victorian Matrimony', *Melbourne Review* 2, (1877), 390 ff.; *The Argus,* 17-1-1860.

[16] *The Argus,* 24-5-1861.

[17] *The Argus,* 7-4-1859.

[18] *The Argus,* 12-6-1860 and 20-6-1860.

What am I to do? I have no means of support. I might take a situation as a governess, but what am I to do with my little boy, four years of age?' 'Marry, stitch, die or do worse'.

Was prostitution all that Victoria could offer to women such as this? It was an intolerable solution – especially as there was another ready to hand: husbands. Men were laid on. The Census of 1861 showed that marriageable men outnumbered eligible women 7 : 2. It is true that the marriage rate had declined between 1857 and 1860, from 12 per 1,000 to 7 per 1,000, probably due to males leaving the Colony and to economic distress, but there were still plenty of males marrying and plenty free to marry deserted women, could they but be divorced.[19] 'The true relief which the [deserted] women needs is to be permitted lawfully and decently to provide herself with another husband. . .'.[20] But to facilitate this, a Clause 13 reflecting Victoria's social needs was vital: 'How else could a deserted married female, left by her husband to push her way in the hard world for herself. . . accept the lawful protection of another husband?'[21] Our particular condition provided a 'good reason to depart from the English law', pronounced *The Argus* firmly, and warned that failure to implement a liberal Clause 13 in the legislation currently under consideration, would drive women into de facto relationships.[22]

'We look to our adopted country to relieve us from a state of bondage', cried a deserted husband, appealing on behalf of all abandoned spouses in Victoria.[23] 'The tearful good wishes and prayers of hundreds of miserable women' attended the successful passage through the Victoria Parliament of the legislation which would free them – so declared *The Argus*, which further stated, with rather firmer knowledge, that it had received many letters 'on this deeply interesting question' of desertion, 'all urging us to help the writers to some relief from our present marriage laws'.[24]

[19]Balls-Headley was still worried about the declining marriage rate in 1877.

[20]*The Argus,* 12-6-1860.

[21]*The Argus,* 8-6-1860. Letter to Editor.

[22]*The Argus,* 12-6-1860. So did Mr. F.A. Corbett, in 1860, in his article, 'The Conjugal Position of the People of Victoria, Considered in Relation to the Laws of Divorce' in *Journal of the Royal Victorian Society* 5, (1860), 108; *The Argus,* 12-6-1860.

[23]*The Argus,* 24-3-1860.

[24]*The Argus,* 20-6-1860. Mr. Horne, MLA, suggested on 20-6-1860, that 'large portions of the community were daily and hourly looking out with intense anxiety for the passing of this bill'. Vic. *Hansard,* 6. 1358; *The Argus,* 20-6-1860. Mr. Greeves, MLA, referred on 20-6-1860 to 'a great many letters and editoral articles in the papers on the subject', Vic. *Hansard,* 6. 1356.

Allowing for the paucity of hard evidence, I think we may say that desertion, especially of women, was clearly a very real contemporary problem with which Victoria was ill-equipped to deal, but which might have largely been offset, given a Clause 13 clearing the way for remarriage of the deserted.

I incline towards a mixture of morality and expediency as prime movers underlying the Victorian Parliament's desertion ground of 1860. But were there other reasons? How important, for example, was incipient Australian nationalism in stimulating Victoria's legislators to deviate in essentials from England's Divorce Act 1857? How many Parliamentarians, some of them schooled in the assertive Melbourne City Council, felt, like *The Argus,* that 'to the colonies of Australia [would] fall the solution of many of the social problems which baffle the skill of the home politician and philanthropist. . .'?[25] Already Victoria had shown the way with political problems – and had, by 1857, introduced manhood suffrage and the secret ballot, with a degree of success that inspired *The Argus* to hope that Victoria would 'take in hand some of our social ones'.[26]

A spirit of pride in Golden Victoria was continually expressed in the late 1850s, and a sense of independence. *The Age,* at various times, and in a variety of contexts, insisted that Victoria had 'passed the limits of national babyhood', was 'not a child in leading strings' and that 'a mighty gulf [separated] us from the Old World, in all feeling but affection. . .'.[27] How many legislators shared this sort of outlook? Some did: Mr. Don, MLA, made his doughty declaration on 20 June 1860, urging Honourable Members to 'do as they thought fit'.[28] Mr. Don 'did not think it right that the terrors of the Imperial Parliament should be held over the House'. He thought 'the House should once and for all assert its independence in this respect'. Mr. Don and others would have applauded *The Argus,* in 1860, when it mocked Lord Stanley's 1858 instructions to the Governor of Victoria to reserve any Victorian Divorce Act 'varying to an important degree from the present law of England'.[29] Scotland had desertion as a ground for dissolution of marriage: 'Let the Secretary of State set himself to reconcile one side of the Tweed to the other, before he comes to the end of the world to enforce an act of conformity.'

[25] *The Argus,* 9-9-1859

[26] Introduced in 1856; *The Argus,* 9-9-1859. There are traces of this spirit in debate. Vic. *Hansard,* 6 and 7 *passim.*

[27] *The Age,* 4-8-1858. Context of defence; *The Age,* 1-10-1857. Context of the law; *The Age,* 22-1-1858. Context of unlocking the land.

[28] See, e.g. Mr. Johnston, MLA, Vic. *Hansard,* 6. 1360.

[29] *The Argus,* 21-6-1860.

Yet perhaps it was not so much a sort of emergent nationalism, or colonialism, as mere headiness felt by the majority of legislators, that led them to pass their wayward Clause 13: a giddiness from their newly-won responsible goverment and their role in it.[30] Although there is no evidence extant of what one might call organised popular demand for Victoria's type of bill, merely a few letters published in the press, a few leaders and pronouncements by *The Argus,* and, less specifically, a resolution at a meeting on prostitution in 1859 that the law of divorce needed reform, the Victorian Parliament probably believed that it had the support of the mass of the electorate and of the adult population for its legislation.[31] *The Argus* was convinced that the people of Victoria had a 'very decided opinion' on the subject, and so was 'Expectant' writing after the withholding of assent had condemned Victoria to a narrower Act based on Britain's: 'I believe it is the universal wish of young and old, rich and poor, legislator and constituent, to see a different divorce bill in Victoria'.[32]

The local Anglican Bishop and twenty-one clergymen had opposed the desertion provision, the General Assembly of the Presyterian Church petitioned against remarriage after divorce and damages from co-respondents, and the Roman Catholic Church rejected the bill in toto.[33] Nevertheless, it survived. Most legislators must have rated the degree of religious opposition not destructive of their political destinies. Undoubtedly most of them knew of unhappy cases of desertion, though no Parliamentarians seemed to have a domestic interest in the success of the Victorian Act, Mr. Fawkner commenting, in the Legislative Council, that 'he had lived with his own wife very comfortably for forty years and did not think the Bill was likely to be of use to him or any of his friends'.[34] Professional self-interest, however, was hinted at by *The Argus* in 1860, jibing that 'the desire of married couples to be unyoked [might] prove to colonial lawyers a fertile source of emolument'.[35] The legal profession was overcrowded in 1860 and business was slack; but most Members favouring a wide Clause 13 were not lawyers of any description.[36] Again, a resolution of the 1859 meeting on prostitution already mentioned claimed that

[30] The elections of late 1856 were the first held under responsible government.

[31] See Mr. Wood, Vic. *Hansard,* 5. 790; *The Age,* 18-6-1859.

[32] *The Argus.* 22-4-1861; *The Argus,* 24-5-1861.

[33] *Votes and Proceedings, Legislative Assembly,* 1859-1860, 1, E 34, p. 327; *Ibid.,* E 33, p. 313; One-fifth of the population of Victoria in 1860 was Roman Catholic, per Mr. Barton, Vic. *Hansard,* 5. 791.

[34] 7-12-1858, Vic. *Hansard,* 4. 489.

[35] *The Argus,* 3-1-1860.

[36] Analysis of Members.

214

the non-availability of divorce in Victoria led not only to 'gross vice' but to 'frequent murders'.[37] Did this persuade the legislators that their Clause 13 was needed? Or had some of the oft complained-of assertiveness of colonial women brushed off on them?[38]

Whatever the compound of reasons which produced our vigorous and sensible proposal in 1860, the men responsible for it, albeit constitutional greenhorns, deserve praise. Less impressive was their collapse in face of Britain's withholding of assent, their meek passing in 1861 of a Divorce Act defrocked of all irregularity, and their shelving of Mr. Snodgrass's subsequent Bill to make desertion for five years a ground for divorce.[39]

Victoria was thus stuck with its 'barbarous and unjust' divorce law for twenty-nine years, with adultery the sole ground for dissolution of marriage and a double-standard for men and women.[40] Only from 1890 was divorce available to the long-suffering deserted.[41]

[37]*The Argus,* 18-6-1859.

[38]E.g. *The Argus,* 8-2-1861. A letter by 'Materfamilias' on female servants.

[39]This Bill, introduced later in 1861, was simply allowed to fade away.

[40]*The Argus,* 22-4-1861.

[41]The Divorce Act 1889. Reserved 25-11-1889; Royal Assent proclaimed 13-5-1890.

INDEX

Bramwell, 49
breach of duty, action on, 44
Brew, Prince, 186
Brian, C.J., 32-5, 37
Bristol, 74
British jurisdiction overseas, 162-98; in the Gold Coast, 162-3, 168-
    84, 187-91
Britton, 13, 118-20
Brooke, Robert, 13-14, 35-6
Brookland (Kent), 60
Broom, Herbert, 18-20
Bryan, H., 190
Bulstrode, Edward, 37
Burlamaqui, Jean, 23
Burrough, 41
Bury St. Edmunds (Suffolk), 111
Butler, Charles, 23

Cambridge, 112
Cambridgeshire, 109, 124
Cambridge University, 149, 151, 156-7
Campbell, 46
Canada, 206-7
canon law, and Chancery, 78
Canterbury, 56, 62, 116
Cape Coast Castle (Ghana), 169
capias, writ of, 98
Caribbean, British, *see* West Indies
Carlisle, Earl of, governor of the West Indies, 193-4, 197
Carnarvon, Earl, Colonial Secretary, 177
Carpenter, Matthew the, 122
Carpenter, William, 60
Carriers Act, *see* Statutes
carriers and the law, 39-49
Case, action on, 32-8
case-books, 28
certiorari, writ of, 88, 90
Chalmers, Sir Mackenzie, 25-6
Chamberlain, Joseph, 181-2
Chancery, equitable jurisdiction of, 68-71; 78-9, 80-6, 88, 90-2; its
    use of arbitration, 9, 84; Chancery decree rolls, 92
Charles I, 193
Charles II, 195

Moore, 37
moral offences, in 17th-cent. Kent, 55-8, 62-3
More, Sir Thomas, 6, 84
Morley, John, 61-2
Mortmain Act, *see* Statutes
Municipal Corporations Act, *see* Statutes
Mylener, Stephen, 62
Mynge, Henry, 62

native law and custom, and British colonial jurisdiction, 177, 185,
    188-9
negligence, carriers', 41-8
Nelson, 21
Newcastle-under-Lyme, 97
Newcastle-on-Tyne, 106
Newport (Essex), 111
Nevis (West Indies), 193
Norfolk, 119
Norfolk, New (Australia), 203
Normandy, 117
Northampton, 104, 107, 113, 121
Northamptonshire, 104, 108, 113
Northamptonshire eyre, 117
Northumberland eyre, 117
Norwich, 96, 109, 111
notices, carriers', 39-49
Nottingham, 106
Nottinghamshire commission, 96
Novae Narrationes, 31
novel disseisin, certification of, 85
Noy, William, 18

O'Brien, William Smith, 199-203, 205-7
O'Donoghue, Patrick, 199-200, 206-7
O'Laughlin, Colman, 199
Oakham (Rutland), 113
Oldcastle, John, 96
Orders in Council and British jurisdiction overseas, 164-8, 174-5,
    185-6
Osborne, Roger, 194
Oswestry (Salop), 103
outlawry, 98-9, 121-2
Oxford, 105-7, 113-15

Oxford, university of, 22, 151, 156; Balliol College, 151; Christ Church, 151; Merton College, 106
Oxfordshire, 105, 107, 112-15

Papinian, 27
Park, 24
Parke, 44, 47
Parlebien, William, 123
Parliament, at Leicester, 95-6, 102; barristers as members of, 149, 151-3
Patterson, 47
peace, crimes against, in 17th-cent. Kent, 53, 55-8, 61-2
peace rolls, 96-7
peine forte et dure, 116-25
Peirson, Henry, 59
Perkin, H.J., 154
person, crimes against, in 17th-cent. Kent, 53, 55-8, 60-1
Peterborough (Northants.), 113
Pinkaman, Thomas, 59-60
Placita Corone, 109, 118
pleading, and the Hilary Rules, 41, 46; refusal to plead, 118-25
Plowden, Edmund, 13
Plucknett, T.F.T., 3, 12, 20
Podmore, William of, 123
Pollock, Sir Frederick, 2, 25
post-mortem examination, 131, 139
Powell, John Joseph, 24
presentments *coram rege*, 96-7, 103
Prest, W.R., 19
principles of common law, 24, 27, 29; *see also* maxims
prison forte et dure, 118, 121
Priscot, John, 32, 36
Pronay, Nicholas, 81-2
property, crimes against, in 17th-cent. Kent, 53, 55-60, 65
Prosser, William, 27
prostitution, in Victoria, 208, 210-11, 213
protectorates, British jurisdiction in, 164-8, 184-7, 190; Protected Territories of the Gold Coast, *see* Gold Coast
public nuisance, in 17th-cent. Kent, 55-8, 64
Pufendorf, 23
Pulton, Ferdinando, 21, 54
Punchyn, Richard, 62
Purcell, J., 162
Putnam, B.H., 94-5

Talbot, John, 103
Tasmania, *see* Van Diemen's Land
taxation, in the West Indies, 194
Taylor, John, 23, 25
Tetbury (Glos.), 135
Theodosius, 23
Theophilus, 11
Thornhaugh, Simon of, 117
Thurbarne, John, 62-3
Thurlos, Mr., 63
ticket-of-leave, 200-5
Tocqueville, Count Alexis de, 140
trailbaston commissions, 95, 102
transportation, 206-7; for treason, 199-205
travelling expenses, coroners', 134-7
treason, in English and Irish law, 199-200
treatises, legal, 11-29
trespass, action for, 30, 33-4, 36-7
trials, *see* criminal trials, jury trial
Tribonian, 11
trover, action upon, 31-2, 34-8
turnpikes, 39-40
Tylman, William, 62

Ulpian, 18
Union, of England and Scotland, 156; of Great Britain and Ireland, 199
universities and legal education, 149, 151, 155-7, 159-61
uses, in Chancery, 68-9, 80-4; and the common law, 80-1

Van Diemen's Land, penal colony of, 200-7
venire facias, writ of, 98
verdicts, coroners', 127-33
Victoria, Australia, desertion and divorce in, 208-14
Viner, Sir Charles, 14, 21
Vita Edwardi Secundi, 116, 125

Waad, Samuel, 194
Wales, Edward, Prince of, 76
Wales, 142, 147-8
Walker, Edmund, 17
Wallingford (Berks), 104-5, 107, 112-15
Waltham, John, 69-70
Warden (Kent), 59
Warner, Thomas, 194

List of volumes in this series

Copies obtainable on order from
Swift Printers Ltd, 1-7 Albion Place, Britton Street, London EC1M 5RE